THE
SITUATION ETHICS
DEBATE

THE SITUATION ETHICS DEBATE

Edited with an Introduction

by HARVEY COX

THE WESTMINSTER PRESS
Philadelphia

BOOK DESIGN BY
DOROTHY ALDEN SMITH

Published by The Westminster Press ®
Philadelphia, Pennsylvania

PRINTED IN THE UNITED STATES OF AMERICA

CONTENTS

THE
SITUATION ETHICS
DEBATE

I

INTRODUCTION AND PERSPECTIVE

by
Harvey Cox

No ONE knows better than Joseph Fletcher himself that there is nothing very new about the " new morality." No one recognizes more clearly that " situationism " is merely an arbitrary designation for an ethical tradition whose roots reach back to the beginnings of the Western morality itself. Why, then, should *Situation Ethics: The New Morality* by this same Joseph Fletcher have caused such a storm, ignited so many fires, and elicited such a wave of response both negative and positive? Not only has the reaction made possible this whole volume of reviews and criticisms. The present essays had to be culled out of bushels of material written about the book. They are merely representative. Why such a fuss?

Victor Hugo once said that nothing is more powerful than " an idea whose hour has come." In the lively discussion about ethics now going on in the world, the hour for the idea so eloquently presented by Fletcher had obviously come. The idea of *Situation Ethics* had, admittedly, come not as something that everyone was ready to accept, as will be all too obvious in the highly critical stance of some of the writers in this volume. Nor had it come as a total synthesis of the various schools of contextualist ethics now available. It had come, however, as an idea that could stimulate, enrage, excite, and fascinate. These essays prove that.

Situation Ethics rang a bell with thousands of readers. It did so because its time had come in the form of a man whose lifelong experience had prepared him for articulating it and because there was now an audience whose readiness to hear it had reached an optimum size. Joseph Fletcher has been stimulating and annoying people for years. He has worked, during his long life, as a coal miner, a laborer in a rope factory, a cathedral dean, a social worker, and a college chaplain. He led his students onto picket lines and called down on himself the wrath of religious standpatters years before the " New Breed " of clergy emerged. His daring books and essays in the once sacrosanct field of medical ethics opened up such previously taboo questions as abortion and the patient's right to die. An admirer and biographer of the late Archbishop of Canterbury William Temple, Fletcher has been a lifelong spokesman for social Christianity grounded in essential piety. Once when I visited some clergymen in the front line of the church's involvement in Mississippi, two of them told me they were there because of an early exposure to " Joe " Fletcher. In his years as Robert Treat Paine Professor of Social Ethics at the Episcopal Theological School in Cambridge, Massachusetts, he has influenced a whole generation of clergy. Not everyone who attends his classes becomes a disciple. Far from it. But no one ever forgets him.

But where did the audience come from, the readers who made *Situation Ethics* a *cause célèbre* and pushed its sales up over 150,000? Whoever they are and wherever they come from, they have demonstrated beyond any gainsaying that there is a large and growing group of readers today who are perfectly ready to cope with theologically and ethically sophisticated material, and who can understand it without difficulty so long as it is not written in arcane or abstruse language. It may be true that church attendance figures are falling off. Conventional piety may be eroding. But at the same time there is a distinct upturn of interest in theological issues even among people who might once have been bored or over-awed by such things. Study groups and discussion circles have multiplied in churches. College students crowd religion courses. There has been a distinct improvement in the coverage of religion in the mass circulation magazines and on TV. Sales of paperbacks on religious topics have soared. The audience for *Situation Ethics* was ready and waiting.

Why has all this come about? In part it is due to the simple fact that Americans as a whole are better educated and they reflect this added sophistication in their ethical and religious attitudes. In part it may be that we are now in the midst of a kind of third generation reverse religious backlash. People whose grandparents were orthodox this-or-that's, and whose parents rebelled by ditching religion altogether, are now coming into maturity and showing an interest in religious issues once more. The current generation of college students and young adults, for example, is neither devout nor deviant. They are open, curious, and in earnest about the religious questions they are asking. They suspect anything that looks either like a canned answer or like a glib attempt to be oh-so-up-to-date. This is one group to whom *Situation Ethics* speaks with such persuasive power.

Quite apart from the actual ideas it advances, *Situation Ethics* has made an important contribution to what might be called the " democratization " of the theological conversation. In this accomplishment Fletcher's book shares credit with such other events as the publication of Bishop John Robinson's *Honest to God,* the so-called " death of God " controversy, and the widespread impact of the Second Vatican Council. These events were both the cause and the effect of the burgeoning new interest in religious and ethical issues. They were all matters on which everyone felt entitled to have an opinion and to

express it. What had happened, sometimes to the chagrin
of theologians and church leaders, was that theology had
ceased to be an elite activity. Although it still requires
its specialists and its carefully prepared scholars, theology now seems somehow more accessible, more open to
comment by the man in the street or the man in the pew.
It was never quite the case that the experts withdrew
behind the walls of professional specialization, formulated the principles of ethics, and then announced them
to the throngs assembled in the streets below. Still, the
idea that those throngs not only had something to contribute but that their contribution was indispensable to
theological and ethical consideration is somewhat novel.
Now many Catholics who never took much interest in
how Catholic teachings or doctrines are formulated are
demanding that the layman's voice in such things be
heard and counted. This demand for increased participation of the laity was eloquently expressed in the Catholic weekly *Commonweal*, on October 28, 1966:

> A central part of reform has to be a whole new
> way of looking at the layman — or, more accurately,
> a return to an older and better way. The bishops
> have to face the fact that their office has, in a sense,
> been overemphasized since the Protestant Reforma-
> tion. . . . What we need now are efforts to achieve
> a proper balance and to restore the layman to his
> true dignity and function. . . . We need structures
> that will make it possible for the layman to share
> more fully in the deliberations of, and responsibil-
> ity for, the Church.

This call for the restoration of the lay voice is a valid
one even when it takes unexpected forms. Whatever else
it did, the now somewhat deciduous " death of God " controversy interjected into American religion at least one
question on which everyone felt he had the right to
speak his mind. It was a lively controversy and it made
clear that the aristocratic bias of theology and ethics had

been broken. From now on those writing in these fields would have to do so with the uncomfortable feeling that lots of people were looking over their shoulders, people who might not like what was being written and would say so.

Situation Ethics contributed immeasurably to this democratization process. Most of its readers were people who had not attended seminary. Many, indeed, who were not even church members found its items stimulating. Still, it was the kind of book professionals in the field felt they had to notice, respond to, denounce, acclaim, or refute. Some of the essays in this book represent this sort of professional judgment.

To illustrate the wide variety of sources from which responses to *Situation Ethics* have emerged, the material in this book has been divided into three sections, sandwiched by the present introduction and Professor Fletcher's reaction. Part III contains a baker's dozen of short pieces entitled " Reviewers and Pundits." Part IV contains the more lengthy and scholarly material under the rubric " Assays and Estimates." Part II, in some ways the most interesting, brings together a sample of the reactions of churchmen, housewives, editors, students, and the judgment — for whatever it is worth — of those two infallible arbiters of American morality, *Time* and *Playboy*.

What strikes the reader of these diverse expressions of opinion most forcibly is the high emotion, vivid language, and wide variety of difference of opinion that *Situation Ethics* elicited. How long has it been since a single book has been called " racy " (Lehmann) , " blood-chilling " (Langford) , " frightening and ruthless " (Roleder) , " sprightly " (Gustafson) , " a watershed in the history of moral theology " (Cross) , and " another example of the rebellion of fallen man against his creator " (Wagner) ? Yet amid this babel of critical and celebrative voices some major lines of questioning do emerge. Paul Lehmann rightly wonders just what is the relationship between what Fletcher calls "situationism" and Christian ethics as such. At times Fletcher seems to use the two terms interchangeably, at other times separately, and at still others he speaks of "Christian situation ethics" which, on his own terms, could be a redundancy. Both John Bennett and Wilford Cross believe the book fails to tackle the dimension of social ethics. This, incidentally, is a criticism Fletcher has taken seriously: he has promised that his next book, growing out of the 1967 Merrick Lectures, will focus on social ethics. More seriously perhaps, both Bennett and Milhaven press the question of how we are to know what love does require in a given situation. "What determines whether an action is loving," Milhaven asks, "or how 'love is served'?" Bennett puts it even more sharply:

> Is it correct to say that love as such provides any illumination concerning what is good for the neighbors? To use love as the great simplifier of ethics is to place too much emphasis on the motive of the one who acts and not enough on the sources of illumination concerning what is good for those who are affected by the action.

Most critics are also dissatisfied with Fletcher's simple equation of love with justice. They ask why we should have two separate concepts if they are really the same, and wonder just how love becomes justice in a particular situation. Again we may hope that in his future work on the more specifically social axis of ethics, Fletcher will cast some light on these questions.

Some of the same criticisms and questions emerge in the lengthier and more scholarly reviews in Part IV. Edward LeRoy Long, Jr., does a masterful job of placing *Situation Ethics* both in the unfolding history of theological ethics itself and in the context of those newer movements in theology that have appeared since the frazzling out of neo-orthodoxy. In fact, Long's essay is so comprehensive and discerning in its placement of the book that it could well have served as an overall introduction to this volume. The serious reader who wants to see Fletcher's work in a clear historical and systematic frame of reference might well turn to the Long essay first of all. The polemical barrage fired off by Robert Fitch is fun to read, as are all his fusillades. But his effort to designate everyone with whom he disagrees, including both Fletcher and the writer of this introduction, as mere symptoms of the " sickness of Protestantism," may not strike all readers as overwhelmingly convincing. We may, in fact, be symptoms of something quite different — a newly vigorous and rejuvenated Protestantism that still has something to say even to the " secular man." Much more judicious is Henlee Barnette's careful and systematic analysis of situationism, an investigation that is able to give credit where it is due and thus to make its critical comments much more plausible. Richard McCormick, a Roman Catholic commentator, states, no doubt to the astonishment of many readers, that " Catholic moral theology is quite as situationist as Fletcher at his best." He feels that Fletcher challenges Roman Catholics to close the serious gap between moral theology and the other theological disciplines. Wilford Cross believes that " the new morality here is the old morality verbally confused." Elton Eenigenberg, on the other hand, contends that " the New Morality is, after all, quite new." And so it goes. The perspectives are so surprisingly various that the reader is occasionally reminded of the hoary old story of the blind men and the elephant. This in itself, however, says something for the importance of Fletcher's book. It takes a mighty big animal to be perceived as a wall, a rope, a leaf, and a snake. It takes a many-faceted book to be interpreted in such contrasting ways. Some might urge that this merely indicates the basic confusion and ambiguity of the book itself. I disagree. Fletcher knows what he wants to say and states it with consistency and candor. If he has a weakness, it is not ambiguity but overstatement, not ambivalence but a certain steely certainty that sometimes annoys while it is stimulating. The fact that the essays in Part IV will also annoy while they stimulate is a tribute both to their writers and to the book itself.

I have spoken earlier about the democratization of the theological and ethical discussion to which *Situation Ethics* made such an important contribution. There is still another important tendency in present-day religious life to which the book makes an equally important, if less immediately noticed, contribution. It might be called the "rediscovery of experience." This is closely related to the process of democratization since what most ordinary people have to contribute to the ethical discussion is *not* a knowledge of the Western moral tradition nor a high degree of skill in thinking through tangled ethical issues. Rather, it is their own *experience,* their own moral failures, successes, hopes, and fears. Situation ethics, which Fletcher rightly describes as " a new form of casuistry " in that it tries to take particular cases into consideration, gives experience a central place in ethical method.

This rediscovery of the place of ethical experience comes at an opportune moment. For thirty years we have been passing through a period in theology in which the place of experience has been minimized. Overreacting perhaps to the somewhat sentimentalized and exaggerated notions of religious experience that were so widespread during the first two decades of the twentieth century, neo-Reformation theology, especially as it was influenced by the early writings of Karl Barth, moved its focus of attention away from the *experience* of God and toward the *Word* of God. Theology became " objective," and theologies based on experience such as that of Herrmann in Europe and Macintosh and the religious education theologians in America fell into disrepute. Bultmann in his theology now stressed absolute obedience as the single appropriate response of man to God's call. Reinhold Niebuhr warned how prone we are to self-deception in our ethical thinking and how an emphasis on the immanence of God in human experience could easily topple over into sanctified arrogance. During the height of the neo-Reformation impact on American theology anyone who talked about "religious experience" was looked upon as an old-fashioned liberal or a vague sentimentalist. The Word of God was transcendent, concrete, and uncompromising. To allow ourselves to wallow in our own experience would invite disaster.

Again such things as Second Vatican Council and the "death of God" controversy ended that chapter. People who belonged to the Catholic Church had for a long time heard its pronouncements, and seen the church's official version of how things were. But somehow their own experience did not always confirm what they heard. Protestants heard what the preachers said about God and morality, but within their own experience it did not ring wholly true. When the "death of God" theologians appeared they gave voice to the inner feelings of vast numbers of people. Notice also that if one examines the methodology of the radical theologians, it is clear that they rarely make any appeal to Scripture, tradition, or doctrinal history. They appeal to *experience,* their own and that of the people to whom they speak. History has shown that experience cannot be the sole basis for theology, but it has also shown that when experience is left out completely, theology can stray a long way from the faith it is supposed to nurture and clarify.

If the occurrences referred to above brought experience back into theology, the situation ethics discussion brought it back into ethics. In reading Fletcher's book, people rightly felt they were not being handed a position to apply, that they were not being imprisoned within a system. They were reading about a *method* to illumine their own experience.

Meanwhile in the halls of academe a new philosophical method was gaining ground, one that comported well with the renascent attention to human experience. Technically it was called " phenomenology." Springing from the work of such men as Edmund Husserl and Martin Heidegger, it turned away from the abstractions to which philosophy had devoted so much of its attention to a new interest in the experience of things as such. Some have called phenomenology a new and radical form of empiricism. Others saw it as a way of exploring human perception without worrying too much about the ultimate ground of the experience. Like Fletcher's version of situationism, phenomenology provided an open-ended method, a tool that could be used by people with widely disparate religious assumptions. Both the atheist Jean-Paul Sartre and the Catholic Gabriel Marcel are in their own way exponents of the phenomenological method. Some saw in the method a return to the commonsense analysis of the way things really appear to us that was so characteristic of William James, whose pragmatism Fletcher sees as one of the components of his own thinking. Others saw in phenomenology a parallel to the increasing interest on the part of many philosophers in " everyday language " as this fascination was demonstrated by such diverse people as John Wisdom and Ludwig Wittgenstein. In any case the mood was ripe for a " return to experience," and *Situation Ethics* arrived just in time to encourage that mood and deepen it. Whatever else now happens in theology and ethics, the renewed attention given to the experience of concrete human beings in history can no longer be overlooked. This is a gain.

In an earlier portion of this introduction I emphasized the very broad and disparate points of view the reader will discover in the essays that follow. There is a remarkable heterogeneity in their total impact that will be hard to miss. Yet the range of opinions is still limited. There are other perspectives that might have been included but do not appear. If we could have found it, we might have included an opinion from someone like the late Frantz Fanon, the author of *The Wretched of the Earth*. Fanon felt that all the talk about " love " in Christianity is so much hogwash and that what oppressed colonial peoples must learn to do is to hate. His own call for a kind of therapeutic violence, a violence that will restore to the " native " a sense of selfhood and dignity, presents a challenge to Christian ethics that is more radical than most are ready to admit. Black South Africans and Rhodesians might well ask Fletcher whether love can ever express itself in violence, not just in necessary or tactical violence, but in violence for the sake of achieving a new mental outlook. This is a serious question. Christian treatments of violence in the past have generally focused on it as a sometimes necessary evil, required at times to achieve a larger good. Fanon insists that colonial and black peoples should utilize violence not just to achieve independence but to gain new identities. If the end alone determines the validity of the means, as Fletcher teaches, then are hatred and violence sometimes required to purge the brainwashed psyches of the wretched? Or is Fanon's whole point mistaken? In a world of postcolonial turmoil and wars of national liberation this is a point that simply cannot be left undiscussed.

There is another point of view that might well have been represented but is not. Speaking about the arguments into which he was so frequently drawn as a leader of the Free Speech Movement at the University of California a few years back, Mario Savio once said he was " tired of people who always need a reason to do what they know is right." Savio speaks as a voice from the so-called " New Left " in America. In saying what he did, he was articulating a criticism of modern moral philosophy that would apply almost equally both to Fletcher and his critics. He was pointing to the cool rationality and lack of regard for gut feelings which characterizes most ethical theory. This point is alluded to once or twice in these essays, but never really dealt with. Gustafson, for example, suggests that Fletcher's approach would profit from Paul Lehmann's suggestion that " sensitivity, the affections and the imagination " have a real place in ethics. This same reservation may underlie Hiltner's belief that Fletcher leans too much on a voluntaristic willpower type of love and overlooks the close connection between feelings and the moral will in the human psyche. It may also explain Norman Langford's accusation that Fletcher's book is " Ethics in Cold Blood."

If Mr. Savio, or someone with a similar viewpoint, had contributed an essay to this collection, it might well have argued that Fletcher is just too far over thirty and very conservative indeed. In contrast to the anonymous correspondent from Maine who calls Fletcher a " wolf in sheep's clothing," Savio might find him an unfeeling hawk posing as a radical, or a dinosaur decked out as a hippie.

Whatever else Fletcher is, he is not a hippie. Like the gentle people, he does talk a lot about love, but his " love " is so unsentimental as to be nearly devoid of feeling. This may be the danger that is always involved in separating *agapē* too much from *erōs* and *philia*. William Miller comes close to making this criticism in his *New Republic* review of *Situation Ethics* when he asks whether, in the age of Norman Brown, it is still fruitful to explore these fine distinctions between the various forms of love.

Fletcher often appears to have a doctrine of man that leans way over to be rational. He overlooks an insight that has been stated recently by Howard Radest in

Center Diary 16, a publication of the Center for the Study of Democratic Institutions:

> The classical statement is that man is a rational animal. In the light of computers or so-called thinking machines, newer techniques in logic, etc., I suggest that the distinctive character of the human being is not his logical ability but his psychological ability, that is, his ability to entertain without apparent discomfort the novel, the bizarre, the unexpected, the contradictory, the making of non-logical connections.

Why is Fletcher so hesitant to allow for the spontaneous, uncalculated act of love that often inspires our admiration even when it fails to accomplish its stated purpose? As a decorous Anglican is he apprehensive about unsorted feelings? Has he been spoiled for spontaneity by too much sticking to the Prayer Book? As an academician and scholar is he nervous about dimensions of the self's decisional life that defy calculation or at least make it difficult? As a man is he insufficiently open to the idiosyncratic and affective sides of life, those aspects which women are supposed to feel more intensely? As a New Englander is he too caught up with the "religion of the head" to give due weight to the "religion of the heart"? For whatever reason, Fletcher's version of love does appear at times to lack passion and avidity. Those earnest elders who hesitate to let the youngsters read this book because it might lure them into illicit acts should really not fear. It will probably cool rather than overheat. This may be why Mario Savio would probably not like it. Still it might be the best reason for him to read it.

There are other positions that have not been included either. There is no atheist to ask why we should love anyway. There is no Marxist to keep bringing up the need for conflict in attaining justice. There is no simon-pure existentialist who sees man making decisions at every moment without even the equipment Fletcher wants us to bring with us. Still, just because these points of view have not been included in this book, most often because such people do not read and review books such as *Situation Ethics,* there is no doubt that any ethical perspective will be sharpened by a careful coping with *Situation Ethics* and with the critical responses collected herein.

By its very nature, situationism can never become a system. It seems to me that even the suffix " ism " is misleading in this case. The method advanced by Fletcher must be tested again and again. These essays merely begin a process which will fail utterly unless it is extended into the reader's own experience. It is the editor's fond hope that every reader will be drawn more deeply not only into the debate about *Situation Ethics* but into that ongoing controversy about choices and decisions which is the substance of human life itself.

II

LETTER WRITERS, EDITORS, AND PREACHERS

THE HUNDREDS of readers who have written to Professor Fletcher or to newspapers, magazines, and journals about his situation ethics, plus editorial treatments and sermons in churches of all traditions, are evidence of some success for his book's attempt to interest a wider range of people than just professional thinkers in the growing debate about "how to do ethics," the question of methodology in the formation of conscience. Most were hostile, but it is well known that people "write in" more quickly out of protest than out of approval. Stacks of letters, clippings, and sermons have been saved, and from them the following are selected as fairly representative Yeses, Noes, and Undecideds in various religious, cultural, and regional groups.

Time, January 21, 1966

"Situation ethics" is rapidly gaining ground in U.S. divinity schools as a way of systematic thinking about morality, and it claims an impressive array of advocates. In Europe it has found a home in the thinking of Karl Barth, Dietrich Bonhoeffer, Rudolf Bultmann. Its chief American exponents include Paul Lehmann of Union Theological Seminary, James Gustafson [who wrote to

Time to say he did not want to be classed this way] of
Yale, and Joseph Fletcher of the Episcopal Theological
School in Cambridge, Massachusetts. . . .

Fletcher argues that situation ethics avoids the pitfalls
of other approaches to morality. In both the natural-law
morality of Roman Catholics and the Scriptural law of
Protestantism, he argues, principles become inflexible
and "obedience to prefabricated 'rules of conduct' is
more important than freedom to make responsible decisions." On the other hand, the antinomian, or non-
principled, approach of the existentialists leads to anarchy and to moral decisions that are "random, unpre-
dictable, erratic, quite anomalous."

The situationist agrees with Bonhoeffer, the anti-Nazi
Lutheran pastor who decided that it was his Christian
duty to join the plot on Hitler's life, that "principles
are only tools in the hand of God, soon to be thrown
away as unserviceable." . . .

Situation ethics does admit to one absolute: love. In
any moral decision, Fletcher argues, the key question is:
"What does God's love demand of me in this particular
situation?" By stressing the demand of love, situation
ethics is at once more lenient and more stringent than
law morality. It can command hard decisions as well as
easy ones — acceptance of martyrdom, for example, when
law morality would permit surrender or compromise. It
can also say that certain acts are immoral which law
ethics would consider technically valid. To the situationist, says Fletcher, "even a transient sex liaison, if it
has the elements of caring, of tenderness and selfless
concern, is better than a mechanical, egocentric exercise
of conjugal 'rights' between two uncaring or antagonis-
tic marriage partners."

Situation ethics has been sharply attacked by Protestants and Roman Catholics alike. President David Hub-
bard of California's Fuller Theological Seminary complains that "we can talk ourselves into a lot of things in

the name of love unless we have some ground rules to play the game." Princeton's Paul Ramsey argues that traditional Christian moral principles are authoritative and that " how we do what we do is as important as our goals." In 1956 the Holy Office condemned situation ethics for Roman Catholics as an illicit brand of subjectivism. Attacking Fletcher's presentation in *Commonweal,* Dominican Theologian Herbert McCabe argues that the new morality has no criteria to distinguish love from what is really self-interest. "How do you know that what you are doing is loving? " he asks. McCabe also charges that situationism fails to consider that man is always acting within a community that cannot exist without law.

Fletcher argues that his approach is applicable to social policy and is no different from that of Jesus, who rejected the complexities of Jewish law and reduced his own ethical teaching to a twofold command to love God and neighbor. Situationism, claims Fletcher, is also implicit in the thought of such formative Christian thinkers as Augustine (" Love with care and then what you will, do ") and Luther, who stated: " When the law impels one against love, it should no longer be a law." He feels that situationism, new or old, " is a reflection in the field of ethics of the pragmatic, open-minded thinking which is characteristic of an age of experimentation, inquiry and question-asking."

> — From " Between Love and Law,"
> in *Time,* January 21, 1966.
> Used by permission.

Letter from a Parish Priest

A small discussion group of eighteen men and women in my parish have spent six weeks (two hours a week) on *Situation Ethics.* It has been the most exciting and successful group I've ever had. The old guard and the new frontier, the middle-aged parents of college kids and some graduate students, made the composition of this group very interesting indeed. We have struggled with your concepts and feel that we at least have improved our decision-making facility.

The purpose of my writing is merely to say thanks for a great book. It has opened so many new avenues of thought; it has motivated many of us to live in the freedom of the gospel and attempt to practice the deep and searching love which we, after great turmoil, have finally accepted as the only absolute.

A Protester Against Protestantism

I have just heard an interview you gave on your views on ethics and religion on *The Voice of America* and though my opinion and comments will not win friends nor influence you, I feel the urge to express myself.

It seems to me that you failed to throw any light on the present situation of the so-called new morality. One of the most important facts, which you being a clergyman could do nothing else but to ignore, is the tragic and colossal failure of religion to make man an ethical and peaceful being, a failure that is written with blood and tears in the pages of history and in the heart of humanity. Religion had failed because its teachings and doctrines rest upon the sand of dogma and so-called divine revelations which in reality are but rantings and wild speculations about the nature of man and of the universe which have been proved wrong and misleading by science. These false teachings and unnatural ascetic morality have bred hypocrisy and cynicism and disrespect for the law. The youth of today is sick and tired of lies and hypocrisy and demands a new code of ethics and behavior that is in harmony with the biological needs of man and woman. But their elders are totally confused and incapable of meeting their challenge and just beat around the bush with platitudes and pious nonsense that never did any good.

An Editor's Opinion

Situation Ethics: The New Morality, by Joseph Fletcher, continues the challenge to older ways of thinking which began with Bishop Robinson's *Honest to God* and has been extended in many books and by the whole array of those who assert that " God is dead." The book is learned, in that the author is privy to almost everything written since ancient times on the subject of morals; and it is composed with a sparkling zest for its thesis. The latter is that we must be frank, grow honest, and dispense with laws, codes, and rules of behavior; substituting for them the judgment of Love in every human situation.

The author's handling of his subject is not cheap, nor an invitation to lawlessness. But, above all things, he is determined to break free from the fetters of convention, which are often embarrassing and must frequently be compromised.

While many may welcome this new creed of individual freedom and responsibility, many more will be dismayed that this " new morality " offers a ticket to unbridled moral anarchy. The weakness of this " situational ethics " is the presupposition that the majority of people are sufficiently grounded in the decencies and rights of the neighbor and are mature enough to respect these rights. Dr. Fletcher appears to have more faith in the average man than some of us have in ourselves, which enables him to believe that no such coercion as the " Law " has always exercised is needed.

— *The Southern California Presbyterian,*
June, 1966

Another Editor

Will you please give me even one instance of an extraordinary circumstance that would make it all right, in your eyes, to covet another's property, to kill, to commit adultery. I can conceive people's inventing excuses for their weaknesses . . .

> SCENE: A hood is caught with his hand in the First National Bank safe. He says, "Ordinarily I don't covet the bank's property, but income tax is about due — and look what happened to Al Capone."

> SCENE: A couple who are married (to two other people) is surprised in *flagrante delicto*. CHORUS: "We wouldn't ordinarily dream of committing adultery, but Agnes is tired and Chuck wanted to go bowling . . ."

> SCENE: Mrs. Doe calls police to report she has just killed her husband. She says: "Ordinarily I don't approve of killing people, but John had the most annoying way of blowing on his soup. I just couldn't take it anymore. Know what I mean?"

To some degree we all doubtless spend time daily trying to justify our acts that we know are wrong. But we *do* know when we are wrong. I cannot imagine the purpose of a theologian who is also a professor of ethics in discouraging the function of the conscience — or in vitiating its development.

From a Cathedral Pulpit

I have spoken at some length about my own disturbed reactions, not because my personal reactions are important in themselves, but because in dealing with questions of this kind the first requirement is truthfulness, and it would be wrong of me to pretend not to be disturbed when I really am. But having said that, I have several things to say on the other side of the question.

The first of these is that the very disturbance that most of us feel about the new theology and the new morality can cloud our judgment. To speak for myself, I am never so likely to come to hasty conclusions as when I am disturbed, and my hasty conclusions are almost invariably wrong conclusions. That, I think, is true of a good many of us. It is particularly true of us when we are threatened. Let us see a threat to something we hold dear, be it our country, our family, our church, or our cherished principles of conduct, and we are immediately thrown on the defensive, both emotionally and rationally. And once on the defensive, the voice of our emotions is apt to be so loud that we cannot hear the voice of reason at all.

My first reaction to the newspaper article about Dr. Fletcher and the college students is a case in point. When I read that article I expressed my feelings rather sharply to one of my colleagues. "That," I said, "is nothing but a general license for promiscuity. Doesn't Joseph Fletcher realize that the more you want to do a thing the easier it is to persuade yourself that your motive is one of love? And even if he doesn't know that, doesn't he know how easy it is, especially for the young, to mistake puppy love for the real thing?" I went on at great length, with certain further trenchant observations that I will leave unquoted. When I had finished, my colleague said: "Charles, as is very frequently the case when you are most positive, you don't know what you're talking about. If you will take the trouble to find out what Joseph Fletcher really said to those students, you will discover that he told them that love that is based on respect for the one you love as a whole person is the only possible basis for sex, and while it is conceivable that this kind of love might justify sex outside of marriage in a very few exceptional situations, in normal situations it dictates just the reverse, because love forbids you to make use of another person as a means to an end. You mustn't imagine that the breakdown of morals was caused by the teachers of the new morality. It came about because this generation no longer accepts the old prohibitions of its elders, it no longer reads the Bible, and it no longer believes it will be punished in hell if it breaks the commandments. In plain words, young people no longer accept the rules that you lay down for them from the pulpit, because they don't think you have the authority to tell them what to do. On the other hand they do understand respect for persons. And while they may not listen to you, they will listen to the man who speaks a language they can understand."

It was a rebuke, and I deserved it. For what my colleague said is true. The moral confusion of this generation is not due to the new morality. It is due to the breakdown of the old. Perhaps the law of love is not the final answer. But it is the kind of answer to which this generation will listen, for this generation must have reasons of its own. And I notice that young people seem to be willing to take the new morality more seriously than they can take the old preachments.

— Sermon by Dean Charles H. Buck, Jr.,
St. Paul's Cathedral, Boston, Massachusetts,
October 30, 1966

From a Southern Gentleman

There seems to be much on the side of logic in your views. One must ask, however, if you consider yourself a Christian for certainly no one could call Christ a situationist. The question then becomes, Will I follow my imperfect knowledge and personal logic in the place of the perfect knowledge of Christ? If this is my choice, I feel that it is contrary to Christ and that I could not consider myself his disciple.

It is my position that Christian ethics and *man-discerned* ethics will be different in this wise: Even the best in man, taken alone, allows him to vary his ethical stance to suit the given situation and prevent him from making more sacrifice than he feels he can afford or which will be greater than what *he believes* to be worthwhile for the good to be gained. (This is the type ethics which keep men from constant conflict.) On the other hand, Christian ethics go an important step farther, I believe. Christ calls the individual to be perfect, as a goal. If a man sets his goal, no matter how unattainable, at less than perfection, he doubtless will become something less than his best.

A Pennsylvania Disciple

There are many people who feel as you do about morality, but never came up with a name for it — situationist!

I admire your courage for speaking out — most of us do not, or have tried it and met with complete rebuff, even from those who secretly agreed with our ideas. I no longer express my opinion on the issues of religion and morality.

I've worked as a farmer, oil-field worker, restaurant waiter, social worker, newspaper reporter, French interpreter, Chamber of Commerce manager, city manager, public relations man, and public information specialist — and in all these fields I found some people who agree with us.

A " Mini-Christian " Label

Dr. Joseph F. Fletcher, professor of ethics at Cambridge Episcopal Theological School, Cambridge, Massachusetts, is one of that new breed of free souls who does not believe that man should abide by rules or laws — not even the laws of God. " For me there are no rules — none at all," Dr. Fletcher announced recently.

He pointed up his new-found freedom by offering the Ten Commandments as an example. He would amend these to read this way:

" Thou shalt not covet, ordinarily.

" Thou shalt not kill, ordinarily.

" Thou shalt not commit adultery, ordinarily."

" In other words," Dr. Fletcher declared, " for me there are no rules."

That statement has a familiar ring. Many extremist racial leaders obey only those laws which are convenient for them to obey. There are educators and clergymen who teach young men how to dodge the draft, who defy civil ordinances. Each in his own way is teaching the dilution of our laws, regulations, customs. Witness the recent trends in some churches to include jazz music — all part of the effort to "modernize" religion which, according to the enlightened clan, has grown obsolete — has not kept up with the " in " times.

We must suppose that as a replacement for old-fashioned followers of Christ, these modernists would convert us all to mini-Christians.

Or atheist Christians, as Dr. Altizer of Emory likes to call it — whatever that may be. An atheist Christian is about as subject to definition as a fascist-Communist.

Getting back to Dr. Fletcher's commandments, he says that anything and everything is right or wrong according to the situation — he calls it " situation ethics " — and what is wrong in some cases would be right in others. We would like to hear Dr. Fletcher's explanation for a rape case, or the mass murders of the nurses in Chicago a few months ago. What he is saying is that in some situations, those crimes would be right.

" And this candid approach is indeed a revolution in morals," he says.

What it is, is a deterioration in morals.

Fletcher goes on with his woolgathering: " What is good? Good is first and foremost the good of people. The good is what works. Apart from the helping or hurting of people, ethical judgments or evaluations are meaningless."

He is saying that there are no absolutes in good or evil. "Goodness is what happens to a human act, it is not the act itself," he claims. Situation ethics has been criticized, especially by Roman Catholics who uphold certain absolute moral laws. An American Jesuit, the Rev. Robert Gleason, said: "It is not in Christian tradition to present love as the exclusive motive for moral action."

Unfortunately, Dr. Fletcher's sophistry attracts many young people. It is always tempting to take the easy way out. Thus, when people like Dr. Fletcher downgrade the Commandments, cast aside the Bible, make a mockery of the church and all it has stood for, we can always expect a rush of followers, who try to rationalize their own moral deterioration by saying what they are doing is in reality a "modern" approach to religion.

The dictionary has an apt definition for the sophism employed by Dr. Fletcher:

"Sophism — An argument used for deception, disputation, or the display of intellectual brilliance; an argument that is correct in form or appearance but is actually invalid."

That's Dr. Fletcher and his "situation ethics."

> — Editorial, *The Rocky Mount* (N.C.) *Telegram,*
> January 13, 1967

A West Coast Sermon

. . . Here in America at least, it is the coherent moral philosophy developed by Dr. Fletcher that is having the greatest, most widespread influence on moral dialogue, both inside and outside the churches. All over the country, in universities, in colleges and theological schools, and in popular magazines as well, "situation ethics" is

being heavily discussed. This is so because situation ethics constitutes a more or less systematic answer to all of
the major moral questions that plague our people here
and now.

Hence, it might well be wise for us to have a close
look at this new situation ethics and see whether or not
it has any relevance for the moral decisions that we ourselves are called upon to make each day in this somewhat uncertain time.

. . . The system of situation ethics has a great deal
to recommend it: it is simple; it is humane; it is oriented
toward the needs of people rather than toward the demands of principle; it is life-affirming rather than life-
denying; it encourages individual freedom and responsibility; it permits more joy and levies less repression; it
allows greater flexibility in the fixing of moral standards
in order to accommodate individual differences; it is
accepting and forgiving, rather than rigid and condemning.

. . . So Dr. Fletcher, with his freshly conceived situation ethics, presses for what might be labeled a " love-
morality " as opposed to a " code-morality." Fletcher
has, without doubt, shed a great deal of light on the dim
darkness of contemporary moral discussion. He makes a
strong case for love as the sole guide in moral situations; and on the face of it, indeed, it would seem self-
evident that a " love-morality " is infinitely preferable
to a rigid old " code-morality."

However, I find that while I agree wholeheartedly with
much of what Fletcher has to say, I have also some grave
reservations. I find, on one hand, that his exposition of
the meaning of love, while somewhat scattered and frag-
mentary, when brought together in one place is most
illuminating. It clarifies and deepens the understanding
of this complex old concept. On the other hand, I find
Fletcher much less illuminating when he discusses (and
largely dismisses) the value of moral codes.

I also find him somewhat behind the times in his understanding of the problem of sexual morality in our culture. You may remember that he was vigorously outspoken against what he called "the reigning ethics of American middle-class culture." This strikes me as an outstanding example of "beating a dead horse." What Fletcher refers to as middle-class morality began to decay rapidly after World War I, and the rate of decay was accelerated after World War II. Before World War I, it is true that the hypocrisy and prudery of middle-class morality were real, live enemies to be combated; but that battle has long since ended. The enemy now is not the rigid, hypocritical repressiveness of the old middle-class morality, but rather the absence of any moral structure at all. Meaninglessness, uncertainty, anxiety, and apathy are the enemies now — not middle-class values.

. . . Furthermore, any man who knows himself to any important degree, any man who freely admits and accepts his limitations knows all too well that he has a marvelous capacity to deceive himself and an ingenious ability to find sure, certain reasons for doing whatever he impulsively wishes to do.

This, again, is not a matter to be taken lightly. It points, I believe, to the severe limitations of situation ethics as a moral guide. It points to the reasons why a well-framed moral code, humanely interpreted, is indispensable to any civilization. The fact of the matter is we simply do not, any of us, neither you nor I, know ourselves well enough or deeply enough to be able to judge at all times (or even much of the time) whether we are behaving in loving ways or not.

Fletcher says only love is unconditionally good and only "malice or ill will is unconditionally evil." This is absurd as a personal moral standard, for hardly any of us are willing to admit or even to be aware of the fact that, we personally, act out of malice or ill will. We see our own acts as righteous. Personal malice on our part we invariably interpret as righteous wrath.

Or again Fletcher says: "What is right is revealed in the facts" of any situation. How ridiculous! As though moral decisions were quantifiable, were merely problems in logic. To be sure, it is essential that we be as rational as ever we can; but if we accept the world as it is, we must confess that not only are the objective facts in any moral situation often extremely obscure (even when available), our own subjective perception of them will frequently, almost inevitably, fall short of exquisite clarity.

If we are going to relate to others in love (and it is true this is precisely what is required of us morally), we need help. All of us. This is what moral codes are for. We need the help of others (apart from ourselves) to be able to decide with wisdom what love requires of us in any given situation. Where our own interests and our own impulses are involved we simply are not very perceptive about what will serve the ultimate well-being of others (or even ourselves).

— By John A. Crane, # 4, June, 1967,
Unitarian Church, Santa Barbara, California

By a Church Magazine Editor

We can accept the definition of legalism as the turning of maxims into rules, but we say that *the commandments of God are not maxims.* To illustrate: "Thou shalt not covet" is a commandment of God. "Virtue is its own reward" is a maxim. Maxims are debatable; divine commandments are not, for the Christian. We reject the implication that the person who obeys God's commandments out of love for God and man is a legalist. . . .

Our fundamental difficulty is with Dr. Fletcher's "ethical personalism" as he defines it. ("The doctrine that persons or the welfare of persons is the highest good.

They who hold this doctrine have theological reasons for it; e.g., a creationist belief that God is 'personal' and man is made in His image, and a redemptionist belief that God incarnated His self-disclosure to man supremely in the personhood of Christ.") No Christian will quarrel with these theological bases of this philosophy. But there is a tragic dimension of the human situation which ethical personalism does not embrace at all: the Fall and its consequences. This moral philosophy would be sound, if man were capable of deciding, all by himself, what will truly help the other person. But the Lord's word spoken to and through Jeremiah long ago is still only too true: "The heart is deceitful above all things, and desperately wicked" (Jer. 17:9). Christ comes to man to help him to overcome the power of Satan in his own being, and He proclaims that he comes not to destroy the law of God but to fulfill it (Matt. 5:17). The laws of God are instruments of his love and healing power. Only in obedience to him can our love for him and for others be truly exercised and expressed. We do not see how we can possibly help another person, in any conceivable situation, by disobeying God. In his service alone is both perfect freedom and true helpfulness to others.

— *The Living Church,* November 21, 1965

An Oxford Scholar's Reply

In your editorial comment on *Situation Ethics,* which has just reached me by surface mail, you rightly said: "Maxims are debatable; divine commandments are not." You implied that Dr. Fletcher disagreed. I am sure he does not. He carefully said that his views were not antinomian. This means that he acknowledged at the outset that God is a lawgiver and that his law is to be revered.

This does not mean that there is no debate between

him and you. It simply means that you chose to break lances with him over the wrong issue. The real problem is that you assume that all of the articles of the decalogue are " divine commandments " and he does not.

You could contend that the weight of tradition backs you up. The doctrine of " divine positive law " teaches that God's law can be put into acceptable written form and that this has been done infallibly in holy Scripture. Nevertheless, I wonder whether it is congenial with our Anglican ethos to consider anything other than Christ himself infallible.

My main point is that there is grave danger of idolatry when we look for governance to anything except Christ. This is why Bonhoeffer has suggested that the business of Christian ethics should be delineation of the " form " of Christ, and Richard Niebuhr has taught that our prospective actions should be appraised in accordance with whether they constitute a " fitting response " to Christ.

Christian situationists would say that positive law is, at best, only a precipitate out of the past experience of encounter between Christ and his people. Some situationists, including Dr. Fletcher, consider it a useful precipitate. It keeps us from having to face new situations *ab initio*. The laws, principles, and precedents which are our inheritance from the past may have no business governing us, but nevertheless they may be a useful guide, *in situ*. Probably they will be a reliable guide most of the time, but there is always the possibility that the Holy Spirit may say to us, with reference to some question in hand, " New occasions teach new duties; time makes ancient good uncouth."

Thomas Wood says, in his book *English Casuistical Divinity in the Seventeenth Century,* that some of the Caroline Divines thought that the Ten Commandments constituted " an imperfect code and digest of the natural law." Do you take them to be more than this? If so, with what warranty?

— A Letter to the Editor
of *The Living Church*

From a Colleague

I hope you will take it as a compliment to your book — I mean it as one — when I say that, quite contrary to your intention, you have given me a new insight into the importance and function of law in Christian ethics. To make it clearer, you have shown me the relation of form to action, of the structure of a relation to its dynamic, of the summarized and objectified experience of mankind living in response to a judging and redeeming God, to the freedom and future orientation that this life gives. My criticism in the review is my own program of study in this area, not an answer to you! I regard your book as a free-wheeling experiment starting from a base we all (even Paul Ramsey when he gets all through talking) accept. But to me it is not a success. By trying to throw out law altogether you have made it clearer to me what is baby and what is bath. Or, a better image, in tossing this problem so cheerfully about, you have shown me what is wheat and what is chaff, though I don't think your threshing instrument (or mine) is yet adequate for the job ahead. . . .

From a Former Student

This letter is about a conversation I had with a key layman from St. James' Church, Columbus. Before turning off the lights late at night on the first day of the conference my layman friend was telling me about something he had recently read in *Time* magazine (I'm quite sure he saw it in the Columbus *Dispatch,* not *Time*).

He was bothered because the article was about some theologian who has been tampering with the Ten Commandments. It suggested that this new and " obviously young " (so my friend said) theologian thought that it was time we changed the commandments. You know, " Thou shalt not kill — except occasionally; Thou shalt not commit adultery — except occasionally; etc. " Well, he wondered just what we were coming to. God's law cannot be changed. So, after listening to him expound for a while, I told him your story about Mrs. Bergmeier and the friendly Volga German camp guard. And I asked my friend what he thought about that. He said, " Well, I really think that in the Lord's eyes *that* would not be adultery." And to top it off, he was unable to make the connection between that expressed view and his own legalistic interpretation of the commandments. . . .

From a Positive Californian

So you would change the Ten Commandments? I've heard of a lot of egotistical people, but you top the list. You know more than the God who made this universe and everything and everybody in it, including yourself!

I wonder what is on his mind as he looks down here on you — pity, I hope. I'm sorry, I can't even pity you — disgust comes about as close as any charitable feeling I can muster up in your behalf.

What a multitude of sins you must carry in your heart to try to alibi your way by changing God's laws.

I too have broken many of the Ten Commandments, but I don't have to try to change them. My God sent a Savior to die for my sins — and yours too, if you'd let him.

Of course it's the twentieth century — but God hasn't changed — only people.

A Woman in the Southwest

I am a young married woman working to put my husband through school. There is little time for study but every spare moment is spent reading and thinking. My life is somewhat lonely in the sense that it is difficult to find people among those around me who care to think and discuss past the ordinary everyday concerns of earning and spending money and such. I am young, but my years have been filled with unusual experiences of love, of life, and death unknown to most my age and I suppose it is these experiences that have caused me to attempt to view life as a spectator rather than always as a participant — to think and question.

I look around me and it brings sadness to my heart to see the lack of happiness in my fellowman. There is so much plodding along, taking life for granted with never a spark of zeal for living and doing — to rise up and pull oneself out of the rut one is in if one wants to badly enough.

I feel that love is and always will be the most important element in the life of man. Love is not limited by time or circumstance. Love can face and endure anything. Yet — how distorted are man's views and interpretations of love, and how few people experience the highest form of love in its truest sense!

Your " situation ethics " discards rigid rules of action saying " always act with loving concern according to the situation, for the well being of others." If only men could be encouraged to take this rule to heart. However, difficulties lie in the fact that a man living by this rule would have to be a person of responsibility — with inner strength and courage of conviction—a man true to himself, and how many such people can be found these days? Far too few — sad as it is! Why are men so untrue to themselves — always looking back regretting their actions — afraid to launch out toward new things for fear of failure? . . .

I refuse to allow anyone or anything to take away my desire to think and to search out new things. There is such a wealth of ideas of life and how it could be so much better inside me, and I have a deep desire to try to help people to draw them out of themselves, to impart to them the importance of thinking and living each moment and each experience, never taking for granted there will be a tomorrow — to make people see the value of looking past a man's actions into his heart and soul to see what prompts him to be the way he is.

Thank you, Doctor Fletcher, for taking time to read my thoughts, for your beautiful ideas of love and life, and most of all for not being afraid to speak out amid criticism from many. You have given me added strength of my convictions and incentive to keep thinking and questioning. . . .

From a Bible Student

You are a Bible fool. Turn to the verse and see what a Bible fool is. You know that the man who says in his heart, " There is no God," is a Bible fool.

When a man of this world gets so high in education, and so selfishly smart, that he can take it on himself to publicly amend the laws of God, he so says there is no God.

In your position you do more harm in advancing confusion in the minds of honest people than a down-and-out liquor sot.

Of course, no Christian is wishing you harm, we would all like you to see the truth, as it is Christ Jesus, but we deplore your condition. We pray for you, but God may be using you for his glory, like he did Pharaoh, in hardening his heart ten times. If so, we waste our breath in prayer to him for you. So all we can say is, " God's will be done." Why do you see the name of God and claim to be a Bible teacher when you know you are a Bible fool? May it please God to help you see what he says for your righteousness, Isa. 64:6. In his sight your goodness is as filthy rags.

A New Jersey Minister

Your book is the kind that makes me wish that I had written it first. What you say in your book, I think, is pretty much what the New Testament is trying to tell us. Unfortunately, this message is being continually obscured and debilitated by good and well-intentioned but fearful people.

Anonymous, in Maine

"You wolf in sheep's clothing."

A Philadelphia Clergyman

I thought you might be interested in what happened at a study session on your book *Situation Ethics* this past Tuesday. A retired priest was the so-called keynote speaker. He very brutally and very concisely dismissed your book as a work of the devil. Then after lunch we discussed some "ethical situations." The man who had dismissed your book in favor of "the moral and ethical principles of the ages" ended up, along with everyone else, by using the situational method which you talk about in your book. Often he had very vehemently declared that he was ruled by a strict set of fixed moral laws; he never once made reference to any and always ended up saying we must rely on our own judgment.

The only conclusion I can draw from all this is that if we were all honest about it, we would realize that the point you make in your book is a very valid one indeed.

A Christian Reader Amazed

The new morality is a movement in modern ethics for governing conduct in the seventh decade of the twentieth century. It repudiates the Ten Commandments, especially the Seventh on adultery; it denies the absolute authority of God; it advocates " permissiveness with affection," it is relativistic and situational in theology; it is the church's accommodation of its teaching to the American sex revolution.

One amazing aspect of the new morality is the support it is receiving from some church leaders. This perverted interpretation says the New Testament teaches freedom from the law, that love is the sole criterion of action. On this ground premarital and extramarital sex relations are regarded as legitimate and right.

At the Harvard Colloquium on " The Church and the New Morality," Prof. Joseph Fletcher openly sanctioned the provision of contraceptives to a gang of unmarried boys for use with their " molls." Prof. Paul Ramsey held that an unmarried couple, committed to each other, was not guilty of fornication if they practiced premarital intercourse, because they were already the same as married, but without the state or church ceremony. And Yale Chaplain William Coffin, in describing most couples who came to him for marriage, declared his concern not about their sleeping together, but about their guilt complex. The same teaching is advanced by Prof. Harvey Cox, Jr., and others.

This teaching is the result of new theology that portrays God as " the Other " who is outside and beyond us, that denies propositional revelation as valid, and that eliminates prescriptive ethics. With the rejection of Biblical theology on God, man, sin, retribution, and redemption, all that is left is human reason and will. Hence the derivation of ethical rightness or wrongness from circumstances. To cling to the concept of *agapē* or love as giving some eternal reference to the temporal problem is a fiction.

— George MacDonald, *The Christian Reader,* December–January, 1966–67

A New Mexico Mother

I am a housewife and mother of three children and I feel that we have something in common: the molding of young minds, directing seeking hearts, and the enjoyment of seeing new ideas being developed.

I feel your stand on morals is quite dangerous to plant in the minds of our children and even though I know you are a scholar and you are considered America's leading exponent of " situation ethics," I feel as a Christian I have to object to this " new morality."

I hope you realize what you are doing and I sincerely hope you will pray more earnestly concerning this matter.

I realize, Dr. Fletcher, that this letter will probably seem very unimportant to you but it is my privilege and heritage to voice my God-given right as a child of God. My prayer is that somehow you will read this letter yourself and consider the contents as seriously as I have considered them.

A Good Question Asker

Your basic thesis, as I understand it, is that *any* legalistic system of ethics will sometimes lead to conclusions that are simply nonsense when judged by the standards of *agapē*. I for one am completely convinced; your examples alone would pretty well make your case. But some questions still remain.

1. Your examples are, in just about all cases, crisis situations. Am I right in assuming, as I think you have said implicitly, that in most everyday situations one could

go by a set of simple rules, without thereby becoming a legalist? Surely the answer will be " yes," but in emphasizing the needed corrective to legalism I wonder if you may not have left open the possibility of a misreading of your intent.

2. You have emphasized the "immorality" of rigid rules. But what if love demands rules? I am thinking, for example, of my children. My son operates your way; he has an inner gyroscope that works beautifully most of the time. My daughter, on the other hand, simply comes unglued if required to make all her own decisions from first principles; without precise rules of behavior she either dissolves before the requirement for decision, or takes a completely selfish course. We haven't given up, and she's only eleven, and all that — but the situation frequently demands of us that we make it possible for her to get through her day with the help of some very precise legalisms. Putting it otherwise, for her the Grand Inquisitor was absolutely right; are you not moralizing, maybe applying rigid standards, in saying that people shouldn't be like that?

3. And what about children generally, that is, how would you go about religious education? Even if all adults could accept the demands of making all their own ethical decisions without rules, are you satisfied that children could be taught from earliest years to do the same? I think of a nephew who was brought up precisely that way, and he's a mess: it takes him twenty minutes to decide whether to blow his nose, and like as not he'll decide to let it drip. How would you visualize a family and church program to produce the kind of adult you would like to see, bearing in mind the lesson of child psychology that you don't necessarily produce an adult with a given characteristic just by giving the child a watered-down version of it?

Playboy's Difference (Editorial)

Yes, there are indeed similarities *and* differences in Fletcher's and Hefner's ethical codes. Both men know each other personally, are acquainted with each other's ideas (for which they share a mutual respect), and agree on the following:

They both accept a situational, or relativistic, approach to ethics. This rejects both absolutism (rigid rules) and antinomianism (absence of rules); it accepts rules as valid generalizations gained by human experience, but subjects them to change or rejection according to concrete circumstances. Similarly, both Hefner and Fletcher regard dogmatism as an evil, because it leads to absolutism. Finally, they both regard the individual conscience as the supreme arbiter of ethical descisions, eschewing all attempts at organizing a *systematic* " new morality " in opposition to the " old morality."

While the similarities between Hefner and Fletcher can be attributed in large measure to their common opposition to the imposition of authoritarianism on individuals, the differences lie in what constitutes for each the basis of human happiness — in short, what man is to do with the freedom of decision. This difference is a reflection of two separate traditions; Fletcher, as a theologian, is in the tradition of Biblical Christianity with its emphasis upon happiness as doing God's will through actively seeking the welfare of others. Hefner, a secularist in the tradition of rational democratic liberalism, sees happiness as resulting from the free pursuit of a full and pleasurable life for the individual.

The Christian and the humanist traditions are similar in their concern for individual happiness, but differ somewhat as to what is involved in happiness. Therefore, since Fletcher and Hefner are spokesmen for these two traditions, it is not surprising that they would agree on some points, disagree on others. We never pretended otherwise.

— In the Forum, *Playboy*, December, 1966

A Vermont Catholic

Thought you might be interested in learning that only one out of thirty-nine students in a sophomore class refused to advise the eating of the Blessed Sacrament, "if human hunger cries for help." On the other hand, none among the thirty-eight thought such an action would be the "desecrating [of] the Holy of Holies."

I must admit that if such a question were posed to them as freshmen, there would have been more dissenters. This year they had been subjected to the influence of McKenzie (particularly his address to the Canon Law Society last fall), Weber-Kilgallon, Schmackenburg, etc. Perhaps Roman Catholic theology has made greater progress than Anglo-Catholic. It would be interesting to discover the results of such a question in other Roman Catholic institutions.

From a Parish Weekly

"Situation Ethics"

If you like new morality drowned in
    quotations,
You'll hail this new book on life's
    situations,
Written by Schopenhauer, Descartes, and
    Kant,
Hegel, Bonhoeffer, Oldham, and Rand,
Scotus, Schiller, Bacon and that isn't all;

For the most cogent phrases belong to
  St. Paul,
The Apostle who left so much wisdom
  behind him.
Doc Fletcher's there too, if you only can
  find him.
But follow the book and you can't help
  but win;
For there just won't be any way you can
  sin.
You may lie, cheat, steal, murder, — live
  the life of a hood.
You never, but never, have had it so
  good.
Even marriage, the state we were taught
  to revere,
Is due for revisions I won't mention
  here.
If these novel precepts grow very much
  broader,
We'll need new beatitudes written to
  order.
But so long as your casuistry's obedient
  to love,
You'll have nothing to fear from the
  powers above.

  — Jack Young, in *The Spire,*
    Christ Church, Bronxville, New York

III

REVIEWERS
AND PUNDITS

THE FIRST great spate of reviews of a new work are always the most revealing and in some ways the shrewdest. They go straight and fast to the point. The later ones are more apt, pundit fashion ("judgments in a solemnly authoritative manner"), to tailor their opinions with sidelong looks at others' reviews and due obeisances to their own reputations. Following are fairly early reviews, sampled from anti-, pro-, and inter- or semi-opinion.

1.
SEWARD HILTNER — in *Pastoral Psychology*

Ever since 1932, which saw the publication of Brunner's *The Divine Imperative* and Niebuhr's *Moral Man and Immoral Society*, ethics as a discipline has been in ferment among Protestant scholars. Most of the leaders — including, in the U.S.A., Reinhold and H. Richard Niebuhr, Paul Lehmann, Paul Ramsey, Paul Tillich, John C. Bennett, and others — have been agreed on what must be rejected about the old Christian ethics, i.e., that which reached its peak in the 1920's. In various ways,

Book Club Review by Seward Hiltner in *Pastoral Psychology*, May, 1966. Used by permission.

they have renounced legalism, moralism, perfectionism, provincialism, pride, and oversimplification. They have done so in the name of the Biblical message itself, along with realistic observations about people, cultures, and institutions.

Our Protestant scholars have, however, been less clear and less unanimous in what they are *for* in terms of Christian ethics. To be sure, all of them have been for love in the Christian sense as somehow focal to ethics. But how love is related to justice, to freedom, to law, and to cases — on all such points there have been divisions. With due respect to the minister of First Church on Main Street, I wonder if he has mastered these differences sufficiently to see the extent of the convergence that has been emerging about Christian ethics? Like the rest of us, he mostly gets worked up about specific issues, not about the general principles. And by no means all the leading thinkers have been competent at demonstrating what their principles mean in actual situations. Thus, I suspect, it has taken a Madison Avenue phrase like "the new morality" (with its vaguely sexual connotations) to make the rest of us look behind specific ethical areas to the basic principles.

In this book, Joseph Fletcher has tried to take this new look on ethics out of the realm of highbrow discussion; and without any diminution of scholarly penetration, make it available to readers who are intelligent but not necessarily expert. His writing is sharp, clear, crisp, and colorful. From the first sentence he argues a thesis, and subtheses, without apology. He states flatly, but appreciatively, where he agrees with other interpreters and where he does not. He uses many concrete situations of "ethical decision" to show how principles and attitudes are related to actual situations. The reader never has to guess where Fletcher stands, or why, or what are the implications of his position.

The author's own summary statement of his position is

as follows, " Christian ethics or moral theology is not a scheme of living according to a code but a continuous effort to relate love to a world of relativities through a casuistry obedient to love; its constant task is to work out the strategy and tactics of love, for Christ's sake." Love — which is interpreted as an attitude and neither as feeling nor as impossibility — and nothing else is " the ruling norm of Christian decision." Arguing this case — what it does and does not mean — constitutes the subject matter of the book.

Fletcher's title, *Situation Ethics*, achieves its provocative intent. It does intend to allege that there are no rules which can be applied apart from the complex nature of the particular situation, " objective circumstances "; but it intends equally to suggest that it is the interplay between situation and " the ruling norm " of love in the Christian sense. Tradition is never cast aside, is always used to illuminate the problem; but the final test is whether " love seems better served " by heeding or setting aside whatever tradition has said. Fletcher tells of a Republican cab driver who said, about his vote at the forthcoming election, " There are times when a man has to push his principles aside and do the right thing."

I intend honor to the author in comparing the probable effect of his book to Carl Rogers' *Counseling and Psychotherapy*, although in a different content area. Rogers had pulled together much that was emerging in counseling, had synthesized it and written convincingly about it. Everybody had said, " I don't give advice." Rogers drew out the full implications of the principle. The result did not vindicate every word Rogers wrote, but the resulting discussion and controversy proved to be highly constructive. I believe that Fletcher's book will similarly stimulate much wider ethical discussion, with equally constructive results. He is sure to be called names, most of them false, by many kinds of people. In a more scholarly and careful way than the Bishop of Woolwich, he has nevertheless given us a kind of ethical *Honest to God*.

Despite my warm sympathy for the author, for his thesis, and for his gift of radical penetration, I am not without criticism of his book. All my main questions center, I see in reflection, upon his use of the will. If love is attitude and *not* feeling, and attitude is " conative " and the right attitude is love or " benevolence " in its inherent sense, has the author then slipped back (under other terms of course) to a " will-power " kind of psychology without realizing it? Joseph Fletcher knows the complexities and intricacies of inner psychic life, and of interpersonal relationships, at least as well as I do. And no one can do everything in one book. Still, I wonder if a critical analysis of will (and decision and attitude and conation) would not compel some changes in the present argument, and not merely be an extension?

From the point of view of pastoral psychology, one of the great contributions of the author is his reconception of " casuistry " or " neocasuistry." In rejecting one kind of casuistry, Protestantism impeded any kind of " case " approach, which pastoral care and pastoral psychology have finally got around to. Fletcher suggests that we need to extend this to moral questions. Such an extension can draw upon pastoral psychology, and also enrich it.

2.
PAUL L. LEHMANN — in ETS *Bulletin*

This provocative and racy volume cuts an impressive swath through the tangled and thorny thicket of contemporary discussion and debate in Christian ethics. Professor Fletcher's lively and informed mind is accompanied by a singular capacity for imaginative and concrete analysis and formulation. In not a few instances,

Book review by Paul L. Lehmann, in the Episcopal Theological School *Bulletin*, September, 1966. Used by permission.

the formulations seem almost too neat. But in a field of thought and inquiry in which traditional ways of thinking are in notable disarray and the range and complexity of problems are both baffling and confusing, the risk of epigrammatic formulations is worth the taking. Its defects — and there are some — are the defects of its virtue. Many readers will find in these vigorous pages a clear and cathartic identification of their own ethical perplexities and concerns and a clarifying candor about decisions to make and directions to take. As a teacher of Christian ethics in a distinguished school of theology, Professor Fletcher sets about his task with the equipment provided by a wide reading of the literature in Christian, philosophical, and social ethics and by an extensive and varied involvement in the problems and the processes of ethical decision-making in our time. He knows what he is about and he wastes no time setting about it. . . .

Professor Fletcher frankly and enthusiastically declares the situational approach to ethics to be his own. He distinguishes this position from legalism and from antinomianism. He explains that he has been led to adopt "situation ethics" because the nature of ethical reality has been decisively shaped, if not changed, by four factors that have made "situation ethics" inescapable. These factors are: pragmatism, relativism, positivism, and personalism. . . .

The book concludes with a "postscriptum" which undertakes to persuade the reader that situation ethics has characterized Christian thought and practice from the beginning but only in "our era's pragmatism and relativism" has situation ethics become "a matter of rational and professed method" (p. 147). The argument here is that the Christian conscience and neocasuistry belong together. This "neocasuistry is, like classical casuistry, case-focused and concrete, concerned to bring Christian imperatives into practical operation. But unlike classical casuistry, this neocasuistry repudiates the attempt to anticipate or prescribe real-life decisions in their existential particularity." (P. 148.) As one of Professor Fletcher's neat formulations puts it: "The indicative plus the imperative equals the normative." It is not unimportant to bear in mind that Fletcher thinks that all men — whether Christians or not — engage in this "critically shrewd tactical . . . strategy of love" (p. 151). It is not unimportant because the reader is prepared in this way to bear in mind that what is distinctive about Christian ethics is not this love, and not this strategy but its *reason*. "The Christian's love is a *responsive* love." (P. 155.) If, then, one asks what it is to which the Christian responds?, the answer is "to God for what he has done for us, for mankind, especially in the life, death, and resurrection of Jesus Christ. . . . What is unique about the Christian ethic is *Christ*" (pp. 155, 157) . . . .

Professor Fletcher is in a hurry and has neither time nor patience for the question whether, if his "postscriptum" had been offered as an "antescriptum," his argument might have gained in subtlety as well as in cogency. In short, if "what is precisely and exactly and starkly unique about the Christian ethic is *Christ* (italics are Fletcher's)," how can an Appendix express this difference other than as coincidentally, inferentially, and vaguely? It does indeed! In this respect, Professor Fletcher is consistent. What is less obviously cogent is the subtlety overlooked by Professor Fletcher in his apodictic and situational hurry. Does he really wish us to think that this starkly unique Christ functions in Christian ethics by dissolving complexity both in the analysis and in the actions that go into the making of a decision? If so, then the proposition: "Situation ethics is Christian ethics" and the proposition: "Christian ethics is situation ethics" are interchangeable propositions. If so, the stark uniqueness of Christ functions in decision-making by a simplistic love reductionism both as regards its "nothing-elseness" and as regards its "neo-casuistical" occasions. Such a reductionism seems strangely akin to the pietism, moralism, legalism, anti-nomianism which Fletcher rightly abhors and strangely impervious to the pragmatism, relativism, positivism, and personalism which he affirms. For these movements, Christ was indeed superfluous, and love a normative value arrived at by reason, and functioning by the utili-tarian rule of reason which Fletcher, like Paul Ramsey, also adopts. In the case of Fletcher's abhorrents, Christ was "desituationalized" by disconnection; in the case of Fletcher's adoptions, Christ was "exsituationalized" by being ignored. Fletcher tries to avoid both distortions by substituting one of his own. In this account of situation ethics, Christ is made to fit into the vestigial mold of an "Appendix."

The point, of course, is that the propositions "Situation ethics is Christian ethics" and "Christian ethics is situation ethics" are *not* interchangeable. The fact is that situation ethics is *not* Christian ethics. Nor does it become so by the semantic device of absolutizing love upon the simplistic authority of the New Testament. Similarly, Christian ethics is *not* situation ethics, al-though it may be understood and interpreted "situa-tionally." In this case, "situation ethics" is as useful and as expendable as were Platonism, Neoplatonism, nat-uralism, and idealism of other days. But, as I say, Pro-fessor Fletcher is in too much of a hurry to pause over these subtleties. The extent to which he does not manage to validate his case is neatly exposed by the semantics which speak of "situation ethics," of "Christian ethics," of "Christian situation ethics" indiscriminately. Fletcher himself is not unaware of this as he candidly admits at the outset. "The basic challenge offered by the situa-tionist has nothing to do . . . with theological over against nontheological faith commitments. . . . (This is not to say, however, that one's faith is without an important bearing upon the situationist's action and decision-making.) " (P. 15.) The parenthesis is the author's. It should alert the reader to the consideration that " faith " like " Christ " is extraneous — *not extrinsic* to Professor Fletcher's methodological concern. Such an evaluation would not mean a relapse into reification as against predication, into " property " thinking as against functional thinking, into intrinsic as against extrinsic ethical analysis. It means that Professor Fletcher's candor takes a questionable advantage of those who are eager for light on these matters and whom he purports to instruct in Christian ethics. . . .

More puzzling is the declaration that love is both a principle and a predicate (p. 60); the " only principle " (p. 60) yet a " *hyphenated* principle " (p. 163). If, " the indicative plus the imperative equals the normative," why reverse the order — *as a situationist* — in explicating the maxim? (p. 151). However well taken the argument of the fifth chapter is, does it really make serious sense to say that " love and justice are the same " (p. 87), or that " love is justice, justice is love " (p. 89)? Why make the distinction, if they are the same? Why, in an ethic of predicates not properties, could justice not be a function of love; and so stated, without the overstated " third proposition "?

Most serious, however, is the misreading of Dietrich Bonhoeffer. Bonhoeffer's distinction between " the penultimate and the ultimate " is not parallel to " the ' penumbric ' concern of situation ethics " (p. 135). Bonhoeffer's distinction endeavors to express the freedom of the Christian for concrete cases owing to his ultimate justification, i.e., being set free by God in Christ. It does *not* mean the " gray areas " of ethical decision-making.

One could continue. But this would be unfair to the very real merit of these pages. With Professor Fletcher's strictness against legalism, antinomianism, pietism, and moralism we agree. His effort to relate pragmatism, relativism, positivism, and even personalism to Christian ethical analysis is a tribute to his sensitivity to the cultural factors in contemporary decision-making. What he says about the importance of keeping love and justice together, about ends and means, and about the situational factors in decision-making is not only timely and clarifying but of first importance in a constructive account of Christian ethical theory and practice. Not least, his singular capacity to focus upon concrete ethical situations and dilemmas with clarity and candor is an invaluable contribution to ethical reflection and discussion today. As an ethical tract for the times, these pages will be illuminating and liberating for many people who are genuinely perplexed, uncertain, and confused. When, however, these readers begin to make the decisions for which this tract so vigorously tries to equip them, they may begin to share the disappointed expectations which have ruefully marked my own reading of its pages. Thomas Jefferson, in presenting his draft of the Virginia Constitution to the General Assembly of the Commonwealth, urged upon them the caution that they refrain from " deluding themselves in their objection to some of its provisions through the integrity of their own purposes." One's admiration and respect for Professor Fletcher's learning, mind, and spirit intensifies the wish that this account of Christian ethics had been heedful of that admonition.

3.
NORMAN F. LANGFORD
— in *Presbyterian Life*

. . . A reviewer is tempted to use the caution of Gamaliel when he advised his colleagues to leave the apostles

Book review by Norman F. Langford, in *Presbyterian Life*, April 15, 1966, pp. 10–11. Copyright 1966 by *Presbyterian Life*. Used by permission.

alone, arguing that if the gospel were of God, it would prevail, and if it were of men, it would come to nothing. Although Gamaliel is often honored for his prudence, his policy of " wait and see " was after all a convenient way to evade the issues. But the reviewer must say something, without waiting until the votes are in.

. . . Although touches of homely language dot the book here and there, no flashy title is given and none needed. The ground has been well prepared by Bishop Robinson's immensely popular *Honest to God.* " The New Morality " was used to designate one of the chapters in *Honest to God* — a chapter which leans heavily on earlier writings by Professor Fletcher and quotes him at length by name.

Presumably, however, the sure success of *Situation Ethics* does not rest solely on Robinson's identification of Fletcher. Robinson opened the door to many writers who wanted to expose their fresh ideas to the general public. A large audience felt itself " liberated " by *Honest to God,* and by other influential if less noted volumes that either admit that church doctrine needs updating or assert new doctrines intended to make theology intelligible to the man in the pew. Many such readers felt free to acknowledge their own doubts, to express their own conviction that classical theology is a thing of the past, and to take hold of new formulations considered more understandable and/or more appealing.

Situation Ethics has been publicized as taking up where Bishop Robinson left off. Certainly this claim is true in respect to ethics. It is perhaps safe to surmise that the reader will look for at least two benefits from the book: a liberation from the moral precepts, maxims, rules, and regulations by which the Christian has felt himself bound in theory if not in practice; secondly and more positively, guidance in making the ethical decisions that confront him every day.

The liberation will certainly be available to him.

Fletcher's face is set against all rules of thumb, whether derived from traditional moral systems or from specific teachings of Scripture. For this reason his book will doubtless be foolishly caricatured as justifying " the new immorality " of a lax and wayward age.

No criticism could be more irresponsible. The anti-legalism of the New Testament ought to be (but unfortunately is not) apparent to any student of the Bible. Fletcher has the right to take this for granted. Beyond this, it is obvious that the author desires to suggest a method of making genuinely Christian decisions in the concrete dilemmas of man's moral life. To be sure, his examples of ethical problems are on the whole extraordinary, and often grotesque. But he aims not to dissolve morality, or even to disregard Biblical precepts as irrelevant, but to make Christian action possible by a conscious and orderly application of love.

Anyone longing for liberation from the dead hand of the law will be encouraged by this book. But although Pharisaical morality is ever with us, and must continually be combated, it is not exactly news that grace is not law. Professor Fletcher, moreover, does not seem to be claiming this as his unique message. If the reader, caught in the various moral predicaments that affect us all, looks for positive help, he must move beyond the mere renunciation of rules. He must discover the ethical method that Fletcher proposes and decide whether or not it offers the practical guidance that he needs to make his everyday decisions. It is at this point that the impact of the book upon the church, the question of what kind of appeal it makes, will be significant.

The premise that there are no rules to cover every dilemma of life sweeps Christian ethics into muddy waters. In recent years one school of thinkers has devoted itself to the exploration of " contextual " or " situational " ethics. Not to oversimplify, but to state the elemental problem, these thinkers have sought to discover what is involved for the Christian in the fact that " circumstances alter cases." In other words, problems of ethics arise from the need to determine what is right in a particular situation, and especially when no possible line of action appears to be unquestionably right. It must be stressed that no two thinkers are likely to have identical opinions. To the knowledge of this reviewer at least one member of the " contextual " school has already objected in print to Fletcher's habit of speaking of the " situationist " as though all other explorers in the field shared his expressed views. But it is in connection with this type of exploration that the term " new morality " occurs.

Fletcher proposes that one must abandon any effort to set up a *system* of values. Rather than rely on a system, one must use a method. This method calls for a person to do that which is *loving* in a given set of circumstances. Love is not a quality or " property " within ourselves or even within our actions. Only God *is* love; but as for us, what we do is expected to *serve* love. *Law* will be brought into play only when it answers to the purpose of love.

. . . The estimate of what help the volume actually furnishes cannot be accurate if enthusiasm is not guarded by careful reflection. Many reasons for cautious reading could be suggested. This reviewer will concentrate on one basic question: Does Professor Fletcher, in the development of his thought, ignore or undermine the basic concept of grace? More specifically, what becomes of the forgiveness of sins in the light of Fletcher's method?

At the very outset, Fletcher acknowledges that the so-called " new morality " is not really new. The effort to make love applicable to specific situations, even in contradiction to " law " when the situation demands a contradiction, calls for the sort of moral decision that Christians have always had to face. In his Foreword, however, he asserts that his method is " an old posture with a new and contemporary look." It does indeed have a new look. What this turns out to be is a singularly objective, even blood-chilling application of love by a process of cool reasoning. Fletcher does not hesitate to dismiss the conflict between love and justice, and to say that justice is simply " love distributed." He is not disconcerted by such a question as what to do if you must choose between rescuing your father or a medical genius from a burning building. The " calculus " of " agape " dictates clearly that the genius must be saved. This is " love using its head." Referring to a decision of the British intelligence service in World War II, " when they let a number of women agents return to Germany to certain arrest and death in order to keep secret the fact that they had broken the German code," he continues blandly that " situational casuistry could easily approve their decision."

But a question remains. Does this " calculus " of love, not, in effect, dehumanize love? Is love, even when it is that unique New Testament love called " agape," so remote from human feeling that it can be exercised with such detachment?

There are many instances of ethical aplomb throughout the book. Fletcher is in various contexts out of humor with Barth, John C. Bennett, Bishop Pike, and even with Bonhoeffer because they fail to pursue his own untroubled logic — because they recognize that in specific situations that which is *wrong* must nevertheless be done. In Professor Fletcher's system, if an act is ethically the better choice, then the act apparently ceases to be wrong. Rightness is never " intrinsic " — that is, inherent in an act — but only " extrinsic," in relationship to the balance of rightness or wrongness in the outcome of a decision. If love is otherwise interpreted, it becomes sentimentality. At one point only does Professor Fletcher relax this remorseless logic. With reference to an incident in the novel *The Cruel Sea,* when a commander must decide whether or not to drop a depth charge that will cer-

tainly kill hundreds of his own sailors and might only
possibly destroy a U-boat, Fletcher observes: "As the
C.O. said, there are times when all we can do is guess
our best, and then get down on our knees and ask God's
mercy."

Most of us have had to make decisions where nothing
that we could do would be immune, as we saw it, from
evil. And most of us, in these ambiguities, could only do
what we could, and then bring our decisions to Christ
that he might cover them afresh with his forgiveness.
Perhaps, on the basis of the solitary illustration from
The Cruel Sea, we may suppose that Professor Fletcher
does not by his theory rule out in practice the conscience that needs consolation because among our decisions none was good. Seldom does he refer to grace except
in parenthesis, when he identifies it with freedom to
make responsible decisions. Perhaps, though the evidence
is meager, he has really seen more in grace than the freedom to make decisions — decisions that, as he seems to
be insisting, may lead to regret but not to the agony of
remorse.

A favored phrase, much used throughout the book, is
Luther's famous *pecca fortiter* — which, translated, means
"Sin bravely." But, if memory serves, Luther's full
thought was, "Sin bravely, but believe and rejoice more
bravely still!"

4.
GEORGE ROLEDER
— in Augsburg *Book News Letter*

This is a frightening book. First, because it seems to
endorse behavior which most Lutherans consider immoral. The reader can take a quick conscience measure-
ment by reading first the open-ended "situations" in

Book review by George Roleder, in *Book News Letter* of Augsburg
Publishing House, June–July, 1966. Used by permission.

Chapter 10. They range from "sacrificial adultery" to the high command decision to drop the Hiroshima bomb. Each calls for an ethical choice. The author, an Episcopal professor of social ethics, hopes to give the reader a framework within which to make the proper "loving" choice.

It is frightening, secondly, for its ruthless insistence that the only norm for ethics must be Jesus' command to love God through one's neighbor. All other generalities are at most only maxims, never rules. For the situationist there are no rules — none at all. Fletcher shows a terrifying seriousness in applying his new morality in political situations often sidestepped by pietists (their religion does not meddle in politics or business) ; to situations in morals (moralism is safely busy with petty disciplines and church attendance but never makes daring demands upon men of goodwill).

Legalism likewise is too rigid, says Fletcher. It does not give love first place and often requires unloving decisions. Religious antinomians (the Pentecostals) and philosophical antinomians (existentialists) claim a sort of built-in radarlike Spirit which gives them guidance in decision-making. Therefore they feel no need for love as a norm, according to the author.

Something must replace the four foregoing corruptions of Jesus' ethics, states Fletcher. His "situation ethics" does this by putting love first, laws second. Laws are to be followed only if they bring about neighborly love. This is relativity and a kind of neocasuistry in morals. The author not only admits this but openly advocates the approach. Six basic assumptions of such "new morality" are outlined as the major content of the carefully documented and illustration-studded book.

Civil disobedience of the Martin Luther King variety finds theological support in these pages. Citizens interested in easing abortion laws are given an ethical framework within which to justify their reform movement.

Premarital and extramarital intercourse may be " right " if entered into with neighborly love.

The author supports his method by thirteen references to Jesus, eleven to Luther, eleven positive but three negative references to Brunner, nine positive and three negative to Bonhoeffer. William Temple and Paul Tillich are called upon nine times each, followed by H. Richard (not Reinhold) Niebuhr with seven. Most contemporary theologians are cited. The Lutheran Joseph Sittler is described as a sympathetic situationist. Unsympathetic name-callers in America are John Bennett, Paul Ramsey, Robert Fitch, Clinton Gardner, and Edward Long. (Pope Pius XII banned all situation ethics from Catholic academies and seminaries.)

Fletcher's brand of Christian ethics is either an incarnation or Luther's " sin bravely," or it is Evil quoting scripture for its own purposes. This reader feels that Luther would have felt " strangely warmed " by this book. It is the radical decision-making necessary to make religion walk and talk in the streets, shops, and homes where people do their living.

5.
JOHN C. BENNETT — in *Religious Education*

Situation Ethics will have two major effects. It will introduce many kinds of readers to central problems of Christian ethics. It plows up the field and a great variety of issues are brought to the surface and are made interesting and relevant. Its other main effect will be to popularize one way of dealing with ethical decisions. It will force readers to come to terms with the author's own position and I am sure that some of the weaknesses of " situation ethics " will be widely exposed in the process.

Book review by John C. Bennett, reprinted from November–December 1966 issue of *Religious Education*, by permission of the publisher, The Religious Education Association, New York City.

If the author had indicated some of the limitations of his position, he would have written a better book but a less striking and probably less popular one.

Fletcher distinguishes his position not only from legalism but also from antinomianism. He does provide a place for principles if they are not hardened into laws or rules. In one place he uses the phrase " principled relativism " to describe his position. That is a much more promising phrase than " situation ethics." All principles are under the rule of love which is understood as *agapē*. Love is the only intrinsic good, the only ruling norm. " The situationist follows a moral law or violates it according to love's need." (P. 26.)

I agree with most of what Fletcher says about the need of flexibility in dealing with the changing and distinctive elements in situations. I have two major criticisms.

The first has to do with the use of love as the only good and the only norm. Since love seeks the welfare of all neighbors affected by what we do or leave undone, ethics must have more to say about what constitutes that welfare. Doubtless Fletcher thinks that the generally valid principles which he does emphasize provide for this. But is it correct to say that love as such provides any illumination concerning what is good for the neighbors? To use love as the great simplifier of ethics is to place too much emphasis on the motive of the one who acts and not enough on the sources of illumination concerning what is good for those who are affected by the action. In one chapter he says: " Love and justice are the same, for justice is love distributed, nothing else." What does it mean to speak of the distribution of love? Fletcher sees clearly that love must be prudent in seeking justice but I doubt if it is helpful to go on to say that justice is nothing else than love. If we do not accept Fletcher's simplification, we would have a more obvious place for ethical guidelines concerning structures of justice that would provide correctives for the judgments of the most loving. If we say that a society of mutual love is better than a society in which there are just structures, we may be ultimately correct but also we may prepare the way for self-deception. There is a role for the pressures and counterpressures which preserve openness and justice in society even though those who take part in these processes are not governed by *agapē*. *Agapē* may cause those who write books on Christian ethics to favor the existence of these processes because they are good for neighbors, but Fletcher does not help us to make judgments about motives or values within the processes themselves where *agapē* in fact is not dominant.

My other major criticism is that I think that Fletcher takes most of the tension out of Christian ethics in practice. He says that " the situationist follows a moral law or violates it according to love's need." But usually when we subordinate an important principle that guides conduct to some other consideration, that principle should still help to correct what we do and should not be " set aside." We may decide that under some circumstances it is essential to use force but love needs to be guided by principles that involve the limitation of force while it is being used. Indeed in the whole area of social ethics this method of Fletcher's is likely to be far too simple and to reduce the range of the " situation " that is recognized. In an incredible sentence Fletcher says that " on a vast scale of ' agapeic calculus ' President Truman made his decision about the A-bombs on Hiroshima and Nagasaki " (p. 98). Truman needed to remember that increasing callousness about the destruction of populations during World War II had robbed him of an essential moral corrective. This sentence almost reduces the position in the book to an absurdity. Fletcher has no patience with those who stress the evil that remains in an action that on balance may be necessary according to some calculus, but this is to destroy sources of restraint and almost certainly in times of conflict it will lead to too heedless destruction of some neighbors for the sake of others. Love in such a situation tends to fall apart. The same lack of tension is seen when he says that "once the relative course is chosen, the obligation to pursue it is absolute" (p. 143). If so, for how long? Who is going to keep the relative course under criticism and remain on the lookout for the stage which may come soon when it should be changed? To say that no acts have any evil in themselves — not even the bombing of populations nor the torture of an individual to get necessary information to protect other individuals — is to destroy essential sources of restraint. There is another trend in the book that appears in a few places, as in his approval and slight modification of Alexander Miller's statement that "if killing and lying are to be used it must be under the most urgent pressure of social necessity, and with a profound sense of guilt that no better way can be presently found" (p. 124). Fletcher prefers "sorrow" to "guilt" but even in this he gives away his case for the view that there is no intrinsic evil in some forms of action.

Professor Fletcher has fought long and hard against moral laws in medical ethics and to some extent in sex ethics, that made forbidden actions that were inherently evil out of actions which seemed in human terms to be beneficial, and he has experienced so great a release from the idea of inherent evil in these contexts that he has moved too rapidly to provide the same release from all conceptions of inherent evil in the most complex social situation. To judge that a particular action is in some situations not the greatest evil does not rob it of all inherent evil. To keep alive awareness of this evil is essential for moral wisdom about the total situation. I realize that Fletcher intends to keep in mind all of the consequences, direct and indirect, those that would usually be regarded as evil as well as those that are more readily seen to be good or natural. But his method tends to rivet attention on what is immediate and most relevant at the moment of decision. This may not be as serious in the case of an abortion as it is in the case of the bombing of a city. Also one should give more weight than Fletcher does to the effect of precedent, when in a situation a moral inhibition is broken down which in all but the most exceptional cases is a desirable source of restraint. I am conservative enough to think that this is true of adultery but I know that it is true of torture.

6.
JOHN G. MILHAVEN, S.J.
— in *Theological Studies*

. . . According to F., the general orientation of situation ethics is not that which has occasionally gone by the name and been condemned by Pope Pius XII and the Holy Office, namely, an existentialist antinomianism. Antinomianism is the approach with which one enters the decision-making situation armed with no principles or maxims and relies exclusively upon the situation of itself, there and then, to provide its ethical solution. The true situationist, on the contrary, brings to the situation the ethical maxims of his own experience and of his community, and respects the maxims as illuminators of his problems. On the other hand, however, unlike the " legalist," the situationist is prepared in any situation to set aside his principles if love seems better served here by doing so. Thus, for many people it is wrong to have sex relations outside marriage because experience has shown that they would thus hurt themselves, their partners, or others. But it is quite possible that for other people, in certain circumstances, extramarital sex relations might hurt no one, further love, and therefore ought to be had. Only love is always good and right, just as only hate and indifference are always bad and wrong. This sole abso-

Book review by John G. Milhaven, S.J., in *Theological Studies*, pp. 483–485, September, 1966. Used by permission.

lute, love, the situationist seeks empirically, pragmatically, relativistically to concretize — "to find absolute love's relative course." To this purpose, experience may yield cautious generalizations, but the situationist will always be ready for exceptions.

Even if he be an atheist, any man who strives unconditionally to love his fellowmen has Love, God, the Holy Spirit working within him. The man of religious faith has the advantage of recognizing this divine dimension. He sees thereby more fully why he should love: to imitate God and (in certain faiths) to respond in gratitude to God's love for him. The motive is more concretely determined for the Christian situationist: all his love is a grateful response to God for what he has done for men in the life, death, and resurrection of Jesus Christ.

As F. rightly points out, the "new morality" is basically not new except in that it brings out more consciously and consistently something that has been essential to Christian ethics, classical casuistry, and, in fact, most human ethical reflection. Moreover, this conscious and consistent reduction of ethics to "the strategy and tactics of love," the planning how to incarnate love in the concrete situation, has undoubtedly been a preoccupation of many twentieth-century thinkers. F. invokes, as representing this orientation to a greater or lesser degree, Emil Brunner, Karl Barth, Dietrich Bonhoeffer, H. Richard Niebuhr, Joseph Sittler, Paul Tillich, Bernard Häring, Joseph Pieper, Jacques Leclercq, and others. But, F. admits, very few have applied this approach across the board and permitted exceptions to *all* ethical maxims except love itself. We touch here the nerve of the question today: Can one permit this? Are there no absolutes but love alone?

To evaluate F.'s affirmative answer, one would have to raise certain questions which, in the judgment of this reviewer, F. barely touches on and certainly does not answer with adequate clarity. What do the maxims, the

" cautious generalizations," tell the individual? How do they illuminate the problem? And how are they adduced from experience? Only after one answers these questions can one see whether the maxims always permit exceptions or not. Furthermore, what determines whether an action is loving, whether " love is served "? What, specifically, does love strive to bring about in the loved? Is there a hierarchy of goods which the " good will " of love should effectuate in the loved? Perhaps F.'s vagueness on this object of love explains why he is vague on the content and formation of the practical maxims. F.'s strange silence on both these points may arise in part from a lack of an intrinsic humanism. As he sees it, man should love himself, not for his own sake, but for the sake of other men. Other men he should love not really for their own sake, but for God's. To love a person is not to respond to his unique value as a person, but to imitate God in caring for this person independently of his deserts or worth. This extrinsicism will surely rebuff most thinkers in the Catholic tradition and indeed most humanists.

The book is evidently aimed at a wide range of readers and will in places strike some readers as too popular in tone and superficial in treatment (e.g., in certain Scriptural exegesis). Elsewhere it will strike other readers as pedantic and overtechnical (e.g., in expounding the " nominalism " of the modern mind). The varying nature of the lectures from which the book is derived may account for this unevenness, as well as for some repetitiousness and overlapping and inconsistent use of terms (e.g., in describing the situationist's attitude to " law "). Yet these minor defects do not prevent the book from being a welcome and substantial contribution to present-day ethical discussion. It will have served well indeed even if it does nothing more than curb the current inflation in ethical absolutes and hasten the review of the process by which the absolutes are determined. And hopefully, subsequent discussion will deal with the questions F. does not touch and thus bring out to what extent Christian ethics can assimilate positively the method of F. and his fellow situationists. One should add that F.'s abundant footnotes provide valuable references to much of the literature, Catholic and Protestant, on the question.

7.
WILFORD O. CROSS — in *The Living Church*

This is the sort of book that provides a watershed in the history of moral theology and the importance of its appearance cannot be overstressed. It follows, of course, a great deal of groundwork already accomplished in England by Bishop Robinson and others. Still, it is far more analytical and exploratory than the earlier writings of situationists. What Professor Fletcher's book really does is to offer a method for the solution of many of the vexing problems of morality brought to crisis by the changing patterns of our culture and our social order. The method, as it appears in this pioneering work, is as yet incomplete and capable of revision, but at least a new approach to problems of conscience and casuistry has appeared.

One objects, at times, to the polemical character of much of the writing, and its prophetic but sometimes rather tedious attack upon " legalism," especially since no effort is made, really, to distinguish between the uses of law as guidelines and the imposition of legalistic requirements in morality. One objects also to the radical oversimplification of human personality that is present in the method in that it largely disregards values, virtues and conscience, and the human structures by which we usually make our moral decisions. Indeed, the method tends to reduce moral problem-solving to an application

Book review by Wilford O. Cross, in *The Living Church*, May 22, 1966. Used by permission.

of love, as " the most loving thing to do," to a situation. This is indeed a reductionism of the complex mechanisms of psychological decision. It results in an oversimplification of moral problems by scaling down to two elements: love and the situation. Love is rather carefully defined, and it turns out that it includes the classic virtues of justice and prudence, so that love is a calculus rather than an emotion. Those familiar with the history of Chinese philosophy will recognize here the classic battle between Mohists and Confucianists in which Mohism claimed an absolute, unqualified love as the basis of ethical motivation, while the followers of Confucius insisted that love must be proportionate, governed by common sense, and subject to reason. Fletcher is far more a follower of Confucius than of Moh and he incorporates prudence into the ethic of love. He uses the word " calculation " so that his situationist position is not an irrationalism dedicated to the emotional aspect of love. Indeed, love is defined so widely that it incorporates both justice and prudential calculation. In this way Professor Fletcher preserves much more of the classical structure of moral theology than his own innovating genius might be willing to recognize.

At times, in situationist ethic, one is never quite sure what ought to dominate, the sheer determinism of the situation or the cognitive-affective attitude of love. There seems to be an ambivalent shift between the pressures of the situation and the motivations of love. For instance, in the case of a wife who is most unhappy with a husband with whom she cannot make any sort of emotional or personal accord, and who is hungry for companionship and love, does the situation of lovelessness become the determining answer to whether one should respond to her need, or does prudential love, concerned with justice, dictate the answer? Situationist ethics, as it is so far developed, does not provide a precise answer. Clearly in this case a love that destroys the relationship between wife and husband, or the possibility of relationship, would be destructive and therefore is not the creative, fulfilling love that Fletcher is writing about. Does this understanding of love as creative dominate or does a situation of obvious need and sexual hunger dominate? If you are going to deny the validity of all lawful guides, such as the notion of "adultery" and talk only about love-applied-to-situation it seems to me that contradictions between the physical and psychological demands of the situation and the just, prudential following of love-alone do arise. And Fletcher does not allow us to seek guidance from the crystallized experience of moral and civil law, which would be, in his terms, "prefabricated morality."

Once you have set aside as irrelevant the guiding structures of law on the objective side and conscience and values on the subjective side, and reduced morality to an issue of love applied to situations, you are navigating in channels which have not been mapped and buoyed. It is quite true and relevant that certain "earthquakes" in our social and intellectual environment have altered the old channels and shoaled them. Situationist ethic is a morality designed to bring men to harbor in channels that have been disturbed and obliterated. It is true that the whole approach to sexual morality has been altered profoundly by the pill and by methods of treating social diseases. No doubt old sexual legalisms were based to some extent on perils of pregnancy and disease and upon a certain marketable value of marriageable chastity. In the knowledge of current changes, premarital sexual intercourse and promiscuity need to be reevaluated. That they should be evaluated in the light of the axiom that persons should treat each other as persons and that every situation should be judged on its own merits rather than by a legalistic, univocal standard, is admissible, certainly, providing that one is willing to admit that any moral generalization or maxim that epitomizes human experience should not be set aside without sufficient reasons.

There is also some doubt as to whether situation ethics, at its present stage of development, is able to handle social questions. It tends to gravitate to personal issues and especially to sexual ones in its illustrations, for here love and situation are determinants. Applied to strikes, the racial issues, Vietnam, it seems at the present to have no firm definition of justice since justice has been swallowed by love. It resorts, apparently, to a pragmatism, at least in Fletcher's analysis, that makes it vulnerable to power politics, though perhaps Fletcher's affirmation of the utilitarian good of the greatest number might serve for a definition of justice. Situation ethic can deal with the sexual revolution but can it deal, in social context, with the cybernetic organizational revolution of modern industrial society? This side of the ethic calls for far more attention than Professor Fletcher's book has given to it.

There is perhaps little that is new, save in emphasis, in the current concern that morality be aware of the concrete situations in which it works. In moral theology circumstances have always been regarded as altering cases. There are, however, certain so-called " circumstances " which have always been held by moral theologians to be inherent functions of certain acts, such as the inherent function of a lie to deceive and the inherent function of killing to take life. These inherent functions of certain acts have sometimes been called intrinsic evils. Situationist ethics, however, denies that there are any evil acts or intrinsic immoral deeds. It argues quite rightly that acts of lying and killing can be in certain situations the best acts that can be performed and are therefore relatively good. This attack upon the intrinsic morality or immorality of certain acts, however, is not quite convincing. There are some acts which by nature are so remote from " the most loving thing to do " that one would have to scratch up very far-out cases in which these destructive acts would be the " best that one could do."

Rape, murder, adultery, mayhem, sodomy, and other dangerously uncreative actions carry inherent destructive functions. The effort of situationist ethics to declare that no acts are intrinsically wrong seems to contradict common experience.

In any case, a great majority of people are going to have to be guided by prefabricated morality for the simple reason that they are not sufficiently mature and their values are insufficiently personalized (in the sense of being conventional and not authentically their own). There arises also a problem of the moral education of children and the molding of the conscience. Despite the stifling effects of taboos and legalism, man becomes a socially successful creature under the tutelage of law and value.

Despite the necessity of pointing out these dimensions where situationism is inadequate in its pioneering stages, it is obvious that Fletcher's book places its emphasis and discovers the spring of morality precisely where a Christian moral system should discover its first principle. This is the primacy of love in Christian ethics. Its second axiom, the flexibility warranted by the situation, is equally essential. Given these guiding principles, and with a lessening of reductionism and oversimplification, situationism can work out the problems of its inadequacies in time. At any rate, Professor Fletcher has written a book that cannot be disregarded in all subsequent writing and development of Christian morals.

8.
JOSEPH F. GREEN
— in *The Baptist Sunday School Board Release*

There is a certain temptation to review Fletcher's book by professing holy horror. Yet this approach cannot do justice to a complex discussion of a complex subject. To understand Fletcher we must recognize at least two things — he is strongly opposed to *Playboy* ethics and he is conscientiously Christian.

It is necessary, in fact, to admit that certain of Fletcher's main emphases are sound and right: (1) love is the one and only foundational principle of Christian ethics; (2) any kind of legalism that makes rules into ends is anti-Christian; (3) Christians should apply love in the light of certain subordinate principles or guidelines; (4) the application of guidelines requires a judgment in each situation.

In spite of this much agreement with Fletcher, there is still a necessity to criticize his outworking of his system. Basically, it seems to this reviewer, his defect lies in directing attention too much to the immediate situation and not adequately to the larger or total situation.

The New Testament not only stresses love as the foundation of ethics, but it repeatedly and emphatically goes beyond this to say: Love works by respecting four things — human life, truth, marriage, and property. Fletcher would agree with this, but he concentrates on immediate situations that seem to him to justify exceptions. The New Testament leaves room for exceptions, but it does not emphasize them. Rather it emphasizes the larger situation that demands a stable moral order. In the larger sense, we can claim to love others only as we sup-

Book review by Joseph F. Green in the February, 1966, release of The Sunday School Board of the Southern Baptist Convention. Used by permission.

port systems that protect life, truth, marriage, and property.

Fletcher fails to recognize adequately the difference between legalism and law. Legalism is mean-spirited; it seeks revenge for the wrongs of the past. Law is constructive; it seeks to prevent wrongs in the present and the future. The New Testament clearly supports law in both religion and civil government. Texts are too numerous and too clear to call for citation.

Law is necessary for both the guidance of those who love and the restraint of those who do not. Love calls us to accept the validity of law and place ourselves under its yoke. More than this, it even demands that we impose law on those who are unwilling or unable to accept its validity for themselves. Here is a burden that we would rather evade, but we cannot evade it in the name of Christian love.

Judgment, of course, is called for. Rigid legalism is not adequate. It is right for Bonhoeffer to plot to kill Hitler. Yet the exceptions are quite extraordinary. Fletcher's mistake lies in implying that they are relatively common. The larger good calls for consistency, and the New Testament is on the side of the larger good.

9.
JAMES M. GUSTAFSON
— in *The Christian Century*

Among many reasons why Fletcher's situation-plus-love ethic appears to be radical, a few are of great importance. First, he is passionate in his distress at any sign of legalism, actual or potential. His reasons for this are sound enough: he does not want the moral subject to avoid per-

From " How Does Love Reign? " a review in *The Christian Century*, May 12, 1966. Copyright 1966 Christian Century Foundation and reprinted by permission.

sonal responsibility by taking recourse to rules or tradition; he does not want the openness and fluidity of life to be straitjacketed into rules. The effect of this antilegalism is to make Fletcher appear radically relativistic. Thus for the moment one loses sight of a possible " modified act-agapism " which is in effect a " modified rule-agapism."

Second, he states that the situation is determinative. However, he is never very careful to designate what constitutes a " situation." Most of the occasions for the most radical of his statements are strictly and narrowly interpersonal; the time and space span of relationships is highly limited. If the situation is to determine what love requires, it is terribly important how one understands his situation. Is it boy plus girl between 1 A.M. and 3 A.M. after a number of drinks in a motel room who feel affection for each other stimulated by proper knowledge of erogenous zones? Or is it boy, responsible to others than the girl, and responsible to and for her over a long period of time under a covenant of some sort, plus girl concerned not only for the present moment but for the past and future relationships as well, in a human community for whose vitality and order they have responsibility and which in turn has to seek its common good? When Fletcher moves from the interpersonal to social ethics he becomes a straight utilitarian. He does not argue his point; here, as elsewhere, he simply asserts it (p. 95).

Third, he seems to want an ethic that omits any possibility of a bad conscience. He has unwarranted confidence in the directing and informing power of love. He does take back, however, some of what he seems to give in this regard, for much of his book stresses the fact that love calculates, it extends itself in prudence, it uses principles (not rules) to illumine the case at hand. He wishes to distinguish himself from " antinomian " or " existential " ethics as well as from legalism. He really wants to modify his " act-agapism." But he does not want people wallowing in guilty feelings for having made moral mistakes. . . .

Fletcher says that persons are to be valued most highly, that love is the only intrinsic good, but also that the situation determines what is to be done. "Love," like "situation," is a word that runs through Fletcher's book like a greased pig (if I may be excused an allusion to my rural county-fair past). Nowhere does Fletcher indicate in a systematic way his various uses of it. It refers to everything he wants it to refer to. It is the *only* thing that is intrinsically good; it *equals* justice; it is a formal *principle,* it is a *disposition,* it is a predicate and not a property, it is a ruling norm, etc., etc. One finds nothing like the delineation of love that H. Richard Niebuhr gave in *The Purpose of the Church and Its Ministry* (pp. 35–36).

If one says that the situation plus love makes for the right action without being clear about what love is and is not, one has a simple formula, a radical ethic in both substance and method. If one says that love uses its head, etc., one may not have such a radical method and substance. Fletcher wants it both ways, and he cannot have it both ways. A much more careful set of distinctions than he is willing to use would modify the shock effect he wishes to create. He wants to simplify and complicate at once, while generally professing to simplify. On each specific judgment he makes about each specific case he uses, one can argue whether he has rightly considered certain factors, other "principles" than love, the complexity of the situation, etc. He suggests that distinctions moral philosophers make between deontological and teleological ethics are unduly complicated, and yet in the end he says "only the end validates the means." He also uses distinctions like "realist-nominalist," "intrinsicalist-extrinsicalist" and others that lend no argumentative weight to his assertions. . . .

If Fletcher is not as radical as he sounds in method, or

in substance, what makes him appear radical? Partly verbal pyrotechnics. But finally in specific cases he makes what many would believe to be a radical judgment. For example, an abortion: " No unwanted child ought to be born." Whose wants are considered? Is " wanting " always the same thing? Many a mother on a day of misery during pregnancy wishes she were not having that child. Is that the day she decides for an abortion? What if one says that the formal principle of love is significant even when one does not feel like loving? Fletcher says it is. Then that fetus that I may not feel like loving now is yet to be loved, has a right to exist.

Here Fletcher would probably say the fetus is not a person; indeed on this kind of case as well as in euthanasia — which Fletcher advocates elsewhere — everything hinges on when a being is and is not a person. All ethics are " happiness " ethics, he says at one point. This may indicate more of Fletcher's basic moral commitment than many other things he says. Does the right come out of an equation "situation plus love using its head equals our happiness in the moment "? This is too simple. But gone are obligation, duty, self-denial in discipleship to the crucified Lord, concern for order (Fletcher almost equates having this concern with legalism — which we have seen is bad). Gone is the daily repentance of man under God's judgment — man who knows he does not do the good he ought to do.

10.
WILLIAM ROBERT MILLER
— in *The New Republic*

What is " new " about the " new morality " in a Christian perspective is the recognition that " that old-time

Book review by William Robert Miller, in *The New Republic*, September 3, 1966. Reprinted by permission of *The New Republic*, © 1966, Harrison-Blaine of New Jersey, Inc.

religion" is ephemeral and recent by comparison with what Jesus was talking about. Underneath the encrustations of dogma and the accretions of pious sentimentality, there is a Jesus who is at least worth taking as seriously as Socrates — which is to say, a secularly relevant Jesus whose notion of agapeic love is the key to equity in law and much more.

What is "situational" about the situation ethics by which the new morality operates is the recognition that decisions cannot be made in the abstract; they arise in a context of circumstances, and this "situational" context not only modifies the application of law but defines the issues that are involved. One thing the churches learned from the struggle for racial equality was that in some situations civil disobedience was preferable to the loveless use of law. Fletcher's book abounds with terse situational vignettes about military and political problems, problems of abortion, artificial insemination, divorce, and unmarried sex, testifying amply to the need for a wisdom higher than the law if true justice is to prevail. Sometimes his examples point to an easy solution, choosing love rather than law or pointing up the absurdities to which a rigid application of law may lead. More often, they show the inherent ambiguity of the situation, where for instance one faces a dilemma of hurting one person to help another, and indecision or inaction might hurt both. Doing the right thing often depends more on presence of mind and adequate knowledge of the facts than on purity of heart. Not surprisingly, Fletcher's doctrine of love comes closer to Bentham and Mill than to Francesco d'Assisi, and he has some pretty harsh words for Tolstoy's myopic perfectionism.

Fletcher lays down four working principles or ground rules as the basis for situation ethics: pragmatism, relativism, positivism, and personalism. The third of these is where love comes in, for by "positivism" Fletcher means that we *posit* the proposition "God is love" rather than inferring it from nature. It is an article of faith to be tested in experience. One wonders why Fletcher thought it necessary to take this approach when he might, with Niebuhr, have observed that love is ultimate because anything less represents some degree of unresolved conflict. He does not refer to Niebuhr's view but does cite Bertrand Russell's offhand remark that "what the world needs is Christian love, or compassion."

This is not quite fair, and it represents one of the book's two major shortcomings. The first is stylistic. The book is jammed to overcrowding with neatly footnoted quotes from secondary and tertiary authors whom Fletcher happens to like, saying things he could just as well have said in his own voice. The preponderant number of these are Anglican or Catholic writers (safety in numbers?). In his concluding chapter, Fletcher asserts that really the only thing unique about Christian ethics is that "we understand love in terms of Jesus Christ." Yet his concluding paragraph is quoted from the *Ethics* of John Dewey and James Tufts. Much of Fletcher's theologizing appears gratuitous, something performed for the benefit of the Christian reader to relate situation ethics to his tradition. To show that situation ethics are not unchristian is a laudable aim, but in attempting to advance a distinctively Christian situation ethics Fletcher merely assumes a parochial stance. Much of what he says under the heading of "Christian" is also Jewish and, omitting the figure of God, humanistic.

This leads to the second major criticism. In a post-Freudian age, how much sense does it make to keep going back to the linguistics of the Bible? Particularly in the light of Norman O. Brown's *Life Against Death* and *Love's Body*, it seems to me no longer fruitful to ponder the delicate distinctions between *agapē*, *erōs*, and *philia*. Furthermore, there is something decidedly mechanistic about using the nominative of love as an absolute norm. Fletcher carefully avoids the aridity of pietism and moralism, but is the flatfootedness of a Benthamite utilitarianism an adequate alternative? This defect comes through most gratingly in Fletcher's discussion of love and justice, which leads him to the preposterous statement: " Love and justice are the same, for justice is love distributed, nothing else." Having said this, he is quick to distinguish between moral and legal justice, but if we were to take him seriously, we would have to reexamine his earlier discussion of how love transcends the moral law.

A mode of thought which is ready to regard situations as moments of process rather than simple clusters of events (and Fletcher's viewpoint implies this) would have to deal with *loving* rather than love — or it might ask: How does love *become* justice in a given situation? Ethics is a means of determining conduct, and we recognize today that conduct itself is the province of psychology; hence ethics increasingly has to do with some kind of supervising of motives. For the old morality, the solution was simple — motives be damned; man was simply a moral integer in a transcendental equation. Now we know better, and even what is irrational in man is a factor, not in an equation but in a process.

These criticisms are not meant to torpedo Fletcher's book. At its best it is often as provocative as Eric Berne's *Games People Play,* and at a minimum it can be a liberating book, especially for Christians who are still caught up in a Sunday school system of morals which they are too mature to honor in practice but not wise enough to avoid feeling guilty about. To them, Fletcher presents a grown-up version of Christian ethics which, whatever its shortcomings, can help both Christians and post-Christians to make responsible moral choices.

11.
C. PETER WAGNER — in *Eternity*

. . . Evangelicals realize that legalism is a bad ethic, and they welcome any new healthy emphasis on the law of love. But Fletcher takes the law of love to an unhealthy extreme. It seems to me also that Fletcher's ethic is quite vulnerable in several areas.

1. He says that love is the only norm of ethics. But what is love? How is its content determined? Even if we admit that love is *agapē*, it still seems exaggerated to expect each man to be capable of defining its content. We need the rest of the Bible to guide us as to just what the law of love expects from us.

2. Love, for Fletcher, is neighbor love. But this is only the second table of the law. The first is love of God. Jesus said, " If you love me you will keep my commandments." It is impossible for us to love our neighbor properly without first loving God, and we in turn show our love to God by obeying his commandments. To suppose that a man can love his neighbor without first loving and obeying God is folly.

3. Fletcher takes for granted that man is capable of loving. In this he bypasses the doctrine of total depravity and scraps the need for regeneration as the first step toward any meaningful obedience to God.

4. Even if it were possible for Fletcher to know what love is and actually practice it, it would still be impossible for him to define with any preciseness a " situation." The results of any moral decision have their repercussions not only in the exact moment, but in society in general and over a period of time. To be able to predict all involved in a moral decision in every case, especially in a crisis of life, is too much to expect

Book review by C. Peter Wagner, in *Eternity*, February, 1967, p. 59. Reprinted by permission from *Eternity* Magazine, copyright 1967, The Evangelical Foundation, 1716 Spruce St., Philadelphia, Pa.

even of an ethics professor to say nothing of the man in the street.

5. Finally, Fletcher bases his law of love on revelation. But he does not tell us what criterion he has used to select this particular fragment of revelation and reject the rest. There must be some norm which tells him he *ought* to believe revelation when it speaks about love, but he need not believe it when it speaks about lying, fornication, or stealing.

Situation ethics is simply another expression of the rebellion of fallen man against his Creator. Man has never stopped sewing fig leaves together in an attempt to cover his guilt feelings which arise from his unwillingness to repent of his sin and submit himself in loving obedience to the God who has revealed himself and his will in Scripture.

12.
JOHN M. SWOMLEY, JR. — in *Fellowship*

. . . Fletcher, however, takes an extreme position. " The new morality, situation ethics, declares that anything and everything is right or wrong, according to the situation." (P. 124.)

. . . The weaknesses in his position may be summarized in this manner:

1. There are some rules derived from love which can be broken only in the most exceptional cases, such as the rule against rape or not using violence against an invalid, or babies, or the aged. One has to think very hard and long to think of exceptions to such rules that could justify a situational ethic. In how many situations could the rape of an eight-year-old girl be justified? Or the peddling of dope to children? Could Fletcher think of enough real life situations so as to justify the

Book review by John M. Swomley, Jr., in *Fellowship*, November, 1966, pp. 24–26. Used by permission.

abandonment of a rule at these points? . . .

2. It is difficult to understand or define love as Fletcher uses it. He speaks of the rule " Thou shalt not lie " and says " But for the situationist what makes the lie right is its loving purpose." He also writes, " But what if you have to tell a lie to keep a promised secret? "

If we concede that there are occasions when it is better to lie than to adhere rigidly to the truth, there is certainly more to the decision than " a loving purpose " or a " promise." It is possible that the State Department official lied about the U-2 incident out of love for 180 million Americans or to preserve good relations with Russia or to keep a military secret. But the lie was discovered and resulted in greater hatred and difficulty between nations. A rule would help Fletcher at this point. The rule might be: You can lie for love only if you can be reasonably sure the lie won't be discovered and result in more problems than the truth would have created in the first place. The idea that love can be simplistically applied to isolated situations is implied in most of Fletcher's illustrations of situation ethics.

There are often other factors or criteria than love or in addition to love which must be considered in complex situations. Yet it is precisely the complex and highly variable situations that are unique enough to be situational or exceptional in terms of rules.

3. There are few situations or specific acts in life that can be isolated from a whole network of relationships or from one's own personality pattern. It is one thing for a person to assume, as Fletcher appears to do, that a whole range of actions such as lying, cheating, murder, stealing, adultery, are in effect ethically neutral so that each situation determines their rightness or wrongness, and another thing to realize that these are so destructive of personality and of human relationships that the rules about them, formulated from love, ought to

be broken only in those exceptional situations when love requires. . . .

4. There is an overriding element of the subjective and of "rugged individualism" in Fletcher's contention that "Every man must decide for himself according to his own estimate of conditions and consequences; and no one can decide for him or impugn the decision to which he comes. Perhaps this is the end of the matter after all. *This is precisely what this book is intended to show.*" (P. 37.)

He evidently sees little if any value in the long experience of the human race or the judgment of the Christian community, which has been summarized into laws. On his basis, Christian love varies from situation to situation and from person to person so that love can command both a German Christian and an American Christian to kill each other for the sake of love or even destroy each other's children for love.

5. Fletcher discusses love in such an imprecise and unsystematic way as to have it mean justice, prudence, a disposition, a ruling norm, and a host of other things. "Love as prudence helps a field commander who has to decide whether a platoon or company, or even a regiment, is expendable. And if so which one." (P. 88.) Nothing is said about the context of the war or whether the army is by every judgment except its own the aggressor. The situation is narrowed to a prudential military decision and prudence becomes love. He apparently sees no problem in identifying love with the mass use of violence and even indicates that Harry Truman made his decision to atom-bomb Japanese civilians on an "agapeic calculus" which means as a love calculation (p. 98).

Fletcher not only repudiates all rules in the interest of his own rule that one must never be legalistic but he actually refers to his situation ethics as a "nonsystem " (p. 11). This implies an inability to have any understanding of the content of the Divine will or process. Yet this is precisely what the Scripture and the whole revelation of God is all about. There is no such thing as a nonsystem. . . .

6. The rejection of any rules or laws makes situation ethics individualistic rather than social. If it is impossible to embody love, even in part, in any rules or laws, how is a complex society to achieve order or any tolerable justice? . . . The voice may be the voice of a situationist but the hands feel like those of a Christian anarchist. Yet there are times when he reverts to the assistance of principles if they are treated as maxims but not as laws or precepts (p. 31).

7. There is implicit in Fletcher's analysis the idea that each situation is so unique that nothing is discernible in terms of a pattern about similar situations so that the application of love to these can be instructively summarized. In actuality the moral problems presented by a whole host of acts such as rape, killing, adultery, mayhem, child beating, have been with the human race for a very long time, and many people have contributed both specifications and generalizations about the meaning of love in comparable situations. These summary rules ought not to be discarded without careful consideration and then in the most exceptional cases.

8. Children have to learn moral values or principles. They do not naturally make the just or loving choice. Specifically, how is a child to understand that it is all right to cheat in the classroom out of love for a less prepared or able classmate and not expect to cheat himself when he is unprepared. Can we think of enough occasions when cheating in the classroom would be in the interest of love so as to discard the general rule? Can children be taught that love sometimes requires killing (perhaps a classmate who is a brutal bully) and in other cases it requires a nonkilling approach? Can we think of

enough occasions when love requires us to kill our fellow human beings so as to discard the general rule against killing?

At what age or point does the child or adult give up the rules he learned? Are all or most adults capable of applying Christian love to situations without the assistance of moral laws? If they need the assistance of laws, then how do they differ from other nonlegalists in ethics? . . .

Fletcher delights in the familiar illustration of love being evident in Bonhoeffer's attempted assassination of Hitler. Here again one has to make a deeper analysis. Was the persecution of the Jews or World War II or its continuation the act of one man or the result of deeper currents and more complex forces? Should a Negro in Alabama assume that the assassination of Governor Wallace would alter the problem of segregation there or is it possible that it might intensify it? Certainly the assassination of the South African Prime Minister brought into office as successor a much tougher nationalist. The repeated approving use of illustrations such as Bonhoeffer's attempted assassination suggests that assassination of tyrants is useful or good or loving whereas the evidence from history is not that conclusive.

Love does not have to be naïve in social analysis or simplistic in its solutions, which is the impression Fletcher leaves in talking in the nuclear age about just or loving wars, assassination of tyrants and various other " love " solutions to situations.

Fletcher endorses the maxim that " the end justifies or sanctifies or validates the means " (p. 131). By this he means that if love justifies the end in view, it must also justify the means chosen. This is where Fletcher errs, even in his own terms, by making a rule out of ends validating means. It is better to say that the end, however good in its intentions, is conditioned by the means chosen. Woodrow Wilson's war to end all wars or to make the world safe for democracy had a good loving end in mind but the means prevented its achievement.

Fletcher quotes Emil Brunner's statement " the necessary end sanctifies the necessary means." The question of course is, what does necessary imply? Brunner, whom Fletcher quotes out of context in support of his position, says, even though it didn't serve Fletcher's purpose to acknowledge it: " We have no right to believe that our action is approved by God unless we do all that lies in our power to make even these means, as far as possible, conform to the Divine End, that is to Love. The means which have to be used for a definite good end may even be of such bad quality that in this instance we feel it to be our duty to renounce the undertaking altogether." (*Divine Imperative*, p. 246.)

Fletcher's book is easy to read, a popular rather than scholarly approach to ethics. It is a most valuable antidote to legalism. Every legalist ought to be confronted with *Situation Ethics* as a corrective. But it is neither the only nor the best nonlegalist approach to Christian ethics.

13.
HARMON L. SMITH
— in *The Duke Divinity School Review*

. . . I expect this book to be around for a while because the position it takes will probably not be better stated anytime soon. In brief, I suspect that Professor Fletcher has argued the case for situationism as convincingly as one (in our situation) can.

This is not to say that the case is convincing. At least there are several questions which deserve to be raised

Book review by Harmon L. Smith in *The Duke Divinity School Review*, Spring, 1966, pp. 149–53. Used by permission.

and an observation or two to be made.

In the first place, this book does not manage to maintain the mediating position which it claims for itself. Its emphasis is plainly on teleology (cf. p. 43), and a role for deontological ethics is very uncertain indeed. The only imperative which Fletcher acknowledges merely enjoins one to will whatever in the situation may be right; but what is right is to be calculated in terms of a *summum bonum* which, for the Christian, "is neighbor-centered first and last" (p. 31).

This procedure itself, however, is mistaken if one recalls that the *summum bonum,* in Christian thought, has been seen as integral to the *summum esse;* and that, therefore, to ask the question of the highest good is to speak within both ontological and hierarchical categories. Yet Fletcher maintains that the neighbor's good cannot be anticipatorily prescribed by reference to any such *esse* but can only be decided in each "definite, yet unconcluded, unique and transient situation" (p. 33). The reason for this may be got at, provisionally perhaps, by a closer look at Fletcher's understanding and use of *agapē.*

What guides one in willing the neighbor's good in the situation is, of course, "love." But this is love regarded as a "predicate" only, i.e., as nonsubstantive and formal, as a principle which expresses "what type of real actions Christians are to call good" (p. 60). *Agapē,* Fletcher argues, is nothing "given" or objectively real or self-existent in the context of our existence. "Only in the divine being, only in God, is love substantive. With men it is a formal principle, a predicate. Only with God is it a property. This is because God *is* love. Men, who are finite, only *do* love." (P. 62.) With this Fletcher has affirmed a "transcendent form" in the classical Platonic-Aristotelian tradition and, having allowed the rules of the game to be so set, he is beaten before play begins —

unless he can devise some way by which the " real " can be experienced and evaluated without reference to the " ideal."

But what Fletcher wants to do cannot be done in the way he has chosen. He has so defined " situation " as to make it ready-made, a simple " that's how it is," just as Platonic-Aristotelian thought defined the being of man as ready-made. What was nonbeing to Plato, namely, the world of becoming, is simple being for Fletcher; and Fletcher's nonbeing (i.e., that which cannot be structured) is consciousness. But both are ahistorical because both are excarnate ways of thinking about being and value. There is no intrinsic communion between being and nonbeing, or between the decision maker and the situation in which he finds himself. For Fletcher, one is not embodied in a situation; he is simply " up against " a situation. What one does, therefore, " in " the situation has no intrinsic corollary to what the person becomes. The irony of the situational approach is that it is not situational enough! The situation, as " objective circumstances " (p. 14), is really alien; it is " the case " or " what is."

One would want to argue here that love cannot simply be taken or placed outside the world and then brought back via situational ethics. If *agapē* is not " given " in the context of our existence, one must always regard the situation as extrinsic to *agapē;* and if this be the case, then the problem of the " good " can never arise because *agapē* cannot become embodied in acts in which the person, his situation, and his decision are all in deep communion and mutual dialogue.

Whatever else Fletcher's understanding and use of *agapē* may mean, it certainly suggests to me that *agapē* is not a human possibility and that therefore we do not, in any serious sense, genuinely participate in the redemptive love of God. My incapacity for the love of which only God is capable (for which there is no explanation or accounting by Fletcher, but only the positing) thus makes meaningless the command "to be like God, to imitate him" (p. 63). But, in addition, it limits my decisions and acts to a kind of heroic fatalism.

Urgent questions, moreover, are certainly raised about the reality and bearing of incarnation upon this way of doing ethics. Christian ethics has traditionally held not only that the *imitatio Dei* is a distinct possibility for one who acknowledges that God was in Christ, but also that obedience to that prototypal divine love manifested in him is explicitly commanded. If we are indeed incapable of expressing *agapē* particularly and concretely, then it needs to be shown how this is so in view of the incarnation. Meanwhile, it is a more tenable view that love, like consciousness, is always incarnate, that is, it is a being-in-the-world through my being-in-my-body; and, as such, this being is fluid without being groundless, structured and structuring without being substantive and forever the same. The *agapē* of which Fletcher speaks is excarnate and for that reason nonsituational.

To return for a moment to the assertion that love is a principle which expresses "what type of real actions Christians are to call good": Professor Fletcher points out that these actions, as indicative of value, are worthy only because the action "happens to help persons (thus being good) or to hurt persons (thus being bad) " (p. 59). He argues, further, that "Apart from the helping or hurting of people, ethical judgments or evaluations are meaningless. . . . Christian situation ethics asserts firmly and definitely: *Value, worth, ethical quality, goodness or badness, right or wrong — these things are only predicates, they are not properties*." (P. 60.) In other words, situation ethics is nominalistic, but with a twist: whereas medievalists argued that good is good because God regards it as such, Fletcher argues that man makes this judgment. Objective value theory, in whatever guise, is of course rejected.

It deserves remarking in this connection that through-out the book too many basic problems are too easily dismissed. Fletcher regards the ease with which situational casuistry resolves problems as one of its advantages; but it is precisely the ease with which decisions and acts are applauded or condemned that makes me uncomfortable.

There are also other questions which, however awkward, merit asking. One of them is: How does one know that he is doing (or has done) the loving thing (to do) in the situation? What judges decision and action? Given Fletcher's definition and use of principles (i.e., that they are "illuminators" but not "directors"), one wonders whether in this sense they retain whatever it is that denominates them "principles" at all? Situation ethics, it is argued, "does not ask *what* is good but *how* to do good for *whom;* not what *is* love but how to *do* the most loving thing possible in the situation" (p. 52). Is it really the case that one is so entirely void of any notion with respect to what love demands? It is certainly true that every new decision is called for in the light of its own peculiar and unique circumstances and that, therefore, no inflexible rule or guide for right decision-making may be supposed as the sole (or even most important) criterion for determining or shaping duty. But one comes to every new moral decison with the resources of both principles and judgments which have been formulated in previous decisions. Neither value system nor situation can thus be said to be autonomous in the decisive moment; and what love *is* will then shape how one is to *do* it, and vice versa. One may agree with Fletcher that obligation in the situation cannot be identified with objectively "right" acts while insisting nevertheless that one ought to try to decide what is right or good in this objective sense. The "deposit" of value judgments brought to new moments of decision cannot be either dismissed or given inferior status in the decision-making process.

Traditionally, Christian ethics has been thought to be inseparable from a religious milieu in which God has something to do with the meaning of right and wrong, good and bad, and from which the moral norms which assess human conduct derive. Whether the neighbor is helped or hurt, then, may not depend upon reason operating apart from the religious tradition, i.e., whether self or neighbor gets what he wants out of this decision/act. How the neighbor is (to be) treated may rather be formulated and assessed by reference to God's intention for him. That the neighbor is to be loved and what it means to love him are thus, it would seem, antecedent to doing it. The error of the situationist approach may lie in the extravagance rather than the exclusiveness of its claim that "Christian action should be tailored to fit objective circumstances, the *situation*" (p. 14). In either case, it promises more than it can produce. For if alternative courses of action are wholly judged according to the circumstances of the existential moment and my possibility for transcending this limitation be entirely excluded, then freedom becomes only a solicitous platitude and I am victimized by the most brutal kind of contextual and impersonal determinism.

Finally, a quotation will illustrate the functional worth of a value system (as I think Fletcher's " nonsystem " to be) derived from precommitments to pragmatism, positivism, and relativism: " *The situationist holds that whatever is the most loving thing in the situation is the right and good thing.* It is not excusably evil, it is positively good " (p. 65). Thus, if a lie be told unlovingly, it is wrong; but, if it be told in love, it is good.

It has long been recognized that we often are confronted by a limited range of act-possibilities over which we exercise little or no control, but it has not been argued before that necessity in the form of situational problematics can make otherwise ambiguous choices Christianly and positively good! The empirical and casuistical temper of situationism has led it, at this point, to a value theory both unwarranted and untenable.

It is unwarranted because the range of moral understanding is not exhausted by assuming that what appears best under the circumstances can be called " positively good." It cannot be consistently maintained, for example, that " killing 'innocent' people might be right " (p. 75). Killing innocent people, perhaps in wartime, may be unavoidable; it may even seem to be relatively good as the better course to take among limited alternatives; but it cannot be assigned unambiguous moral value. Rather, if " justification by grace " be taken seriously, one need not exonerate from moral responsibility by calling equivocal acts " right " or " positively good." Their contingent and provisional character can be recognized and accepted for what it is, namely, morally ambiguous however necessary! Forgiveness permits us to live without the choices we would have preferred but didn't have. But it is precisely this quality of the moral life that one misses in the situationist's baptism of existential necessity with the waters of normative relativism.

The value theory advocated here is, further, untenable because it establishes the base for the methodological model upon the exceptional case. Although Professor Fletcher introduces the method of situation ethics with deference to the place of principles in the decision-making process, every case which he cites as illustrative of the situational approach demonstrates abandonment of generally accepted maxims. For example, he relates parallel stories of two women whose crying children threatened the safety of their respective wagon trains moving west (p. 125). One woman killed her baby " with her own hands," and she and her companions reached the sanctuary of the fort; the other woman tried unsuccessfully to soothe her baby, and she and her party were discovered and destroyed by Indians. Fletcher's altogether rhetorical question, " Which woman made the right decision? " is much too simplistic in its implied answer. Moreover, he is guilty of doing precisely what he elsewhere condemns, namely, asking one to generalize value judgments without careful scrutiny of the whole range of contextual configurations. But, beyond all else, it is not inconceivable to me that a group of people might deliberately choose almost certain death (whether at the hands of Indians, Nazis, or the K.K.K.) rather than submit to existence bought at a cost which would reduce life to animality.

What emerges from *Situation Ethics* is a way of doing ethics which is certainly a corrective to old-line legalism and pietism. But if it were widely accepted and practiced, both Professor Fletcher and I would be put out of our jobs. For what is offered here requires no reflection from the " professional " moralist and theologian. Indeed, it is plain that the theologizing task is undertaken by anyone who thinks about " God," although this thinking need not be done within the perspective of systematic, historical, or dogmatic Christian reflection. What, precisely, this " God thinking" comes to is far from clear. . . .

IV

ASSAYS
AND ESTIMATES

S CHOLARLY RESEARCH PAPERS and technically competent perspective treatments, unlike reviews, do not put a book and its thesis starkly or unreferredly at the center of attention, somehow thereby distorting or even falsifying it. The papers here, with only the very slightest and unessential parts omitted, manage to put contextual or situation ethics in a frame of reference and under a magniscope which truly contribute to the future depth and reach of the debate. As in the earlier selections in this anthology, the reader will quickly see for himself that these careful assays and estimates fall all along the critical spectrum.

1.
EDWARD LeROY LONG, JR. — " The History and Literature of ' The New Morality ' "

THE TERM " the new morality " has come into popular use in recent theological journalism to refer to a variety of trends in ethical analysis, some of which are very old. It is a phrase which attracts much attention at the din-

From the article " The History and Literature of ' The New Morality ' " by Edward LeRoy Long, Jr., in *The Pittsburgh Perspective*, Vol. 3 (September, 1966), pp. 4–17. Used by permission.

ner table, tea party, and bull session and which has become recently discussed in the columns of popular newsmagazines, but which lacks precision as a theological category. It seems to be of greater interest when advocated by round-collared bishops than when discussed by noncollared campus beats, but neither seems overly precise in defining what is meant by the term. It is sometimes identified with a similar catchy phrase, " the death of God," which has become an object of popular attention in about the same era; but such an identification can only compound the confusion. Many expressions of the new morality presuppose a theocentric world view quite at variance with the outlook of religious atheism. . . .

I

The confusion which surrounds the use of the term " the new morality " stems in part from the fact that it has been applied to three or four distinctively separate kinds of movements in the last forty years. Some of these movements have been antithetical to each other. In 1928 Durant Drake of Vassar College published a book entitled *The New Morality*,[1] which was a thoroughgoing attack upon authoritarian and supernaturalistic ethics in the name of pragmatic naturalism. A few years later, G. E. Newsome of Selwyn College, Cambridge, and Chaplain to the English king, published a book [2] by the same title protesting the libertarian sexual ethics then advocated by Bertrand Russell. In this epoch the term " the new morality " was a product of naturalistic pragmatism and seems clearly to have been at odds with professed Christian thinking.

With the rise of existentialism as a " new " form of philosophy the meaning of the term " the new morality " changed. Existentialism engendered a nonprescriptive approach to ethical questions. It stressed the importance of the specific conditions of each ethical choice rather than the claim of rules and principles. The theological world was influenced in part by this new philosophical outlook. Indeed, it found much of it congenial and made common cause in many respects with its basic intentions. In 1950 the Roman Catholic world was explicitly warned against this alliance in the papal encyclical *Humani Generis* which called existentialism a " new philosophy of error " and declared it equally dangerous to a true theology because like idealism, immanentalism, and pragmatism " it tends to leave the unchanging essences of things out of sight, and to concentrate all its attention on particular existences."

In 1952 a papal allocution, *Acta Apostolicae Sedis,* again warned against moral judgments based upon considerations of situations alone; and on February 2, 1952, the Sacred Congregation of the Holy Office used the phrase " the new morality " in an allocution which condemned this approach to moral thinking and sought to arrest its influence in the academies and seminaries of the church. Bishop John A. T. Robinson therefore attributes the phrase to Pope Pius XII, at whose behest and authority the allocution was issued.[3]

The term as such seems not to have caused insurmountable difficulty for subsequent Catholic writers. Father Ignace Lepp, a French Roman Catholic priest, used it to entitle a book written in 1963,[4] some eleven years after the condemnation was issued. Lepp's book belongs on the left margin of acceptable Roman Catholic thinking and builds in part upon the categories of Teilhard de Chardin. Many of its arguments call for a flexible kind of moral thinking and would find approval among the advocates of the new morality in its more recent and more radical expressions, but the book does not partake of the hostility to principles as such that has been characteristic of the more radical formulations. Lepp considers conditions under which the application of prescriptive moralism creates serious violations of good sense and humane values, but he does not plead the case for an ethic based solely upon considerations of circumstances in the particularity of individual cases.

The allocution of 1952 condemned both " existentialist " and " situational " approaches to ethical thinking. From the standpoint of a traditional moral theology of essences and principles these two approaches undoubtedly seem much the same. But thinkers like Karl Rahner have managed to plead for much that they consider valuable in the existential insights while taking into account the strictures contained in the pope's discourse.[5] Care and caution is abundantly evidenced in Roman Catholic discussions of what may be valuable considerations to be garnered from existential and situational approaches, which the condemnation of 1952 does not seem to have totally erased from the pages of books with the *nihil obstat*. It also has brought forth some newly reinforced defenses of traditional morality.[6]

. . . Many of the most widely read treatments of Christian ethics from the Protestant perspective have incorporated insights which are now dubbed " the new morality," but which at the time of their writing were set forth as careful, deliberate, extensive, and scholarly efforts to spell out the ethical implications of the Reformation principle of justification by faith alone. In fact, the Protestant discussion of Christian ethics has for years been dominated by treatments in which elements of the new morality have been carefully explicated. Emil Brunner's *The Divine Imperative*,[7] Karl Barth's *Church Dogmatics* (especially Volumes II/2 and III/4) ,[8] and Dietrich Bonhoeffer's *Ethics*,[9] are among the Continental statements which soon found their way into the American discussions.[10] That there are very significant differences of structure and emphasis among these books must surely be kept in mind by any careful student of these trends, yet each of them in its own way has taken issue with the ethics of philosophical rationalism and of religiously inspired legalism.

In America the discussion of issues related to these matters did not take place with any fullness until the middle of the 1950's. It was heralded by an article by Paul Lehmann entitled "The Foundation and Pattern of Christian Behavior" in 1953.[11] Nels F. S. Ferré protested against the thrust for rational autonomy in Christian ethics in 1951.[12] George W. Forell brought Luther's ethical thinking to American attention in a new way in 1954.[13] But despite these several efforts the real impact of contextual and situational ethics did not strike the American theological consciousness until just before the 1960's.

At first, the main ingredients of such an approach were well expounded in books which made no mention of the phrase "the new morality." In 1958 Joseph Sittler published his provocative essay, *The Structure of Christian Ethics,* in which the principle-transcending nature of Jesus' teaching was portrayed with the image of "gull-like swoops."[14] H. Richard Niebuhr's posthumous work, *The Responsible Self,*[15] appeared in 1963 and presented the most careful statement of relational ethics as a generalized category yet made. Paul Lehmann's *Ethics in a Christian Context*[16] appeared the same year elaborating and defending a situational approach to decision-making as the single legitimate manner of doing Christian ethics. Almost all of these books claim to call the theological world back to a Biblical and Reformation type of ethic rather than forward to something "new."

The Protestant use of the term "the new morality" is even more recent. In October of 1959, Joseph Fletcher wrote about "the new look" in Christian ethics.[17] In 1963 Bishop Robinson entitled his chapter on morals in *Honest to God*[18] with the phrase "The New Morality," and like many of the other catchy aspects of that book this term stuck in the public consciousness. In 1963 Fletcher again set forth his view, this time speaking about ethics in "a new key." [19] Finally in February, 1966, he broke forth with the phrase itself in *Commonweal*,[20] and later this same year gathered all the previous discussions into a paperback entitled *Situation Ethics: The New Morality*.[21] The phenomenal interest in this book shows with what alacrity the public will flock to a theological catchword which arrives at a particular *kairos*.

Still another aspect of the new morality which must be mentioned is an emphasis upon the validity, authenticity, and importance of man's common social life. This point has been most vividly made, perhaps, by Harvey Cox in *The Secular City* [22] which welcomes both urbanization and the collapse of traditional religiosity as twin developments in the twentieth century. Bonhoeffer, who contributed to an existentially formulated statement of neo-Reformation ethics, began a prolonged discussion of religionless Christianity, a Christianity suitable for men who live in a "world come of age." Other writers have propelled the same theme along its snowballing path, including Ronald Gregor Smith [23] and Gayraud S. Wilmore.[24] John A. T. Robinson coupled these two themes together in *Honest to God,* devoting a chapter to each. Strictly speaking, these are related but not necessarily inseparable trends, since several versions of contextual ethics presuppose the church (or divinely formed *koinōnia*) to be the very locus of Christian decision-making. However, even such a strong advocate of a *koinōnia* ethic as Paul Lehmann has responded with evident enthusiasm to the outlook advanced by Cox.[25]

The extensive popular usage of the phrase "the new morality" has created something of a reaction among even its own innovators and defenders. Robinson has given vent to the feeling of frustration which rightly ought to perturb any careful theologian whose categories have become bandied about more in the marketplace than in the academy:

The phrase "the new morality" has overnight become a slogan — relieving those who use it of any need to distinguish between widely different views, or even to know what they are. Nothing, I judge, could be more injurious to the Church than this kind of blanket thinking. For if the response of churchmen is simply undifferentiating reaction, then it will merely confirm the image which we are constantly told is a caricature. And this would be tragic in an age in which Christian *discernment* was never more necessary.[26]

Canon Douglas A. Rhymes, himself a spokesman for the main tenets of the new morality, apparently would like to disclaim the name. Moreover, he is convinced that its approach to ethics is really not new at all but can be traced back to the mind of Christ himself.[27] Even the enthusiasts for the secular world have manifested second thoughts. In noting the warning cries sent up by critics of the position, Cox has confessed that "we should not dismiss conservative voices with a mere wave of the hand. They will turn out to be right unless we are able to manifest a degree of maturity, accountability, and adulthood which has not yet emerged, at least in the American mentality and probably not in the mentality of most nations today."[28]

II

Given the variety and complexity of ideas combined in the new morality — a variety and complexity often obscured by the quick and journalistic coverage it receives — dare any interpreter define what is meant by the term? It is both risky and difficult to attempt this, but without such an effort any future discussions of this matter will find it almost impossible to focus on the relevant issues. . . .

This approach to ethical decision seems, in the first place, to acknowledge that the claim of the person who stands in the concrete situation, either as recipient or dispenser of neighbor-love, is greater than the claim of any abstract conception of the right. The literature says this in many different ways: often this point is made negatively through a polemical attack upon rules and principles. But the positive implications of this declaration also deserve attention. Rhymes puts it this way: " The goodness of an action will be determined not by reference to some absolute codes based upon a law system of morality . . . but by what is the relevant action for that individual in order that he may live his life in its wholeness and secure the maximum welfare of all concerned in the situation." [29] Robinson complains that the traditional supernaturalist ethic which is concerned about some metaphysical or moral universal thereby subordinates the importance of the individual, who should be dealt with in the context of his personal needs.[30] Fletcher makes the same point when he says: " There are no ' values ' in the sense of inherent goods — value is what *happens to* something when it happens to be useful to love working for the sake of persons." [31] These quotations all presuppose a dichotomy between the claim of rules and the needs of neighbor, a dichotomy which once it is posed quite naturally elicits the judgment that neighbor-claims are prior.

The emphasis of the new moralist upon what hap-pens to persons has much in common with the professional stance of the healing arts. It is naturally suspicious of the judgmental stance of revivalist preaching. Terms like " authentic," " mature," and " therapeutic " convey the mood of this approach better than terms like " judgment," " law," and " guilt." Future statements of the new morality may make more of this contrast than most of the present statements have made, for up to this moment a preoccupation with the contrast between legalistic or principled ethics and ethics of response to particular situations has overshadowed many other potentially fruitful ways of setting forth the distinctive features of this " new " approach. If one examines the ways in which and the extent to which Paul Lehmann uses the term " maturity " in connection with his ethic, the portent of this development can be perceived.

Back of this is a distrust of the authoritarian temper, a distrust which finds frequent open and even more frequent veiled expression in the writings of these thinkers. Rules and principles are considered to be bad, not only because they do not take the needs of individual cases into account but because they are indigenous to closed and rigid moralities. Judgments tendered in the name of natural law as well as Scriptural legalism come in for severe criticism. Distrust of authoritarian legalism is certainly not a totally new thing in Christian ethics. It has an honorable history. What may be new in the new morality is the claim that such legalism can be overcome by revamping the basic structure of ethical thinking.

A second important aspect of the new morality is its willingness to make common cause with the moral practices of its culture. *It regards the moral changes that are taking place in our time as more to be welcomed and transformed than to be resisted or reversed.* It relaxes the tension between Christian faith and culture by moving toward a congenial acceptance of modern mores. Indeed, at times, it even hails modern culture as a more adequate channel for true morality than specifically religious cultures of the past. Kierkegaard may be the inspiration for the metaphysical assumptions of the new morality, but it hardly shares the motivations which prompted his *Attack on Christendom.*

Bishop Robinson begins his discussion of the new morality by suggesting that Christian thinking about morals calls for the same recasting of traditional outlooks in the light of the revolutionary changes in cultural behavior which are necessary with respect to Christian formulations about God's nature. He declares:

> There is no need to prove that a revolution is required in morals. It has long since broken out; and it is no " reluctant revolution." The wind of change here is a gale. Our only task is to relate it correctly to the previous revolution we have described and to try to discern what should be the Christian attitude toward it.[32]

. . . The new moralists have frequently said that Christianity is revolutionary, that it must turn its back upon the rural ethos and town culture with which it is presently identified. The more cautious and conservative spokesmen for the new morality have generally stated this conviction in general terms, as does Ignace Lepp, who declares, " All authentic morality is necessarily *revolutionary,* on the condition, evidently, that the word *revolution* is understood dialectically, the emphasis being put not upon the upsetting and destruction of what is but upon the creation of what must be." [33] In more radical statements of this theme, however, the critical dialectic implied by Lepp tends to relax in favor of an enthusiastic embrace of the revolutionary changes of our era. These are accepted, hailed as the work of God, and looked upon as the channels through which the Christian not only can, but is told he must, work if he is to be relevant in today's world. The culturally *avant garde* become the heroes. Everything from the thrust of colonial nations for self-destiny to campus mores about sex and personal behavior is looked upon as a potentially fruitful development.

It is wrong to think of the new morality merely as a more open attitude toward sex, though many defenders of the position have felt it necessary to counteract a popular tendency to make this identification. To be sure, the new moralists have addressed themselves to questions of sexual behavior, but they have just as often criticized the commercial exploitations of sex in modern culture as they have complained about the unfortunate consequences of religiously inspired prudery. The twofold emphasis which is characteristic of most analysis of this issue by the new moralists is nicely packaged by Joseph Fletcher in this sentence: " We do not praise a technical virgin whose petting practices are sexually unrestrained, nor do we condemn a loving transgressor of the law who is emotionally honest although technically unchaste." [34]

Yet a third feature of " the new morality " is its preoccupation with method. This may not be a self-conscious preoccupation nor a matter of deliberate attention, but who can read the literature of the movement without being struck with this characteristic locus of concern? As Paul Lehmann puts it, " The present analysis of Christian ethics as *koinonia* ethics is an attempt to take with full seriousness the methodological revolution in ethical thinking inaugurated by the Reformation." [35]

We have fallen so naturally into this preoccupation that its subtle effects upon the nature of ethical discourse may escape our notice. The new morality is essentially convinced that the central ethical issue concerns the ways in which decisions are approached and ethical judgments rendered. It blames the difficulties of the past upon faultiness of method and promises a new procedure for dealing with the problems of choice. The new procedure is set forth programmatically but always in terms of the description of the method rather than the specificity of its consequences. This inevitably subordinates questions about the content of moral behavior to questions about the process of moral decision.

There is, of course, no little discussion of the significance of love for Christian ethics in the literature of the new morality. Robinson puts it: " Nothing Prescribed — Except Love "; [36] Fletcher: " Love Is the Only Norm." [37]

This curious willingness to speak of love in terms

which are rigorously eschewed for all other value concepts might send linguistic analysts into a quandary. But this seemingly valuational espousal of love is consistent with the contextualist outlook because love alone always makes judgments intrinsically related to the situation. The Christian can be unreservedly committed to love since love commits him unreservedly to the needs of the person in the situation. It alone can be used to speak of the Christian obligation to meet the situation in terms of the situational demands.

> Love, alone, because, as it were, it has a built-in moral compass, enabling it to " home " intuitively upon the deepest need of the other, can allow itself to be directed completely by the situation. It alone can afford to be utterly open to the situation, or rather to the person in the situation, uniquely and for his own sake, without losing its direction or unconditionality.[38]

Apart from this seemingly valuational discussion of love, which is in reality a paradoxical affirmation of methodological maturity rather than the portrayal of a given quality of behavior, the situationalists concentrate upon a quite different locus of concern. It is a concern for the ways of ethical analysis and the proper way of describing how it should be undertaken.

III

. . . The spokesmen for the new morality can be grouped into those who present an excited, aggressive defense and those who look upon the new morality as a corrective and supplement to traditional ways of thinking about ethics. Likewise, the critics of the movement seem to divide into those who set forth a defensive rejection and those who would subject the claims of the new morality to a careful scrutiny and thorough exploration, raising issues in the process about its adequacy.

Consider first, representative examples of the aggressive advocacy. The front page of the issue of *Commonweal* which presented an interchange between Joseph Fletcher and Herbert McCabe carries the headline " Ethics at the Crossroads." Presumably we are at the junction where we must choose to go one way or the other, with no moderating interchange possible. Fletcher himself once said it this way:

> After forty years, I have learned the vital importance of the contextual or situational — i.e., the *circumstantial* — approach to the search for what is right and good. I have seen the light; I know now that abstract and conceptual morality is a mare's nest.[39]

Joseph Sittler's *The Structure of Christian Ethics* is, if my reading is not faulty, likewise a rigorous defense of a single way of dealing with ethical choices, as is Paul Lehmann's *Ethics in a Christian Context*. The zeal of new enthusiasm is coupled in these materials with the profound conviction that situational ethics has correctly understood the way in which Christians are to approach the making of ethical choices. This is it; the alternatives are wrong and must be replaced.

A different note is sounded by John A. T. Robinson in his *Christian Morals Today*.

> I believe that the " old " and the " new morality " (in any sense in which I am interested in defending the latter) correspond with two starting-points, two approaches to certain perennial polarities in Christian ethics, which are not antithetical but complementary. Each begins from one point without denying the other, but each tends to suspect the other of abandoning what it holds most vital because it reaches it from the other end.[40]

In expanding on this observation, Robinson finds values and functions in the old morality which seem hardly to be acknowledged by many of his fellow thinkers. Taken seriously, this would make for a very different kind of discussion than that which results from setting these two kinds of morality into mutually exclusive camps.

James Gustafson has termed the dichotomy between context and principles a "misplaced debate," and has pleaded for a broader and more empirical way of identifying all the different theological-ethical stances which can enter into various kinds of decision-making.[41] Max Stackhouse has made the same point as follows:

> A truly " historical " theology of history for the new social gospel would not be caught designating one " system," or level of experience, as crucial and call that " the essential one." But, as we have pointed out previously, neither is it sufficient to say they are all important all of the time, for the question of accents is crucial.[42]

In reading Roman Catholic thinkers about these issues, one is always aware of the restrictions under which they supposedly work. Yet, it cannot be presumed that men like Karl Rahner or Bernard Häring seek to combine the insights of the principled approach with those of situationalism simply because they are not free to embrace an unreserved kind of contextualism.[43]

Among the critical responses to the new morality two kinds of objections can be noted. On the one hand there are reiterated ethics of principles, insistent that there is a place for rules and guidelines. Paul Ramsey expresses this sort of sentiment when he declares:

> Theologians today are simply deceiving themselves and playing tricks with their readers when they pit the freedom and ultimacy of *agape* (or covenant-

obedience, or *koinonia,* or community, or any other primary theological or ethical concept) against rules, without asking whether *agape* can and may or must work through rules, and embody itself in certain principles which are regulative for the guidance of practice.[44]

John C. Bennett has given expression to much the same line of reasoning, while Robert E. Fitch [45] has blasted the new morality for substituting the tyranny of the contemporary for the authority of the traditional. These largely polemical responses might very well lead, as they have in the case of Herbert Waddams,[46] to a reaffirmation of the place of moral theology in Christian thinking.

On the other hand, there is a small growing body of literature which questions the adequacy of the new morality in quite different ways. It worries, for example, lest the new morality abandon the sense of judgment and tension with culture in its effort to avoid authoritarian errors. Bernard Meland has given expression to this concern as follows:

One thought that has troubled me in pondering the course of the present concern to secularize Christianity, and now the church's response to the moral life, is that its advocates seem to reflect the same romanticist attitude toward people outside the churches that motivated many earlier liberals and modernists. In their view they are people with whom alert churchmen and theologians must identify themselves. Their ways must be our ways. What is not meaningful to them or usable by them must be discarded. Christian faith must be streamlined to accord with the energetic and practical bent of mind that characterizes the modern person absorbed in the restrictive routines of the technological era, or in the swift-moving sophisticated life of public figures and the professional intellectuals. Is this not trading one mode of conformity for another, being acquiescent to the demands and conditions of a relativistic ethos instead of being puppets in the hands of an absolutistic and authoritarian church? [47]

John Fry has also raised the question whether contextual ethics really get down to the actualities of ethical decisions as commonly carried out by the ordinary individual.[48]

The future direction of this discussion is certainly not clear. Perhaps the issues have been canvassed so thoroughly that there is not much left to be said. On the other hand we have, perhaps, only opened for exploration very complex considerations about the nature of Christian decision. The months and years immediately ahead of us will alone tell whether the new morality is a passing enthusiasm, a truly liberating way of thinking about Christian ethics, or just another partially successful effort to state the truth of the gospel.

2.
ROBERT E. FITCH
— "The Protestant Sickness"

THERE is a Catholic strength, and its name is order. There is a Catholic sickness, and its name is tyranny. There is a Protestant strength, and its name is liberty. There is a Protestant sickness, and its name is anarchy. In the past several years the Roman Catholic Church has been moving to prevent its sickness, and to see that order is impregnated with liberty. Meanwhile, what has Protestantism been doing?

It has been moving in two opposite directions at the same time. On the level of polity, of ecclesiastical struc-

From the article "The Protestant Sickness," by Robert E. Fitch, in *Religion in Life*, Vol. 35, No. 3 (Fall, 1966), pp. 498–505. Copyright © 1966 by Abingdon Press. Used by permission of the publisher.

ture, it has been moving toward an enhancement of order. This is evident in various mergers, or in various
devices of comity or of cooperation. But on the level of
theology and of ethics — at least on the Anglo-American
scene — it has been moving toward an enhancement of
disorder. The current name for this chaos in ethics is
situationism or contextualism; in theology, it is atheism
or Christocentric humanism.

If we look at the Protestant sickness in a relatively be-
nign form, we have Joseph Fletcher's *Situation Ethics:
The New Morality.* This is probably the ablest Protestant
work on basic Christian ethics since Paul Ramsey's volume in 1950. It is marked by an erudition enormous in
breadth and in depth but without pedantry. It gives the
reader a sense of communion with the facts of life as
well as with the lore of learning. It exhibits orderly thinking in pressing a thesis to a logical conclusion. It offers
the impact of a mind in serious and sensitive quest of the
meaning of Christian love in our time. And it is written
with a vivacity that must delight the layman, and with a
lucidity that not even a professional theologian could obscure. I mean to see that all my students are exposed to it.

There is, however, a gentle fraud in the title. There
is nothing " new " in this ethics. For all its neoliberalist
precautions about pietism, moralism, and legalism, it is
pretty well dated back to the respectable liberalism of
the 1920's. Nor is it " situational," really. On the contrary, it is absolutist. It is more absolutist than anything
in Immanuel Kant. The fact that this is a love-absolu-
tism — " Love only is always good " — does not make
things better. It makes them worse. In the hands of hu-
mans, or in their hearts and heads, all absolutes are de-
stroyers. Absolutes are only for God.

Also there is here a lack of realism in social ethics. It
would be very nice to believe that " love and justice are
the same." But historically, contextually, situationally,
they have not often been so. Indeed, they are too often

in opposition to each other. Furthermore, the liberties which are gaily celebrated in this writing require in civil society a constitution, a structure of law, a Bill of Rights, which are not automatically engendered by antinomian orgies in faith and love and grace. Perhaps it is this blind spot in the author that makes him prefer Richard Niebuhr's *The Responsible Self* to the teachings of Reinhold Niebuhr. The fact is, Fletcher's neoliberalism is open to the very strictures against the old liberalism that Reinhold Niebuhr expressed in his famous Introduction to *Moral Man and Immoral Society* (1932).

By the same token, Fletcher's text is semi-Pelagian. It has not sufficiently considered love against the facts of sin and of suffering and in the light of the cross. And in its marvelous contempt for the inherited body of laws, commandments, principles, and rules — which teach us the discriminations of love and of justice — it liberates like a demolition bomb more than it gives birth like an act of creation. Personally I am leery of all love-absolutists. "Dangerous," indeed, is their doctrine, as Fletcher says; but dangerous above all to the works of love. If, moving in such company, I should meet a Joseph Fletcher, then the encounter could be a pleasant and a profitable one. But then, in such company, it is equally possible that I might run into the Grand Inquisitor.

The Protestant sickness derives in part from a myopia of the mind. With its inordinate passion for Christian novelty, it might do well to take another look at profane antiquity. For the first contextualist or situationist in ethics was Aristotle. He had a keen awareness of the existential dimension. Just as he taught that a virtue must be exercised without excess or defect, so he insisted that it must be expressed " at the right times and on the right occasions and towards the right persons and for the right causes and in the right manner." He knew also that there could be a difference between persons, or occasions, as to whether the excess or the defect should tempt one farthest from the mean. Essentially a pluralist (not a relativist) in his recognition of the reality of several values within the larger framework of the good, he insisted that good judgment must be used at all times. Yet with all his sensitivity to assorted situations, he knew there was an inclusive situation — the human one — which gives us standards for testing all local situations. . . .

Finally, there is the critical question as to what really defines the limits of the context or the situation or, for that matter, the character of the koinonia. Certainly the situation is not self-defining, any more than the Christian community. Indeed, I may choose to defy the situation seen in a narrow perspective when I view it in a larger perspective under God and in Christ. There is still such a thing as the generically human situation. There is still, for the understanding of love, the generically Christian context of the cross. But neither the larger context nor the immediate context will be illuminated by rhetorical gestures about love and grace and freedom. Both of them call for a great deal of painstaking analysis which, in its use of a historic resource of laws, commandments, principles, rules, is infinitely removed from any simplistic evangel in ethics.

At the heart of the Protestant sickness today lies an old idolatry — the idolatry of secularism. To be sure, the hierophants of this cult will insist that what they have hold of is something " new " — the very latest thing. It could be described more accurately as the very belatedest thing. And if I were a certain kind of orthodox Roman Catholic, with more of malice in my mind than charity could allow, I should find an ironical satisfaction in this subservience of Protestantism to secularism, since it would be my view that the rise of Protestantism and the rise of secularism are two coincidental movements in modern history. And I should read and then reread, with peculiar relish, Harvey Cox's *The Secular City.*

The subtitle of this book on the city calls us to "a celebration of its liberties and an invitation to its discipline." For instance: the paralysis of power, the breakdown of transportation, the failure of the water supply, newspapers suddenly out of circulation, garbage collection at a halt, the pollution of the atmosphere, the decay of churches and of public schools, the growth of slums, the exacerbation of ethnic divisions, the heightening of distinctions between the rich and the poor, the increase in crime, police corruption or police brutality, the inadequacy of the tax structure, the lack of civic responsibility, the absence of centralized political authority. These are the liberties we are to celebrate! This is the dicipline to which we should subject ourselves!

Perhaps at this point I have to prove that I am not just another barefoot boy from California. In fact, most of my life has been lived in great cities: Hangchow, Shanghai, Lausanne, Paris, London, New York, Los Angeles, the San Francisco Bay area. Indeed, I think I savor and am grateful for the advantages of a great metropolitan area as much as anyone else. But I am not prepared to bow down before this Babylon and worship it. And the heroic mayors or councils of citizens who have wrought significant reconstructions in Boston, New Haven, Rochester, Philadelphia, Pittsburgh, Fresno, Coventry, Rotterdam, have not done so by going into ecstasies over the anonymity, mobility, pragmatism, and profanity of their urban cultures. On the contrary, they have acted more in the mood of Jeremiah — first to pluck up and to pull down, and then to build and to plant.

No doubt Mr. Cox will explain that he, too, is on the side of these heroic mayors and councils of citizens. But I begin to be troubled by Mr. Cox's explanations — both for their ingenuity and for their superabundance. For example, in a debate between Harvey Cox and Andrew

Greeley in *Commonweal* (November 12, 1965) one might think it necessary to choose to believe either what Mr. Greeley said Mr. Cox said, or what Mr. Cox said he said. But after a careful scrutiny of this debate and again of *The Secular City,* I find myself forced to believe what both of them said he said. The fact is, there is a basic ambiguity of outlook, an irreducible uncertainty of perspective, in the writings of Harvey Cox. His idolatry of secularism has in it more of ardor than his vision of God and his church has clarity and conviction. All the erudition, all the intellectual adroitness, and all the literary skills Mr. Cox has at his command cannot cover up this basic confusion. . . .

3.
HENLEE H. BARNETTE — " The New Ethics: ' Love Alone ' "

. . . As TRADITIONALLY interpreted, Christian ethics appear to be inadequate as a moral guide in our complex culture. Indeed, as the editor of *Look* magazine declares: " We are witnessing the death of the old morality. In our world of masses of people, jet-age travel, nuclear power and fragmented families, conditions are changing so fast that the established moral guidelines have been yanked from our hands." [1]

This, in spite of the fact that our century has had great theological ethicists in the Niebuhrs, Tillich, Barth, and Brunner. The ethical thrusts of these men appear to be waning, and the search is on for a new approach to ethics. Not only theologians but scientists are calling for a new morality. Harlow Shapley, the Harvard astronomer,

From the chapter " The New Ethics: ' Love Alone,' " pp. 32–49, in *The New Theology and Morality,* by Henlee H. Barnette. Copyright © 1967 The Westminster Press. Used by permission.

declares: " We need an ethical system suitable for now —
for this atomic age — rather than for the human society
of two thousand years ago.[2]

I. A Trio of Situationists

In response to the challenge of the moral situation, a
group of theologians is emerging who espouse what has
come to be known as the " new morality," " contextual
ethics," or " *Situationsethik.*" This new thrust in Christian ethics stresses the primacy of love without law. It
is a reaction against the old morality of laws, rules, and
moral principles as guides to conduct.

This approach to moral issues is inductive rather than
deductive, beginning with concrete facts of a specific
ethical situation rather than with moral laws or principles. It insists that the demand of God must be perceived in the moment of concrete experience rather than
in principles or laws of conduct abstracted from the
moment.

1. Rudolf Bultmann: " As thyself "

" Radical obedience " in love is the central motif in
the ethics of Rudolf Bultmann. By this he means " *to
listen for and respond to the Word of God speaking
through the situation in which one exists.*" [3] Radical
obedience is an eschatological ethic. God's reign is breaking in now, and impinging now, summoning men to live
now in terms of God's coming reign. This eschatological
content demands radical obedience in the present tense.

Thus in his idea of radical obedience, Bultmann is
attempting to synthesize the older liberal view of the
ethical teaching of Jesus to be applied to problems and
the thoroughgoing eschatologists (Weiss and Schweitzer)
who held that the ethical imperatives of Jesus were " in-
terim ethics." Bultmann holds that the eschatological

and ethical teachings of Jesus cannot be separated.[4] Hence, decision and obedience have their ground in the eschatological teachings of Jesus. For the future forces impinge upon man in the *present*, requiring of him decision for God or the world now. Readiness for God's future demands obedience to his will in the present. The content of radical obedience is love, and no one is ready for God's reign unless he loves his neighbor whom he meets. Man is to live and love his neighbor as if the end, the *eschaton*, were present. Here, " end " does not mean chronological end, but the end of a false understanding of ourselves and history. It is the end time of ultimate judgment and decision.

Bultmann makes a distinction between " formal " obedience and "radical" obedience. Judaic legalism, in which the law had lost its content but retained its form, is characteristic of the former. Formal obedience, therefore, has to do with conformity to external rules. Radical obedience involves the total person, his being and his doing. Man is obedient in his being as well as in his doing.

God's demand, according to Bultmann, is not an abstract system of ethics apart from the demand of the moment, but to be radically obedient in the moment. Man " hears " God's word in the concrete situation. Somehow the demand of the moment is discernible, for God's demand is written into the situation. If we do not hear it, the fault is ours. The self cannot bring with it any standards of the past, for it is a standardless moment, but allows the moment to create its own unique demand. Hence, the moment contains *all* that is necessary to understand the will of God.[5]

However, Bultmann does admit that what the moment demands is made clearer by a knowledge of precedents and consequents. But a moral decision made in relation to one's neighbor in the moment is never determined by such knowledge. Man knows what he ought to do in the moment, but not out of rational analysis or previous ethical knowledge. The morally good action cannot be known until it is revealed in the situation. It is disclosed out of the situation of the moment.

But what does the moment demand? It does *not* demand a *what* (a specific action) but a *that* (that one is to be responsible). It demands that we love in every situation. The *what* or the content of love must be left to the individual in his concrete situation. God does not specifically tell us *what* we are to do, but *that* we are responsible, allowing us to choose how we are to be specifically responsible. For example, the great commandment of love says nothing about the content of love, only that we are to love our neighbor as ourselves. Says Bultmann, " The demand for love needs no formulated stipulations," as seen in the parable of the good Samaritan.[6]

Bultmann argues that everyone *knows* how to love his neighbor because he knows how he wishes to be loved. The love commandment simply tells us we ought to love our neighbor, not what we must do to love him. " As thyself " is the key to the content of the demand of God in the moment. One simply has not heard the call of the neighbor if he legalistically asks the question what he is to do.[7]

For Bultmann, love is not emotion or sympathy, for love does not depend on man's feelings, but on the command of God. Man loves because the neighbor is in need, and his need constitutes the demand of God in the moment. Thus the neighbor is every person who meets us in the moment with a concrete need.

By now it is obvious that radical obedience as Bultmann sees it cannot be the ground for a systematic theory of ethics because it refers to a specific and concrete relation to existence. Once radical obedience is conceptualized, it loses its concreteness, historicity, and existentiality which distinguishes it from other ethics.

As we have seen, Bultmannian radical obedience operates out of an eschatological view of history. It also involves an existential view of man. At this point, Bultmann was greatly influenced by the philosopher Martin Heidegger; namely, his presupposition that *man's being is a possibility of being*. Human existence is not a static being with a "fixed" nature, but a being constantly choosing itself. Man is always in the midst of *choosing who he is*. Therefore, human *nature* possesses no constants that may be relied upon in any given situation. Hence, there can be no systematic ethics organized only on the basis of human nature. Man is always striving toward a goal, but the goal is left undetermined by his ontological structure. Death to the old life and *becoming* is the law of the obedient life. Man's possibility for the authentic life can only be achieved in response to the proclamation of the gospel. This is what he calls *ontic* possibility for authenticity.[8]

Man lives in his *intentionality*. He is in search for authentic selfhood. Man knows that he *is* not what he *ought* to be. He knows that his life consists in a struggle to become an authentic self, that is, to really be himself, to be what he *ought* to be. The theologian sees the demand of God as none other than authentic selfhood. In response to the deed of God in Christ, man becomes a new being, an authentic self.[9]

2. John A. T. Robinson: "Nothing Prescribed — Except Love"

Another contextualist in ethics is John A. T. Robinson, Bishop of Woolwich. In 1963, Robinson published a small volume entitled *Honest to God*,[10] which had a bombshell effect on both sides of the Atlantic. The response ranged from high praise to severe condemnation. The debate about the book continues unabated.[11] Robinson borrows from Bonhoeffer's idea of a "religionless

Christianity," and Jesus the "man for others"; from Bultmann's demythologizing theory; and from Tillich's concept of God as the "Ground of all Being." Theism is gone, Robinson says, because men today do not find God "up there" or "out there." As the "Ground of Being," however, he may still be found in the depth of experience. Thus Robinson abandons the idea of spatial transcendence, concluding that God is the "Ground of all Being." Christologically Robinson follows the New English Bible: "What God was, the Word was." In other words, if one looked at Jesus, one saw God: "He who has seen me has seen the Father" (John 14:9). Drawing on Bonhoeffer, Robinson says "Jesus is 'the man for others', the one in whom Love has completely taken over, the one who is utterly open to, and united with, the Ground of his being." [12] To be in Christ is to be a new being. "It is the life of 'the man for others', the love whereby we are brought completely into one with the Ground of our being, manifesting itself in the unreconciled relationships of our existence." [13]

Robinson's chapter on ethics is labeled "The New Morality," a popular cognate of "situation ethics." It appears that this phrase was inspired by Pope Pius XII in 1952 to describe situational ethics in a radio message, "The Christian Conscience." Here he made the terms "existential" and "situational" synonymous. Four years later "situational ethics" was labeled "the new morality" by the Supreme Sacred Congregation of the Holy Office and banned from all academies and seminaries.[14] For Robinson, morality is situational; that is, response to the specific, immediate grasp of the will of God rather than dependence on rules or natural law. "Man come of of age" demands a "new morality" and Robinson proceeds to provide it.

A rather sharp contrast is drawn between the "old" and the "new" morality. The old is deductive, beginning with absolute standards, eternally valid, remaining unchanged, and to be applied in the midst of change. The new morality is inductive and begins from " the other end," namely, " unselfregarding *agapē* " in the particular situation. *Agapē* is the one constant element in the distinctively Christian response in every age, for it produces in the Christian, however diversely placed, a style of life that is recognizably the same.[15]

The old morality starts with principles, the new with persons. It proceeds empirically from the particular to the general. Traditional deductive morality tends to be *antihumanist,* being oriented to supernatural principles which sometimes take precedence over persons and to which they must conform regardless of the circumstances. The new morality emphasizes " the priority of persons over principles." [16]

Robinson admits, however, that society needs certain laws and rules to survive. Actions such as stealing, lying, killing, and committing adultery are wrong because they are destructive to human relations. But he says that we cannot mean that these are always wrong, as, for example, killing in a just war may be right.[17]

Also there are blocks of ethical teachings in the Gospels and epistles for the ordering of the life of the church, and these come to us through the church. But these teachings for the early church can be a distortion in the church today. The ultimate criterion of conduct is not an ethical code, but selfless and sacrificial *agapē* in the moment of decision. The one important thing that really counts is " treating persons as persons with unconditional seriousness." [18] This is the end at which the new morality begins.

According to Robinson, the *content* of Christian morals changes with changing situations. A change, for example, in biological, technological, or psychological knowledge may modify our understanding of the responsibility involved. He then proceeds to supply several illustrations. Take the problem of divorce. The traditional teaching of the church is that marriage ought never to be dissolved. In the case of Protestants, of course, divorce may be allowed for adultery. Divorce, therefore, is always wrong with the one exception of fornication. The Matthean exception is an addition by the writer (Matt. 5:32) and has been made a law by church and state. To say that all divorce involves adultery is not true. If a wife had already committed fornication, one cannot, technically, make her an adulteress, for this she has already made herself. Any divorce of a wife is to make her morally and not legally an adulteress. Jesus also speaks of *lust* as the moral equivalent of adultery, but no one treats it as legislation. Paul, himself, allows persons who become Christians to divorce their pagan partners if these will not live with them (I Cor. 7:12-16). The practice of cohabitation in celibacy (I Cor. 7:36-38) in the teachings of Paul would hardly be acceptable today. Indeed, cohabitation in celibacy would be considered a scandal — certainly among the clergy! [19]

All of this is to say that while the church must have rules, these rules are not necessarily timeless. Take the problem of homosexuality, for example. Love also is to determine our attitude toward the homosexual. Pressures from the empirical side have already forced us to alter our attitude toward this problem. In 1957, the Wolfenden Report stated that " homosexual behaviour between consenting adults in private should no longer be a criminal offence." [20] In the case of homosexuality, inductive ethics begins with the empirical, with persons, and through love these are to be helped to solve their problems.

At the heart of Robinson's ethics is love. He sums it up:

> Love alone, because, as it were, it has a built-in moral compass, enabling it to " home " intuitively upon the deepest need of the other, can allow itself to be directed completely by the situation.[21]

Love alone is the only ethic "which offers a point of constancy in a world of flux and yet remains absolutely free for, and free over, the changing situation.[22] Admittedly, we must have laws and conventions in society, for these are "the dykes of love" in a world that has lost its way. But they must be defined situationally and not prescriptively, in terms of persons and not principles. His is a plea for the priority of love over everything else. This is the only ethic for "man come of age."[23]

3. Joseph Fletcher: "Love and Nothing Else"

The third person of the triumvirate that espouses "love alone" ethics is Joseph Fletcher. . . . He claims that basically there are only three approaches to making moral decisions — legalistic, antinomian, and situational (a way between rules of legalism and antinomian unprincipledness).[24]

For Fletcher, Christian situation ethics has only one norm — the *agapē* of the commandment to love God and neighbor. All rules, principles, ideals, and norms are only *contingent,* only valid if perchance they serve love in any situation. These may serve as *illuminators,* but not *directors,* in moral decisions. Hence, "*only* love and reason really count when the chips are down"[25] In capsule form, situational strategy is a method that proceeds from one law, *agapē* (love), to *sophia* (wisdom) of the church and culture, to *kairos* (moment of decision, the fullness of time) in which the responsible self in the situation decides whether *sophia* can serve love there.[26]

Four presuppositions are inherent in this approach to decision-making: pragmatism (a strategy which holds that to be correct or right a thing must *work,* but in situation ethics love is the standard of rightness); relativism (love is the constant and all else variable); positivism (theological positivism in which faith propositions are affirmed voluntaristically and not rationalistically); and personalism (people and not things are at the center of concern). Put together, these principles take the shape of action, existence, and eventfulness. Hence, the situation ethic is one of " *making* decisions rather than ' looking them up ' in a manual of prefab rules." [27]

In situation ethics, conscience (moral consciousness) is a function, not a faculty. Conscience is taken into account only when it is acting and deciding. Moreover, situation ethics is concerned with antecedent, not consequent, conscience, " with prospective decision-making rather than with retrospective judgment-passing." [28]

The core of situation ethics consists of six propositions.[29] Proposition one points to the nature of value, the " rock bottom " issue in all ethics — namely, the only intrinsic good is love: " nothing else at all." On the reverse side, the only thing that is intrinsically bad is malice. Love is a predicate with men, and only with God is it a property because God *is* love and finite men only *do* love. No law, principle, or value is good as such — not life, truth, chastity, property, marriage, or anything but love. Hence such acts as lying and suicide are not always wrong, for these are contingent upon the situation.

In his second proposition, Fletcher declares that love is the ultimate norm of Christian decision. Jesus himself set aside the law of the Sabbath for the higher law of love in the healing of the man with the withered hand, and Paul was permissive about circumcision. *Agapē* seeks " the neighbor's good radically, nonpreferentially." [30] Hence, Christian ethics is not " a scheme of codified conduct," but separates " the creed from the *code,* but not from conduct " as some critics charge.[31]

Love is the only norm of conduct. Jesus put his stamp of approval on the translegality of the action of David, who, when he was hungry, went into the house of God and ate the bread of the Presence which was not lawful except for the priests (Matt. 12:3-4). Thus, the ultimate norm of conduct is love and nothing else.

Proposition three equates love and justice, for the latter is love distributed. Love of the generic " neighbor " in the teachings of Jesus and Paul must be converted into a plural " neighbors." Hence, justice is love working out its problems; it is Christian love using its head and calculating its duties.[32] Justice, therefore, is love distributed.

Proposition four embodies the view that love wills the neighbor's good whether we like him or not. Love and liking are not the same thing, for the former is benevolence and goodwill. There is nothing sentimental about love. It is not an emotional but an attitudinal ethic, volitional, and can be commanded.

Proposition five declares that only the end justifies the means. Classical Christian ethics accepted the doctrine that " the end does not justify the means." Fletcher asks that, if it doesn't, what does? The answer is, " Nothing! " [33] But, unless justified by some end in view, any action is meaningless, pointless. Referring to Paul, who says that it is not being " lawful " that makes a thing good, but whether it is expedient, edifying, constructive, Fletcher makes his case for " agapeic expediency," for only love can make a thing " lawful." [34]

To the question, " Does an evil means always nullify a good end? " Fletcher says, " No," for it all depends upon the situation. In this world of relativities, " we may do what *would* be evil in some contexts if *in this one* love gains the balance." [35] For example, if the emotional and spiritual welfare of both parents and children in a *particular* family can best be served by a divorce, then love requires it.

The sixth proposition of Fletcher attempts to validate every judgment within its own context. Hence, decisions should be made situationally, not prescriptively. He accepts Emil Brunner's principle that the divine command is always the same in the *Why*, but always different in the *What*.[36] Christians should not, therefore, underestimate this relativism in ethics. They must put away their childish rules and learn love's tactics.[37]

Fletcher, in his postscript, notes that situationism in Christian ethics is a reaction against legalism. Contextual or situational ethics, he feels, is freedom from legalism and the sense of guilt it engenders. Man is free " when we tailor our ethical cloth to fit the back of each occasion." [38] This is what he calls " neocasuistry." Like classical casuistry it is case-focused, concrete, and concerned to bring Christian imperatives to bear upon practical issues. However, it is unlike classical casuistry in that it repudiates any attempt to prescribe " real-life decisions in their existential particularity." [39] It is always " a casuistry obedient to love." [40] The tactical formula for the strategy of love is: " *The indicative plus the imperative equals the normative.* What is, in the light of what love demands, shows what ought to be." [41] He concludes that Christian ethics is not " a scheme of living according to a code but a continuous effort to relate love to a world of relativities through a casuistry obedient to love; its constant task is to work out the strategy and tactics of love, for Christ's sake." [42]

II. CRITICAL EVALUATION

We have briefly examined " love alone " ethics and three persons who champion it. A critical analysis of their conclusions reveals both strengths and weaknesses. These are suggested below.

1. Strengths of the Situationists

One cannot but be impressed with the ethical seriousness of Bultmann, Robinson, and Fletcher. Christianity is an ethical faith as well as a theological one. It is a way of life undergirded by faith in God as revealed in Jesus Christ. It is always refreshing to read theologians who include both theological and ethical dimensions in their presentation of Christianity.

Love is the central motif of Christian ethics for all three men. In this they follow the New Testament pattern. Jesus laid down no rules for Christian conduct. He was not a new Moses handing down laws to govern behavior. Rather, he presented illustrations and principles of the Christian style of life. Christian morality, therefore, cannot be reduced to a legalistic set of rules applicable to every person in all situations.

Concern for persons in preference to abstract moral rules does have merit. Traditional morality with its " Thou shalt not's " is hardly the approach to take when counseling with people who are in serious trouble. To offer such persons a code without compassion does appear to be " antihumanist." The Christian way of meeting the spiritual needs of men is to be redemptive, and this means to treat them as persons. For example, the notion that chastity is a part of charity, the expression of caring enough for a person not to use him or her, is an excellent one. While this has Kantian overtones, it is also in keeping with the Christian ethic of love. Actually, Robinson does not, as charged, condone premarital sexual experience. His emphasis is upon approaching the problem in the spirit of love rather than law.

Again, situation ethics is largely a methodology of ethics. As such, it will undoubtedly serve as a stimulus for some serious and much-needed research in the area of the methodology of ethics. Here is an area of ethics, particularly Christian ethics, that demands, in the light of the radical social change of our century, some solid research. The confusion that reigns in contemporary moral life is, to some extent, due to a lack of understanding the basis of moral authority, the central ethical imperatives, and how moral decisions are to be made in concrete situations. A long step toward clarification of these issues is the development of a correct methodology in ethics.

Professional counselors and concerned pastors are especially appreciative of the situationalist's emphasis upon the new casuistry and the need for beginning with persons with problems rather than with prefabricated moral laws. From the standpoint of pastoral psychology, Seward Hiltner is enthusiastic about Fletcher's notion of " neo-casuistry." Hiltner is right in noting that in " rejecting one kind of casuistry, Protestantism impeded any kind of ' case ' approach, which pastoral care and pastoral psychology have finally got around to." [43] There are signs now of renewed interest in Richard Baxter's *The Christian Directory* and some concern for a Protestant casuistry. No doubt Fletcher's approach will provide impetus toward a more realistic Protestant study of casuistry.

Finally, the works of Robinson and Fletcher will serve as catalysts for a more serious study of Christian ethics by laymen. Teachers of Christian ethics are always a bit miffed when their discipline is identified in the popular mind with etiquette! Perhaps the situationists may serve to stimulate more study of Christian ethics in depth.

2. Shortcomings of the Situationists

Exponents of situation ethics betray certain basic weaknesses. Already in popular magazines and scholarly journals numerous articles are appearing condemning and praising the " new morality." Some pieces reflect more emotion than elucidation, more condemnation than comprehension. Here we shall attempt to bring the more constructive criticisms to bear upon the situationists.

Bultmann speaks of the " standardless moment " of moral decision. But he cannot escape the use of at least one " principle " — that of loving one's neighbor " as thyself." He assumes, erroneously, that everyone knows how to love in keeping with this moral imperative. What he throws out of the front door — ethical principles — he bootlegs in the back door. His assumption that every man "knows what is good" is, to say the least, highly questionable. His view of love tends toward subjectivism, and his concept of the "moment" is constantly in danger of becoming an abstraction.

Robinson and Fletcher lay themselves open to several valid criticisms. There is ambiguity with reference to the use by both of them of the terms "situation" and "love." One is never certain what they mean by these terms. To lay all stress upon love in the "right situation" is to talk about an abstraction, to raise an issue that is nonexistent. Just what the right situation may be is never described with any factuality.

The word "love" is also confusing as used by the situationists. Nowhere do they describe in a systematic fashion their various uses of love. As James Gustafson notes specifically in the case of Fletcher, love refers to everything he wants it to mean: the intrinsically good, justice, principle, disposition, ruling norm, etc.[44]

Both Robinson and Fletcher give priority to love, but they do so at the expense of the content of love. Love is the fulfillment of the law, but it does not abrogate the law. Love goes beyond the law, and is a higher order of morality for Christians. Paul provides content to love by pointing out that love of neighbor involves the principles of the Decalogue relating to conduct toward neighbor. "The commandments, 'You shall not commit adultery, You shall not kill, You shall not steal, You shall not covet,' and any other commandment, are summed up in this sentence, 'You shall love your neighbor as yourself.' Love does no wrong to a neighbor; therefore love is the fulfilling of the law." (Rom. 13:9-10; cf. Mark 12:29 ff.; Gal. 5:14.)

It is true that both Robinson and Fletcher recognize some need for laws and principles. Robinson appears to accept the law at one end and to deny it at the other. At times he is a proponent of "rule-agapism" and at other times "act-agapism."[45] Fletcher declares that love plus the situation makes for right action. But then he speaks of love as a principle and as using its head. It appears that Robinson and Fletcher want to eat their ethical cake and have it too!

Both Robinson and Fletcher tend to equate the moral law with ecclesiastical law. The law forbidding David and other nonpriestly persons from eating " the bread of the Presence " appears to be as sacrosanct as laws about adultery, murder, and lying.[46] Certainly rules of religion must be set aside to meet human need, but they are not the moral law. Just because such ecclesiastical regulations were set aside by Jesus does not mean that all moral law is to be discarded when it is convenient to do so.

" Love alone," or situation ethics, is characterized by a one-sided methodology in arriving at moral decisions. It is a misplaced emphasis, a false polarization in Christian ethics. James Gustafson, of Yale Divinity School, has convincingly written that the umbrella named " contextualism " or " situationism " has become so large that it covers persons whose views are as different and divergent as some of the defenders of the " principles " approach.[47] He shows that Christian ethics begins from at least four points (situational, principle, theological, and relation to Jesus Christ), and regardless of which one is primary for the Christian ethicist, he moves toward the other three in the extension of his ethical posture with a Christian frame of reference.[48]

All emphasis upon extreme cases, the exception in Christian ethics, plays down the rule, limits ethical perspective, and often determines the moral answer before the existential moment of decision. For example, in 1804 at a logrolling near Louisville, Kentucky, the question arose as to whether or not a man would be justified in telling a falsehood under certain circumstances. This illustration was proposed: " Suppose a man has five children. The Indians come and kill four of them, the fifth one being hidden nearby. The savages then ask the father if he has another child, would he be justified in telling them that he had not?" The dispute waxed hot and finally got into the Long Run Baptist Church and split it into the "lying" and the "no-lying" Baptist churches! [49]

Situation ethicists would, in the above situation, hold that the most loving act would be to lie and save the life of the child. Hence, the moral decision is determined before the ethical problem arises, a flat contradiction of their contention that prior moral decisions must not be made until the existential situation presents itself. Each situation is different and the individual is to do the will of God as it is revealed to him in the moment of decision. Under God, in this instance, the right act may be to say nothing or to refuse to reveal the whereabouts of the hidden child. There could be alternatives, but the situationists dogmatically decide beforehand what the moral decision is to be, namely, to lie and save the child.

Both Robinson and Fletcher are "act-utilitarian" (acting in the way that will likely produce the greatest balance of good over evil) when they move from personal to social relations. Fletcher states that when the love ethic seeks a social policy, it must form a coalition with utilitarianism, taking over from Bentham and Mill the principle of "The greatest good of the greatest number." However, in the coalition, *agapē* replaces the pleasure principle, the hedonistic calculus becomes the agapeic calculus. Happiness is doing the will of God, and utility sets the Christian to seeking his own happiness by seeking his neighbor's good on the widest possible scale. [50]

Fletcher clearly resorts to the principle of utility rather than revelation to relate love to social action. He does this because he knows that it is impossible to derive all our duties in the larger social life from love alone. And he must be aware of the fact that it is as difficult to derive what is the just thing to do from utility as it is from love. Christian theologians from Thomas Aquinas to

Emil Brunner have confronted this problem and have found no easy solution.

Finally, situationists tend to lack theological breadth and depth. Robinson's God is too small, too restricted to provide an adequate dynamic for his love ethic. God may be the " Ground of our being," but he also has other dimensions — " out there," " up here," and " under there," as well as " in here." God cannot be packaged in the neat definition of " Ground of Being." Noticeably absent in Fletcher is any serious concern for repentance, judgment, human nature, and redemption. Robinson leaves the impression that modern man is grown up and therefore has little need for spiritual help outside of himself.

Robinson betrays a naïve view of sin. He admits that there is a whole class of actions (stealing, lying, killing, and adultery) that are so destructive of human relations that no differences of time or society can change their character.[51] But this does not mean that in certain circumstances these could never be right. Yet, he has no answer to the questions of rape and incest. Can they ever be justified by motives, circumstances, and consequences?

III. Toward a More Realistic Morality

Situationism is a needed corrective for overemphasis upon laws, codes, rules, and principles. But it is not a self-sufficient methodology in Christian ethics. Hence, the corrective stands in need of a corrective, for it is too limited a system. The Christian ethic is so rich and varied that it is not a matter of either the freedom and ultimacy of pure act-agapism or pure rule-agapism.[52] Christian ethics involves both *agapē and principles* for its completion. That *agapē* indicates certain norms of behavior, general principles that embody its own nature, may be seen in its qualities and in the statements of what it demands (I Cor., ch. 13). Principles do not restrain the freedom of love, but provide concreteness and fulfillment in Christian action. Principle-agapism furnishes content and guidelines for the direction that love may take in concrete situations. Hence, principle-agapism saves Christian ethics from the twin perils of legalism and antinomianism. It takes into account the situation and seeks the most loving norms of action.

To rule out general principles of conduct in Christian ethics is to limit the freedom of love in determining the right, to impose too heavy a burden upon the conscience in decision-making, and to disregard the past accumulated moral wisdom of the Christian faith.[53]

It appears to this writer that Christian ethics can remain contextual without dispensing with principles. As has been noted, Bultmann, Robinson, and Fletcher are unable to dispense with principles altogether. Bultmann admits that they are helpful precipitates out of past experience, though the decision of the moment is never determined by such knowledge. "Decision is not dice-throwing," he says, and its character is clearer when practical possibilities are understood.[54] As indicated above, he makes love of neighbor "as thyself" a universal principle. Robinson declares that the link "between bed and board, between sex and the sharing of life at every level, must be pressed as strongly as ever." [55] This is, in fact, a statement of principle. Fletcher's act-agapism drives toward principles by falling back upon reason, "neo-casuistry," and the summary rule as truths to be discerned by the Christian in decision-making.

Hence, there is no escape from the use of principles in Christian ethics. The Christian brings to the situation not only his awareness of redemption, Biblical ethical wisdom, and common sense but also the general objectives of order, freedom, truth, and concern as guides to prevent decisions from being blind. Love-embodying principles can serve in an advisory, if not always definitive, role in moral decisions.[56]

There is more — the function of the Holy Spirit in moral decisions, a sadly neglected factor by almost all Christian ethicists.[57] Yet the fruit of the Spirit is presented in ethical terms: love, joy, peace, patience, kindness, goodness, faithfulness, gentleness, self-control (Gal. 5:22-23). Christian character and hope are made possible "because God's love has been poured into our hearts through the Holy Spirit which has been given to us" (Rom. 5:5). Without the energizing and enabling power of the Spirit the Christian ethic is impossible. For it is the Spirit who ultimately informs the Christian in concrete moral decisions and guides him "into all the truth" (John 16:13).

4.
RICHARD A. McCORMICK, S.J.
— "Notes on Moral Theology"

. . . IN AN AGE of mass communications it was inevitable that this discussion would shift from tome to table talk. In the process of its popularization it has lost some of its theological rootage and precision, but none of its liveliness. The three best-known popular exponents of a "situation ethics" are Canon Douglas A. Rhymes,[1] Prof. Joseph Fletcher,[2] and Bishop John A. T. Robinson.[3] Since Rhymes and Fletcher have written during the past semester, my summary will consist of excerpts from their writings.

The first difficulty one encounters in making a précis and comments on Fletcher-Rhymes is the problem of rhetoric. It is here that Fletcher is at his best as a situationist. What he says of acts ("Goodness is what happens to an act, it is not in the act itself") could be applied to his use of words: "Meaning is what happens to a

From "Notes on Moral Theology," in *Theological Studies*, Vol. 27 (December, 1966), pp. 612–617. Used by permission.

word, it is not in the word itself." Fletcher is dangerously close to the absolutism he abhors in adhering to
this. Thus, Gustafson in his rather devastating review
has noted that:

> "Love" like "situation" is a word that runs
> through Fletcher's book like a greased pig. . . . No-
> where does Fletcher indicate in a systematic way his
> various uses of it. It refers to everything he wants
> it to refer to. It is the *only* thing that is intrinsically
> good; it *equals* justice; it is a formal *principle;* it is
> a *disposition,* it is a predicate and not a property,
> it is a ruling norm, etc.[4]

Others have noted this same thing in Canon Rhymes.
Robert E. Fitch, dean of the Pacific School of Religion,
has gathered some of these phrases together under the
rubric of fetish phrases: mature, adult, responsible, relational, provisional, contextual, etc. He refers to it all
as " the flourishing of shibboleths. . . . We look up for
the water of life, but are drowned under a cascade of
clichés.[5] Similarly, Union Theological's Tom Driver,
after calling attention to the neon words in this rhetoric
(" maturity," " responsibility," " love "), asks simply:
" Who can disagree with such statements? "[6] Bernard
E. Meland, formerly of the University of Chicago, sees
" maturity " and " responsibility " in Rhymes as weasel
words. He asks: " Mature in what sense? Responsible to
whom or what? "[7]

The matter of rhetoric is important beyond the fun
poked at it by its critics. It constitutes a kind of methodology by incantation which makes it terribly hard to
know what Fletcher is actually saying. Certainly he is
against legalism; but we all are or should be. Certainly
he is for maturity, responsibility, and love. But are we
not all? The intent, then, is beyond dispute. When he
spells out this intent, he waves before us a series of supposedly clear opposites which are neither clear nor clearly

opposed: " brushing aside moral responsibility in favor of sticking to the rules "; " an ethic of responsible decision rather than obedience to law "; " love not law "; " principles are maxims not rules "; " love people, not principles." Rhymes uses many of the same couplets and asserts that Jesus does " not primarily call men to a code to be applied but to the demanding rule of love as the only absolute, to the working out of what love means in the existing situation." [8]

Obviously such rhetorical gestures cry out for several distinctions and it would be tedious to marshal them here. But their general effect is to jockey one into the position of not loving and caring in the situation if he insists on the validity of an absolute. This is the methodological point Paul Ramsey is constantly making when he talks about getting the terms of the debate straight. It is unsound to begin by defining what he calls " general-rule agapism " or " in-principled love " as readiness to obey a rule even though the action it calls for is seen not to be what love would directly require.[9] It is because in-principled love sees nothing of the kind that it adheres to its principles. It is precisely the love that is in it and which would be violated by departure from it which gives the principle its validity. Or as Ramsey himself puts it: " The fact that nothing other than *agape* makes a thing right or wrong does not mean that nothing is right or wrong." [10] To think otherwise would be to compromise love and actually to risk doing the unloving thing. Fletcher's rhetorical beginnings are, then, only justified if one has established their suppositions.

The only way to get at Fletcher's suppositions is through his conclusions. These conclusions, as I read them, could be stated in two propositions. (1) There is only one absolute: love. In whatever situation man finds himself, it is his call to work out the maximum response of love. (2) No negative principles have absolute validity in describing the character of this loving response.[11]

Thus, practically, adultery may generally be immoral, but there can be the outside instance where it is the loving thing to do. No serious Christian moralist will quarrel with the first assertion. It is the second, or rather its suppositions, which constitute the heart of the matter.

Before one can defend this position other than arbitrarily, he must have answered the question: How does one go about making a moral judgment? As far as one can gather, Fletcher's answer to this would run as follows: evaluate the total situation, then do the loving thing. So far, no problem. But how does one determine what is the loving thing? Here Fletcher is very ambiguous. At one time the loving thing is the sum of the consequences of an act, so that if, by and large, more harm will result, the proposed activity would be unloving. At other times, as Herbert McCabe, editor of *New Blackfriars,* notes,[12] this caring is distinct from the act and its effects and seems to be only an inner psychological state. In other words, judgments of morality are assessments of the caring or loving thing to do in the situation; but it is not clear how one determines this. Obviously Fletcher has not made up his mind on how moral judgments are made. As long as this remains unclear, he can squeeze out of any epistemological corner, because he has none he calls his own. And as long as he has none he calls his own, one can only say that he has adopted a method (and its content-conclusions) without first solving the problems of methodology.

It would be ungracious to imply that no one else is guilty of this. We have all had our turn at it, and undoubtedly far more often than we realize. However, this cannot be allowed to blur the fact that rather than work his way back carefully to his premises, Professor Fletcher has chosen to plug the holes where these premises begin to appear. Even when he unveils a premise, it remains a slippery word (e.g., nominalism) which he would prefer to bandy about rather than analyze. This is not to say that Fletcher is wrong; it is only to say that he has not shown satisfactorily on what grounds he could be right.

In his tightly reasoned *Commonweal* article, Fr. Mc-Cabe sets out to show why Fletcher is wrong in his suppositions. He begins by stating the issue: " Are there some things that you must never under any circumstances do? " If the answer is " yes," then Fletcher is wrong. The Fletcher-situationist says " no." McCabe's answer to this is a kind of *reductio ad dualismum*.

McCabe's basic point seems to be this. The new moralist must contend in principle that every piece of behavior can pass as " loving." Therefore he must deny that any action is loving or unloving as such, specifically that any action is always unloving. McCabe sees this as an attack on the significance of human (bodily) behavior. He asserts: " I think that it is possible for them to hold this only because they believe that the adjective ' loving ' is descriptive not of bodily behavior as such but of something else that accompanies it." If this is true, McCabe sees it rightly as inseparable from a dualistic view of man, a view according to which values attach to events in an interior and invisible life which runs alongside of man's physical life. Love is not behavior; it accompanies behavior.

The accusation of dualism is, I believe, well aimed. If any activity can count as loving, we begin to sense that the word has lost its content, because human actions have lost their significance. To take but a single example — and that is all that is really needed [13] —is there a more disastrous sentence in recent theological literature than Fletcher's " sexual intercourse may or may not be an act of love "? [14] One can only make such a statement if he denies significance to this particular bit of human behavior. What Fletcher should have said (but could not on his suppositions) is: " This *act of love* may or may not be personally accompanied by appropriate sentiments of loving concern and othercenteredness, may or may not occur in circumstances which honor its meaning." Fletcher must deny that sexual intercourse as such is in any sense a loving act. For him it is neutral. It merits description as "loving" only when the parties put their minds to it. That means that ultimately it merits description as "loving" only *because* they put their minds to it. There have always been those who thought that sexual love was better off when confined to the mind. But have we not been battling such attacks on the significance of human behavior for centuries?

McCabe is right on target, therefore, when he points out that for Fletcher there is no such thing as sexual love; there is only sex accompanied by love. "Sex," Fletcher notes, "which does not have love as *partner* is wrong." The implications of this type of talk must be a terrible setback to all who feel that we have made genuine progress in extricating ourselves from the one-sidedness of the past in analyzing human love. For it is quite as effective an attack on the significance of human behavior as a narrow physicalism. On the other hand, perhaps we should not be surprised that our contemporary culture finds it more congenial to ask not *why* coitus is an act of love (an act which therefore makes demands of its participants), but *whether* it is.

But to McCabe's thoughtful essay one might apply the old axiom: *omnia dicta sunt vera, sed non omnia vera sunt dicta.* I mean that though McCabe has felled his demon, he has not shown, and did not really attempt to show, how one determines precisely what activities are always unloving and therefore generate absolute prohibitions. This is a far larger problem.

It would be a serious mistake to treat Fletcher-Rhymes as mere ethical gadflies. I believe that they are saying something very important. First of all, over and beyond their healthy revulsion from mere conformism as the meaning of morality, they are articulating very persuasively what one can easily believe is the implicit moral position of the vast majority of Christian non-specialists, especially when they face desperate situations. These writings, therefore, can speak a message to the theologian who sees his task as more than ivory-towerism. Secondly, they are raising a question for technical moral thought which has not been satisfactorily confronted by Catholic theologians — the problem of Christian moral knowing. Finally, one can suspect that the fact that this question has not received the attention in Catholic circles that it deserves stems at least partially from, and therefore passes judgment on, the working separation of moral theology from other theological disciplines.

5.
WILFORD O. CROSS — "The Moral Revolution: An Analysis, Critique, and Appreciation"

. . . THE SOMEWHAT DISMAL SCIENCE of moral theology has recently come to life. This resurgence of vitality in a theological discipline which has been bogged down in traditionalism or been supplanted often by a highly psychologized pastoral treatment has been motivated, in great part, by the debate over situation ethics. Permissive commentators on the sexual revolution have duelled with traditionalists over the problem of whether morality should be governed by the peculiarities of the situation or guided by codified law. This, indeed, seems the crux of the controversial issue. This crisis is further intensified by the apparent breakdown of Puritanism in Anglo-American culture. Another ingredient in the issue is the emphasis upon the companionate element in marriage which has been stressed by the family-planning issue and

From the article "The Moral Revolution: An Analysis, Critique, and Appreciation," by Wilford O. Cross, in *The Anglican Theological Review*, Vol. 48, No. 4 (October, 1966), pp. 356–379. Used by permission.

the terrors of overpopulation. The "pill" itself is no minor fact in the liberation of sex mores which lies behind the debate. Also, some analysts of the so-called "sexual revolution" think that this area of human activity elicits a special interest because it is a refuge of personal intimacy which is not dominated by mass production and the corporate and collective spirit. It is a province of life where personalism has meaning.

Whatever the complexities of the current climate of eroticism, the entrepreneurs of permissiveness within the Christian tradition claim to be engaged in making moral teaching relevant to a world in which standards and values in sexual matters are in a state of flux. The claim is that Christianity must speak to men and women caught in the turmoils of the sexual revolution. When Christianity speaks, its voice must not be the harsh tones of a purely negative legalism but an understanding effort to guide perplexed people on the road to the attainment of personal fulfillment. In England two centers of Anglicanism seem to serve as the nests — some would say mares' nests — from which changes in attitude are being produced. These two foci of ethical innovation are the divinity faculties of Cambridge University and the Diocese of Southwark, the London of the South Bank of the Thames. Cambridge opinions have been largely voiced by Dean H. A. Williams in the book *Soundings*,[1] while the prophets of the South Bank have spoken in Bishop Robinson's *Honest to God*[2] and also in Canon Douglas Rhymes's *No New Morality*.[3] Stimulated by these iconoclastic works, advocates of a more conservative position have sought to negate some of the advanced claims of the new morality. Lindsay Dewar in *Moral Theology in the Modern World*[4] and Canon V. A. Demant in *Christian Sex Ethics*[5] have replied to arguments of the Cambridge-Southwark situationists. Very acid criticism, inspired by the moral reaction in England to the Profumo affair, has come from the laity, particularly exemplified in *The New Morality*, written by Sir Arnold Lunn and Garth Lean.[6] Habitual writers of letters to the editor have professed a sense of outrage and some bishops have spoken as if their world had come to a catastrophic end. Bishop Robinson's lectures in Liverpool Cathedral were picketed. When an Anglican cathedral is the focus of a demonstration over lectures on moral theology that discipline is no longer a somnolence-inducing couch but has become a powder keg.

In March of this year, in America, *Situation Ethics*, written by Prof. Joseph Fletcher, of the Episcopal Theological School, appeared.[7] This significant book is the most careful and brilliant presentation of situationalism in print so far. It is a painstaking analysis by a competent moral theologian, and while it sparkles with pugnacious thrusts, it is far less journalistic than the pioneering works hitherto mentioned. It attempts to lay a solid foundation in ethical argument for the situationist thesis. (Since I have written a fairly full-scale review of this work in the Spring Book Number of *The Living Church*,[8] I will refer the reader to my somewhat marginal criticisms of it in that periodical.) Professor Fletcher's provocative and scholarly work, and Bishop Robinson's Liverpool Lectures, subsequently published as *Christian Morals Today*,[9] have, in my opinion, given the new morality a right to be considered most seriously and sympathetically as a new method of casuistry. In both of these works the problems of the sexual explosion are faced realistically in the light of the moral implications of Christian personalism.

THE CHRISTIAN ETHIC OF LOVE

Advocates of the new morality are sincere in their desire to make the teaching of the church relevant to our age. Many ask, however, if the situationist sex ethic is merely a libertarian moulding of morality to suit the looseness and indulgence of our times. Is the quest for relevance a surrender to contemporary fads and fashions? Is this concerted attack by some churchmen upon the legalistic guidance of codes simply mounting the tailgate of a bandwagon of lechery? Perhaps the answer to these questions is discovered in the fact that sheer situationism and radical nominalism are not the only guiding principles brought out by the new morality. Situationism is not an unprincipled merging with the erotic trend of Dionysusism, but an attempt to discover positive guidelines for ethical endeavor. Rather than " an ethic of sin " that is a discipline for confessors who must adjudicate past offences according to law, it is engaged in promulgating an ethic for the moment of decision in the heat of personal moral crises.

However ambivalent the new morality may be on this point, its undergirding principle is not the ambiguity of the situation but an insistence upon love as the test of moral worth. The new moralists have drawn heavily upon Bonhoeffer and his tragically unfinished and somewhat unsystematic ethic, but clearly they have drawn with Christian perception of the foundation in love upon which law and prophets rest. This emphasis, of course, has always been central to the Christian tradition, beginning with our Lord's sayings in the Sermon and elsewhere filled with the dynamism of filial and fraternal love. " A new commandment I give unto you that ye love one another " was followed by St. Paul's insistence on the primacy of charity. The founder of Western moral theology, St. Thomas, told us that charity was the form, the root, and the mother of all the virtues. The new morality is on sound ground in its first maxim: " Do the most loving thing that can be done."

Nevertheless, there is in the new morality a perhaps partially necessary but somewhat arbitrary shadow from the light of this first principle. This is the vehemence of the polemic against law which is always labeled by the pejorative term "legalism." Dean Williams and Canon Rhymes most loudly thump the drums of this offensive. Both insist that the Christian moral tradition, after our Lord, beginning with St. Paul, has been uniformly legalistic. This has been most strikingly true, they contend, in matters of sex. In *Soundings,* Dean Williams distinguishes between "inherently authentic sayings" of our Lord and words attributed to him by pharisaically minded disciples. The Gospels must be pared down to the essential dominical word, and everything having to do with jots and tittles and adultery and divorce must be purged as inauthentic. Canon Rhymes also has his own privileged method of Biblical exegesis, chief of which is his interpretation of the word "fulfillment" as meaning the fulfillment of man rather than the fulfilling of the law. This antilegalist thesis implies that Jesus was a radical antinomian and that this antinomianism was destroyed by the institutional church, beginning with the modification of its radicalism by St. Paul. The church sought a paranoic refuge from its fear of sex in a strict, ascetic legalism.

That this thesis is an arbitrary and dogmatic violence perpetrated upon Biblical exegesis and history should be clearly obvious. Canon Demant has been at pains to correct the extravagant assertions of the new moralists on this issue.[10] During its first century, Christianity tended to disregard sex and procreation because it was expecting the end of the age. St. Paul at times tended to speak of marriage as an expedient for mitigating lust, though he could also say that it represented the mystical union betwixt Christ and his church. Some hundred years after St. Paul's time, Manichaean gnosticism, while officially stifled, had rubbed off enough of its dualism into the thinking of the church so that an unbalanced value was given to sheer biological virginity. The Western fathers — Jerome, Tertullian, Augustine — sing hymns to the virginal state. It ranked with fasting and other forms of physical undernourishment. Thanks perhaps to twelfth-century revivals of Manichaeanism in the Cathar and Albigensian heresies, with their aversion to marriage and procreation as the work of the devil, wedlock became, by reaction, the Seventh Sacrament, but at the cost, being paid for by our Roman brethren today, of an overemphasis upon the procreative side of sex and a diminution of the friendship, companionship, and love involved in marriage. In other words, the history of sexual morality in Christianity has been varied and shifting, ranging from the Oriental tantrism of the Massalian heretics to the worship of chastity by Tertullian and others. The word "legalism" is too much of an oversimplification to be really penetrating, though that is not to say that in dealing with sex, Christianity has not often been legalistic in its attitudes and pronouncements. Sex is a torrent, and in ages when the church had an authority rooted in the fear of hell, it attempted to frighten people into " being good " and it brandished its laws like a threat. This side of the situationist reading of church history is true, but I think one must ask, Can St. Thomas with his Aristotelian doctrine of marriage as "the highest form of friendship," or St. Bernard, St. Bonaventura, Abelard, Petrarch, to say nothing of Dante, be considered strict legalists in their view of love between men and women?

I believe the new morality, then, as propounded by both Dean Williams and Canon Rhymes, is guilty of both an arbitrary exegesis of Biblical texts and a distortion and parsimonious interpretation of ecclesiastical history. This weakness in making use of selected proof texts from Biblical sources and rejecting others, and the oversimplification of history, rests upon an a priori dogmatism in which facts are distorted by theory and, indeed, become facts only when they fit neatly into the theory. The major difficulty is that the word " legalism," with its pharisaical connotations, has been allowed to dominate the theory.

Two Situationist Mythologems of Love

Stressing the primacy of charity has led pioneer situationists, and indeed later, more mature confessors, to mount a fiery attack upon any sort of codification of Christian morality. One of the lawful maxims upheld by the traditional magisterium of the church is that sex relationships must be confined to the matrimonial state. The new moralists agree that in about 99 percent of cases this moral law is correct, but they argue for the hard and exceptional cases where sex relationships outside of marriage are creative. Professor Fletcher, for instance, uses the illustration of a German woman in a Russian war camp. She could be allowed to return home to the two young children who needed her if she were pregnant. She therefore induced one of the guards to impregnate her and thus by committing adultery was restored to her family.[11] The implication here is that the legally forbidden act of adultery was used for creative purposes. However, I am quite sure that within the jargon of traditional moral theology an argument could be found for the justification of this woman's irregular conduct on the ground that the copulation involved was an " indirect object of the will " rather than " the direct object " and that, at least, she chose the lesser of two evils. Adultery here had the matter, but not the intentional form, of sin.

The two mythologems in mind, however, are provided by Dean Williams. He offers them as evidence that fornication may be in rare cases a sacrament of healing and redemption. He cites the case of a young sailor ashore in the port of Piraeus who, when he becomes involved with a harbor prostitute, is overcome with anxiety and lack of confidence in his own masculinity. Through the tender mercy of this woman his masculine ego is restored. All this Williams draws from the contrived celluloid of the movie *Never on Sunday*. Williams' comment is: " He goes away a deeper fuller person than he came in. What is seen is an act of charity which proclaims the glory of God. The man is now equipped as he was not before. Can Christians possibly say that devils were cast out of him by Beelzebub? " [12]

All this does seem topsy-turvy. In the first place the young man's precarious psychological condition seems rather exaggerated. Adolescent timidity and lack of confidence in confrontation with bordello professionalism is neither unusual nor something from which one needs to be saved. Williams exaggerates the boy's psychic predicament in order to conjure a redemptive experience.

Williams dscovers in still another movie a second mythologem illustrating the sacramental therapy of the sexual act. In the film *The Mark* a man goes off for a weekend with a mature woman and by copulation is restored to sexual normalcy — at least on celluloid. Previously he has had a hankering for fondling little girls but this weekend experience restores mature desires. Dean Williams says of this: " He has been made whole. And where there is healing, there is Christ, whatever the Church may say about fornication. And the appropriate response is — Glory to God in the Highest." [13]

These illustrations are expected to demonstrate by the case method that the church has legalistic, prohibitory standards which are directly contrary in some cases to the healing influence of Christ. That both cases come from the phantasy of the movie theatre which has developed a facility for glamorizing and sentimentalizing sex does not seem to give Williams pause. I do not know how Williams would have reacted had his young sailor acquired venereal disease along with salvation. Also, it seems rather inconsistent to affirm that no act is wrong in itself and at the same time to insist that fondling little girls is sinful. However, Williams faces this inconsistency by saying that his antihero's penchant is "utterly destructive" and "can do nothing but untold harm," because fondling and molestation is "exploitation to the nth degree." [14] Exploitation is the reverse side of "the most loving thing that can be done." In the new morality exploitation of another person comes close to being the only intrinsically wrong action. Indeed Williams develops this notion of the only intrinsically wrong act — he does not use the term "intrinsic," however — to a rather dangerous conclusion.

A great deal of what Christians often call virtue, on closer inspection turns out to be cowardice of this kind — a refusal to give myself away because I am too frightened to do it. This is most obviously true in the sphere of sexual ethics, because here more than anywhere there seems to be an enormous amount of double-think. If I am to give myself away to another person, I cannot, in any circumstances, exploit her or him. To exploit is to withhold. It is totally incompatible with giving. [15]

Dr. Alex Comfort, a secular advocate of the new morality, puts the implications of this somewhat unclear paragraph bluntly, saying, "Thou shalt not exploit another person's feeling and wantonly expose them to an experience of rejection." [16] There is a great deal of rather thin celluloid and equally thin psychology, it seems to me, in these arguments for a rather wide range of sexual permissiveness.

LOVE AS A COMPASS

As we have seen, the antilegalism of the new morality leads it sometimes to a radical rejection of all norms, standards, and moral generalities. It is then forced to find its guiding principle within love itself. There is a tendency towards an antinomianism of love, but situationists are not altogether in agreement on this point. Canon Rhymes seems to be the most antinomian and nominalistic of the group. He makes no distinction between lawfulness and legalism.

> The answer then to our first question as to whether Christian morality is based on a law-system is clearly " yes." It is an authoritarian morality, a system in which certain things are declared to be right and others wrong; it is a matter of rules in which we are supposed to move with absolute conformity, avoiding what we are taught are sins and seeking what we are taught are virtues.[17]

As an alternative to what he considers and describes as legalism, Canon Rhymes proposes " a relationship which will be based not upon the observance of laws but on concern for the person in the situation of the person." [18] He compares the traditional teaching of the church with the position of the Pharisees. " Thus they must protest against Christ because they found in him a dangerous spirit of antinomianism; a refusal to accept flat laws, however good, as the touchstone by which goodness and morality is measured." [19]

In *Honest to God,* Bishop Robinson claims that love is the sole ethical criterion and that nothing else makes a human act right or wrong. The test of moral action is " the deepest welfare of these particular persons in this particular situation." [20] Lindsay Dewar objects that this overpersonalistic approach isolates persons from their wider social reference and commits situationism to an acute individualistic ethic.[21] Dewar is right, in the sense that this is the path along which situationism has pursued its earliest explorations of personalistic ethic. To shift the metaphor, it has been concerned with blossoms rather than rose trees. There is considerable correction in Professor Fletcher's book, for he insists that there are no unmitigated and uncomplicated personal interrelations but that in any moral issue we are always involved in a multiplicity of claims and a plurality of clients.[22] Though the social ethics of situationism badly needs writing, perhaps with the maturing of the new morality some cues can be discerned among Continental phenomenologists, particularly the Belgian Roman Catholics, who have taken the lead in the attempt to break out of the isolated " horizon " of personalistic existentialism, where each man centers his own horizon and it moves with him, into the wider area of " coexistence " and interpersonal relations. The principle of parsimony is not logically legitimate when it reduces complexity by isolating oversimplified singularity. Canon Dewar, I feel, is correct when he argues that the nominalism of situationism allows it to reduce human relations to a one-to-one formula.

In his earlier and rather hasty work, *Honest to God,* Bishop Robinson seems to lean towards antinomianism. There is no moral guidance save love's own *élan.*

> Love alone, because, as it were, it has a built-in moral compass, enabling it to " home " intuitively upon the deepest needs of the other, can allow itself to be directed completely by the situation. It alone can afford to be utterly open to the situation, or rather to the person in the situation. . . . It is able to embrace an ethic of radical responsiveness, meeting every situation on its own merits, with no prescriptive laws.[23]

Granting that love, defined here as regard for the " welfare of the other," lends wings to the perception of the situation, this statement still leaves many unworked elements that contribute to confusion. Is it the situation or the person to whom one responds with homing love? We have previously noted an oscillation in the new morality between situation and eros, between the objective facts and the subjective, " agapeic " response to the external realities of the situation. Bishop Robinson seems to detect this ambivalence, for his phrases shuffle a little as he writes: ". . . to be utterly open to the situation, or rather to the person in the situation." If love is a response of the whole person, intellect and emotion combined, Robinson is on sound ground when he notes love's homing, intuitive quality. It is the mother eagle who sees the hawk hover over the nest, because love had been motivating her faraway warding of her young. Yet there is confusion here in linguistics, a confusion that we will also see in Fletcher's work, for it is not love that " homes," or is intuitive, or cares, but a person with a mind, a moral history, the moral structure of character, who through reason and conscience operates as a loving person. The tendency of situationism to treat love as a sort of intellectual-emotional substance in itself and give it verbs of action, saying that love does such and such, creates manifold confusion of thought.

This defect in situationism is bred from its antinomian side, for it has been characteristic of spiritist movements, such as early Quakerism, the Familists, and, earlier still, the followers of Joachim of Fiori, to remove the responsibility for human moral acts from the person and attribute action to the Spirit or to " love " apotheosized. Even Peter Lombard, who was not an antinomian, taught that love was the indwelling of the Holy Spirit, thus removing it from the realm of responsible human acts. Fletcher makes the same error when he writes, " Love is not the work of the Holy Spirit, it *is* the Holy Spirit — working in us." [24] Situationist use of the word " love " as if it were an independent psychic force apart from the person who loves and who is morally responsible, tends to destroy an exact moral science of the human act. In Fletcher's book, for instance, this inexact use of language leads to confusion between the moral virtues, for one finds such phrases as "love is prudence" or "love calculates." [25] Bishop Robinson's love that "homes" is a case of uncurried language.

Nevertheless, Bishop Robinson, despite some of his utterances, is not antinomian. In his first lecture at Liverpool he said: "A moral net there must be in any society. Christians must be to the fore in every age in helping to construct it, criticize it, and keep it in repair." [26] The Bishop's metaphor is presumably a cargo net, something well understood both in Woolwich and the port of Liverpool, and though he does not define what he means, he seems to be saying that it is impossible to solve every moral issue *ad hoc* according to the situation and therefore moral generalities that net things together are a necessity. The Bishop also comes very close to certifying a list of intrinsic evils, a thing abhorred by the new morality, for he says, "I would, of course, be the first to agree that there are a whole class of actions — like stealing, lying, killing, committing adultery — which are so fundamentally distructive of human relationships that no differences of century or society can change their character." [27]

Professor Fletcher explicitly denies any traffic with antinomianism and, indeed, in *Situation Ethics* calls it "anarchy." He states that his casuistical method is a middle way between legalism and antinomianism. He makes use of the term "maxims," which he substitutes for the usual term "law," affirming that a maxim is an advisory, guiding principle but not an absolute, binding, legal stipulation.[28] Walking any middle path, of course, is fraught with the dangers of ambivalence and whole sentences of a very decided antinomian texture could be lifted from Fletcher's work, particularly in the context of his attack upon the concept of intrinsic evil. Unlike Bishop Robinson, he does not concede there are classes of actions which are inherently destructive.[29] No act is wrong in its inherent function but only wrong because of the situation or the lovelessness of the act, he affirms. Thus the inherent function of a lie to deceive, which is destructive of human relationships at their very core, the core of communicating language, is not intrinsically wrong to Fletcher, because a lie may be told in love and because a lie in some situations is the best thing that can be done. Nevertheless, the maxim "Thou shalt not lie" serves for Fletcher as a useful guideline.

The distinction between lawfulness and legalism is a critical discernment. The new moralists do not always make this distinction but tend to plaster the word "legalism" uncritically like blind wallpaper hangers. Legalism is a univocal concept in that it imposes upon every situation the full rigor of an unbending legal requirement. Lawfulness, on the other hand, is analogical, for it brings to bear upon ethical decision the guidance, rather than the imperative, of a generalized compendium of human, moral experience. Antinomianism, in contrast, is equivocal, for it denies in a spirit of radical nominalism that any structured, general moral norms are binding or useful. It appeals to the element of uniqueness in every particular situation. These three terms — univocal, analogical, and equivocal — could be replaced without great loss by the more ordinary terms: positive, flexible, unstructured. At any rate, these terms serve to indicate the methodological approaches current in the situationist debate. Radical new moralists, such as Williams and Rhymes, tend to confuse legalism and lawfulness, maxims and absolutes, while Robinson and Fletcher accept the difference between analogical lawfulness and univocal legalism. At the end of the sixteenth century, Richard Hooker, the founder of Anglican moral theology, in his treatise on law in the *Ecclesiastical Polity*, carefully worked out the distinction between positivistic legalism and advisory lawfulness. He defined moral law as "a measure of operation." It is a pity that some of the new moralists have forgotten the wisdom of our Anglican heritage.[30]

In radical situationism, and even in the lurches towards the precipice of antinomianism by the middle-of-the-roaders Robinson and Fletcher, the modern intellectual fad of an antipathy to any sort of structure in morality is apparent. The new morality is somewhat caught up in the current existential fashion of dismissing intellectual structure — constructs, concepts, norms, and essences. This is an intellectual pose, rather than a working device of thought. It is a fascination with *Lebenswelt*. Nevertheless, whenever existential thinkers attempt discussion — whether in sociology, psychotherapy, philosophy, or ethics — the requirements of reason force them, as Tillich frequently noted, to resort to structured concepts. Existence itself in its radical particularity has no language, for language is a way of connecting singular experiences together in typological references. Some sort of conceptualism or essentialism is forced upon us by the neurological structure of memory in the human brain and consequently by language. Every noun, even if it be as simple as " this post," carries an implied classification and typology — in this case the genus " post." The struggle of existentialism with this encapsulation of the human mind in essence, concept, form, and structure leads to the use of such expressions as " in-itself," or " for-itself," " man-as-project," " being-in-the-world," in order to escape the hardened concepts entailed in ordinary language. This haunting of the human mind by form lies at the bottom of Platonism. In every field conceptual apparatus is a necessity, like the generalities of science or the codification of moral experience in ethical and civil laws. Sometimes this conceptual apparatus becomes so top-heavy that a cleansing revolution occurs, like that of Ockam in Aristotelian logic, or that of Husserl within the Cartesian and Kantian tradition, or that of existential psychotherapy within the Freudian technique. Top hamper is cut away to bare masts.

In the light of this description situationism may be seen as a special eddy in the present nisus towards an impatience with conceptualized structure, in this example, the structure of moral law. Situationism begins by cutting away law. But, since generalities are inevitable and undiscardable necessities of human thought, it goes on to restore maxims and moral nets. Unstructured morality, as Professor Fletcher notes, is chaos and anarchy. The new morality is quite right when it recognizes, with St. Thomas, that moral law cannot be an absolute. However, it defeats itself as a moral methodology when it refuses to recognize that the moral experience of men, like the scientific knowledge of mankind, must be codified into capsules of generalization and moral rules of thumb. Moral law is analogically valid as a measure of ethical decison and operation. It enshrines the moral experience of the race.

The new morality is quite right, however, in its recognition that the motivating dynamic that brings life to law is love. The sterility of the legalist, the " square," is due to the want of this fundamental quickening yeast. The legalist has allowed conventions to become duties that are motivated only by a tyrannical, irrational sense of " ought " for ought's sake. Nearly all of the hackneyed debates between love and justice, gospel and law, charity and obligation, are reducible and solvable by this psychological insight. Love provides the dynamic incentive, and justice and right, the channels by which ethical action becomes operative. It is this fact of moral action which forces Professor Fletcher, in his effort to insist upon love alone as the absolute moral guide, to include within *agapē* the virtues of justice and prudence. As we have noted, he does this by making use of doubtful language, such as " love is a calculus " and " love is justice." [31] By putting the burden upon love instead of upon a loving person, he introduces into the radicalism of situational ethics the traditional virtues of prudence and justice. Love, for him, is not sheer emotion, but calculating, prudential, estimating, valuing. For Professor Fletcher love is " care," an attitude combining prudence and the sense of oughtness entailed in justice with the motivation of the spirited emotion of love. By verbally putting the burden of all this upon *agapē,* however, Fletcher fails, I think, to recognize that human personality is basically a cluster of values as well as a person who seeks to relate himself to others by the outreach of love. Man, because he is a social animal, has been able to master this planet largely by the feat of cooperating with his fellows, and, in relevant degrees, primitive taboo, barbarian custom, and civilized law have provided the social sheathing and binding that has made man's coexistence with his fellows possible. Situationism puts its emphasis upon the tendential element of love in man's nature, but this tendential dynamism of social outreach has been creative and constructive in the midst of much cruelty, blood, and barbarism largely because it has been guided and controlled by law. Law as moral guidance and channeling, and love as gregarious motivation, are both necessary to produce order and stability in society. Law and love are as inseparable as body and soul, for they are indeed flesh and spirit to each other. Love, then, is not its own compass if love be defined as an emotional incentive, for love must be taught by reason and intelligence; that is, by prudence and justice how to love ethically — as Professor Fletcher has so wisely recognized in his current book. Indeed, with a stimulating freshness, Fletcher has reissued the claims of the traditional virtues.

The Moral Anatomy of Human Persons

The new morality tends to reduce the human psyche to a one-dimensional person exuding the emotions of

love or of hostility and exploitation. This agapeic parsimony neglects the processes by which human decisions
are in fact made. It leans towards the simplification and
meager description of personality as either agapeic or
exploitative. This oversimplification of human nature
is inherent throughout the new morality. As a matter of
psychological fact, human moral decisions are never
altogether dictated by the objective facts of the situation or by simple incentives such as love-as-care, but by
ingrained, habitual, interior, and subjective moral values.
Human personality is a cluster of values. We cannot
think of human persons apart from what we call " character." Character is a complex of traits and attitudes,
habits, and reactions, developed in the psychological
and social history of the person and to some extent even
determined and shaped by biological inheritance. Moral
attitudes determining decisions are bundles entwining
opinions, habits, tastes, and attitudes. Moral values are
always the product of biographical history. They accu-
mulate in us from infancy forward by the impressions
made by parents, siblings, schools, church, law, teen-age
peer group, customs, movies, television, novels, and a
hundred other sources of influence. Finally self-reflection
and moral examination render, in some cases, these values personal and our own. We digest the inherited,
heteronomous derivation of values, and interiorize and
personalize them, making them intimately our own. This
is the meaning of conscience: a personalization of derived
and institutional moral guidance. As we grow up, values
cease to be infantile and become mature notions of what
we ought to do and what we ought to become. This is a
process of ingestion analagous to the absorption of foreign food stuff into our bodies. The hamburger we ate
yesterday becomes in some part our flesh today. It is
upon the basis of this interior structure of value that
most of our moral decisions are made, and when we con-
travene it because of appetite, passion, or compulsion we

experience the psychic dissonance of pangs of conscience and moral qualms.

Moral values are characterized by a feeling of " ought-ness." The brand, the hallmark, of moral value, as distinguished from purely forensic or utilitarian value, is the peculiarity of this urgent sense of " oughtness." An imperative, a sense of requirement and obligation, haunts value. To go against my sense of value is to work upgrain, to realize a haunting sense of unauthenticity, to suffer a peculiar psychic dissonance. We are able, for instance, to write letters of recommendation largely because we recognize in persons whose character we know this peculiar structure of moral values. A letter of recommendation really says that such and such a person has such and such a character structure and that he would feel uncomfortable if he filched a five-pound note from the till in the local pub.

In thus stressing conduct, character, conscience, and values we have used a lay form of the philosophy of value. The same sort of psychological, anthropological value structure of human persons could, however, be demonstrated within the terminology of depth psychology. Here, however, we would speak of the interaction of the id, the ego, and the superego. The superego is the infantile conscience. It is that part of me that wakes me in a state of shock when I dream that I am preaching naked in a pulpit. Since the baby conscience of the superego resists maturity, Freudians invented other terms for the mature conscience, such as " the reality principle " and the " ego ideal," both of which have critical relevance for ethicists, for one illustrates the ethic of response and the other, the ethic of fulfillment. According to the Freudian analysis, the mature conscience does not grow out of the superego as a tree grows out of a seedling, but the superego, which is very largely a psychic deposit implanted by parents concerning hygienic, sanitary, and nudic concerns, is quite often in

conflict with the mature conscience of the reality principle. Often conflict between reality principle and superego is drastic, invoking neuroticism. The superego is
often an impacted wisdom tooth in the gum of conscience.

Pastoral theologians sometimes note that absolution
and a sense of forgiveness sometimes do not penetrate to
the psychic ache of the superego. It could be that the
sick of the palsy to whom our Lord first said, " Thy sins
are forgiven thee," before he ordered, " Take up thy bed
and walk," was a man suffering from a buried superego
neurosis of this kind. Perhaps this stubborn intractability
of the buried superego of infantile conscience is the
basic reason why the maxim of the new morality, " Do
the most loving thing," creates in some cases a deepen-
ing of conflict, for it demands a mature morality while
the superego is still infantile. The infantile conscience
takes over some tasks, such as modesty, hygiene, and
petty larceny. A child feels different from a dog about a
hydrant on a city street. What concerns us here, however,
is that the oversimplified formula of the new morality
is somewhat parsimonious when confronted with the actual facts of the psychology of those values, infantile or
adult, by which people actually make moral decisions.
Neither love nor situation are quite as important as ingrained, habitual, value responses emanating from the
conscience. Situationism has seriously underestimated
the psychic force of neurological habit and the somewhat constant substance of human character. There is
an " inner legalism " of human character which the situationalists have underestimated. Their understandable
zeal has produced an oversimplification.

LOVE AS A TEST OF LAW

We have claimed here that there are two kinds of
structure which shape moral choices. We have just ex-

plored the presence and value of one of these, the psychic structure of internal, subjective values known traditionally as the conscience. There is, however, an external structure of values: the fabric of moral and civil law. So far, the new moralists have neglected both objective and subjective sources of the determinants of moral decision. The assumption seems to be that no one anymore listens to his conscience and that external pronouncements of law have no relevance. This facile assumption is untrue, for both conscience and law are still, as always, the guides by which decisions, and a sense of guilt over past decisions and actions, are motivated.

External moral law, or maxims, or principles of moral conduct are not absolutes but generalities of human experience which seek to guide conduct according to the empirical, discoverable wisdom of human behavior which was actually and realistically experienced that certain types of action, such as adultery, are not socially creative but destructive. To regard such standards as legalistically absolute is to deny the relevance of human experience. In other words, human beings in their long and painful history have discovered that certain acts are creative and that certain acts are destructive. The new morality seeks to deny the validity of this moral, social experience. It absolves itself from history. In doing so, it cannot, however, absolve itself from the consequence of acts which have been registered in history as destructive and uncreative acts. Its sexual permissiveness in regard to fornication, adultery, and homosexuality does not free its ethic from the negative pronouncement that has been articulated by history upon these specific acts. The new morality is bound to explain why homosexuality, adultery, and fornication are creative acts of love, over against the common, historic, lawful opinion that such acts are destructive. To test every act by the love or care for persons involved in the action creates at once a moral responsibility to prove that such acts have consequences in value. And what values stand as judges over these acts? The only possible value is that of the growth and development of human personality. What fulfillment of personality is implicit in a loving homosexual act?

The test of law by love brings us to the relationship of love to justice. If love be regarded as motivating and justice be defined as a rational description of right, then love provides the motivating energy and justice the rational channel of righteous acts. This is about where Reinhold Niebuhr left it. Professor Fletcher, in his concern to make love a simple absolute, is not content with this accommodation of love as motive and justice as means but seeks to incorporate justice within love. He stretches love to include the Aristotelian virtue of prudence and the Aristotelian virtue of justice, thus reissuing the classic cardinal virtues under the aegis of love. This accommodation of love and justice is accomplished largely by a linguistic conjuring in which love is spoken of as justice. If the sentences involved in this description were reduced from linguistic confusion to meaningful statements, they would all be saying: " A person motivated by love-as-care-for-others rationally seeks intelligent ways in which this sort of care can be effective and operative." That is to say, " Genuine love impels one to be fair and just." Fletcher states this by saying that love is calculating and desires to be just. It is not really love that is calculating but a person motivated by love-as-care. Once the linguistic confusion is cleared up, the traditional relationship held by moral theology between justice and charity reappears. Professor Fletcher has stated the traditional doctrine in a defective linguistic form. The new morality here is the old morality verbally confused. It is, however, encouraging to discover that love cannot be discussed without justice, nor without prudence, and to find that the new morality is still the old morality. However, Professor Fletcher's effort here is in the interest of ethical parsimony. The classical ar-

rangement of love as motive and incentive, and justice
as guide, is thus virtually reaffirmed by the new morality.[32]

The Personalism of the New Morality

The foregoing analysis leads us to the conclusion that
the personalism of the new morality abstracts the riches
of character from the moral formula. The new morality
is rather thin. It is ironic that so often the dogmas of
personalism read like ghostly abstractions. This is as
typical of the *Lebenswelt* of phenomenology as it is of
the situationalism of the new morality. In both instances
the structure of the human person, the essence of man
in all his varied appearances, is erroneously left out. The
new morality seems nakedly unfleshed, having little substance drawn from the wealth of anthropology, psychology, and axiology that is available to us. Man seems to
be some sort of bee exuding the honey of love. The inner
structure of man, his value cluster of habitual virtues
and vices, his ingrained attitudes and responses, his
neurologically grooved reactions are all reduced to the
single undifferentiated attitude of love-as-care. This oversimplification of motive and incentive makes it easy for
new moralists to discuss man as a moral creature involved
in person-to-person relationships, but it is not real. This
sort of etherealism naturally leads to the linguistic confusion we have noted of discussing love as an abstract
and yet concrete noun and forgetting that the assertions
involved are about people who hate and love. In the
name of personalism the new morality tends to destroy
the person, substituting the motive of love, putting in
the place of the complex person the abstract motivation
of care. The reduction of an ethic to love applied to a
situation abstracts from the biographical and historic
values that constitute a personality. The result is a casuistry that is not genuinely personal but an absolutism

that judges conduct simply and parsimoniously by the criterion of love. This is as legalistic in its absolutism as judgment by law. Whatever you do, if you do it from love, you have done rightly. This is the legalism of love.

The objection that we are making here is not that love is not the primary motivation of Christian conduct, but that decisions made by Christian men are motivated and determined by two sorts of structures: one objective and external, the whole fabric of the moral law, and the other internal, subjective, and psychological, the inherent values that motivate and guide men in their decisions. The outer law and the inner conscience tell us what right and wrong is. Situationism merely, therefore, substitutes another method of casuistry to help us in our doubtful and perplexed states of indecision. Professor Fletcher states this when he insists that his ethic is not a system but a methodology.[33] Situationism is a new method of casuistry to be put alongside of tutiorism, probabiliorism, and probabilism. It gives us the guiding maxim " Do the most loving thing," because upon this hang all the Law and the Prophets. This maxim is the test of the rightness of our conscience and of the authenticity of moral law. The primacy of charity has been reaffirmed as the spring of morality.

This is not to say that situationism, even as a methodology of casuistry, does not need to become mature. Its incipient antinomianism must be purged, for it fails to understand that law is an analogical summation of a generalized, historic, moral experience. Its tendency to allow moral decision to be at times at the mercy of the objective situation is a peculiarly perverse " natural law " ethic that allows objective facts to determine the outcome of moral decisons. Its notion of love badly needs the kind of definition that Professor Fletcher has sought to give. The social implications of situationism call for development, for it tends to reduction to a one-to-one personalistic basis. On the whole, however, despite

a weakness in handling language and a curious inno-
cence of history, situation ethic embodies the promise
of a novel, relevant, and penetrating approach to the
perplexing and sordid moral issues of these disturbed
times. At least, the new morality has got hold of our
Lord's insistent emphasis upon the intention of the
moral act, the intention of love which is the fulfilling
of the law.

Its great want and need and crying deprivation is some
understanding of social structure as exemplified by codified moral and civil law and some recognition of that
realm of interior psychological values that constitute the
dictates, or annoyances, of conscience. One ought not,
however, anymore excoriate situationism for its imma-
turity than one can criticize a child for its diapers. It has
begun well, recognizing the critical element of the situation and the obligatory element of the demand of love.
The role of situationism is to insist that all of these
values — stuffy conventionalism, ethereal idealism, and
utilitarian pragmatism — be examined and estimated and
valued by the value of values, the absolute of love. As it
fulfills this role of criticism and estimation, it will prove
its casuistical usefulness and vindicate its vocation as a
new incentive in moral thought. When situationism
comes to terms with moral history, a new moral theology
will be built; when it comes to terms with the structure of
man, a new Practical Divinity will be at hand. When the
new morality is able to speak about social issues in terms
of its primary incentives, a mature, viable Christian ethic
will result.

6.
JAMES B. NELSON — "Contextualism and the Ethical Triad"

THERE IS a double jeopardy involved in attempting to describe contextualism as an ethical method today. On the one hand, the writer can simply rehash " that tired debate " between defenders of principles and defenders of the context. On the other hand, one can err by assuming that all contextualist writers are saying virtually the same thing.[1] Some of the " debate " will inevitably appear in what is to follow, though that is not my major purpose. And, while I am obviously and deeply indebted to the work of H. Richard Niebuhr, James M. Gustafson, Paul Lehmann, Joseph Fletcher, Gordon D. Kaufman, Joseph Sittler, Alexander Miller and others, I shall not make a systematic attempt to sort out the differences that do exist among these contextualists. Rather, I shall attempt to sketch in broad outline one possible contextualist method. I do not believe that this is the only viable method for Christian ethics, but I do believe that this approach can do justice to the major historic dimensions of the Christian faith and also can be particularly helpful for illuminating the decisions of contemporary Christians.

Why has contextualism commended itself to many in our time? The theme of this issue of the *Quarterly*, rapid social change, is one significant reason. Startling technological developments and their social consequences call into question what were once thought by many to be immutable moral laws in such areas as international, economic, and medical ethics. Correlatively (though less obviously) the communal and institutional structures which " live " within the individual have changed at an

From the article "Contextualism and the Ethical Triad," by James B. Nelson, in *The McCormick Quarterly*, Vol. XX, No. 2 (January, 1967), pp. 104–116. Used by permission.

accelerated pace. Thus, the quest for identity and the quest for ordered community become two sides of the same ethical coin. Philosophically, two emphases in the modern period, relativism and the notion of "responsibility," lead toward contextualism, just as does the renewed theological insistence upon God's sovereignty, freedom, and grace.

I

Before the contexts of decison are described, it is important to look at some of the basic assumptions which both lie behind and are part of this contextual method. (Most of these assumptions are held in common by writers previously mentioned.) First, there are several affirmations to be made about the nature of Christian ethics. The task of Christian ethics is more analytical than prescriptive. This ethical methodology cannot prescribe in advance correct moral decisions, but it can assist the Christian to decide and act with greater clarity and faithfulness. Since our decisions are never simply the result of applying previously learned principles to new situations, but always involve the competing claims of social loyalties, it is the ethical task to analyze the ways in which faith is expressed through those loyalties.

Further, Christian ethics is fundamentally indicative and only secondarily imperative. H. Richard Niebuhr has taught us that more fundamental than the question " What is my goal? " or " What is my duty? " is the question " What is going on in this situation? " [2] Similarly, Paul Lehmann insists, " Ethical demands acquire meaning and authority from the specific ethical relationships which precede and shape these demands." [3] And, since what is going on in the relational pattern also involves technical data, the contextualist finds it impossible to draw a sharp line between moral and technical knowledge. [4]

Moral principles are not, by any means, to be eschewed. However, following Gustafson's distinction, they are used more heuristically than deductively; they are understood as illuminative more than as prescriptive.[5] The moral actor does not tend to find a solution to a theoretical problem first and then apply that solution to a situation. Rather he tends to respond to concrete persons, groups, powers, and things, with the guidance of those principles which have, in some sense, become internalized as part of the structure of his personality.

Thus contextual ethics is concerned not only with illuminative moral principles, but also with the understanding of the process of internalization, a process which is always profoundly social. And as both Miller and Lehmann are fond of saying, we are not embarrassed by the recognition that ethics always has a close affinity to *ethos,* and Christian ethics to the ethos of Christian community.[6] The Biblical faith is profoundly social, communal, and historical. Christian ethics, consequently, is rooted in Christian community, for it is here that the individual's selfhood is given distinctive shape, it is here that meanings, values, and principles qualify that shape, it is here that loyalties are generated which are stronger than the rational explanations which we are normally able to give for our actions.

Already it has been implied that the self is dialogic. Yet the dialogue, as Niebuhr has pointed out, is not primarily between the "higher self" (reason, spirit, conscience, or whatever) and the "lower self" (passion, emotion, flesh, or whatever); it is primarily the dialogue between the self and the "other."[7] One develops his sense of identity through his communities of orientation, his "reference groups." The self exists within a plurality of communities, this community apparently influencing this decision, that community influencing that decision. Yet, insofar as the self has one community which functions as "a court of last resort," insofar as the self has a community which embodies or, better, points to an encompassing and transcending loyalty, the self also has a unity. In a word, the question of the church as the Christian's crucial society and the Christian's sense of identity is integral to and not accidental to the ethical question.

A final important contextualist assumption — indeed, an assumption of highest significance — is that of a relational value theory. A relational value theory " defines good by reference to a being for which other beings are good." [8] As Niebuhr emphasizes, value does not exist in and of itself apart from relationships. Value rather is present whenever one being is related to another being in fittingness. Or, in the words of Fletcher, " Good and evil are extrinsic to the thing or the action. . . . Value, worth, ethical quality, goodness or badness, right or wrong — these things are only predicates, they are not properties." [9]

Several implications appear to follow from a relational value theory. While value is not an objective kind of reality, neither is it subjective in the sense of depending upon the *feelings* of persons. Positive value is related to the *needs* of persons or other beings. Hence, some notion of the true needs of others is necessary, and for the Christian this comes in that understanding of others which is transformed by the divine revelation climaxed in Jesus Christ.

Furthermore, relational value theory suggests that an act cannot be defined as good or bad, right or wrong, in itself and under all circumstances. Such value judgments are extrinsic to the act. It all depends upon the relationship of the persons or beings in the particular situation. And, again the importance of empirical knowledge of the social relations, structures, and processes in which beings are joined to beings becomes evident.

Finally, relational value theory suggests that every value system is inherently religious; the valuing person must affirm some " center of value " in relation to which goodness, rightness, and fittingness can be judged, a center which is valuable in and of itself. In Christian ethics we affirm God as the center of value. He alone is absolute; all else is relative to him. Our relativism concerning judgments of worth, moral principles, virtues, and laws then is not simply a relativism stemming from a philosophical bias. Nor does it stem solely from our recognition of our common finitude, historical and cultural particularity, and our sin. It is also and even more fundamentally a relativism which follows from the confession in faith that God alone is sovereign.

II

Making the assumptions indicated above, we can now proceed more directly to sketch a method of contextual analysis. Where do we begin? Professor Gustafson, in a most helpful article, has delineated three different starting points used by different contextualists. Some, Kenneth Underwood for example, appear to begin with an emphasis upon realistic social analysis, insisting upon accurate knowledge of what is occurring in the arena of social action. Others, such as Lehmann and Sittler, become contextualists in the first instance for more theological reasons, especially an understanding of the God whose actions toward and claims upon men are always concrete and specific. Then there are those, such as H. Richard Niebuhr, whose contextualism is rooted in a social and responsive understanding of selfhood; the self responds primarily to persons, events, and things, and only secondarily to goals, laws, and principles.[10]

Perhaps it can also be said that, regardless of the point at which the systematic ethicist begins his exposition, the other two elements of the triad (God, self, neighbor) are immediately involved. If a truly relational thinker begins with God, his thought also involves *at the same time* the self and the neighbor. No one of the three elements of the triad may be reduced to or collapsed into the other. Yet as Niebuhr observes, " The interrelations of self, companion, and God are so intricate that no member of this triad exists in his true nature without the others, nor can he be known or loved without the others." [11] Recognizing that in moral decison and in life itself, the three cannot be sharply separated from their interrelationships, we nevertheless must focus upon each one separately, asking how this element affects the decision.

First, Christian contextualism emphasizes the activity of the living God. Ethically speaking, God is not primarily the giver of goals or laws (in which case his past activity could be considered normative and present activity quite superfluous). He is, in words common today, " the God who acts," the Doer of deeds. Christian ethics, then, is an ethics of response to the divine activity. " Responsibility affirms: ' God is acting in all actions upon you. So respond to all actions upon you as to respond to his action.' " [12]

Now, quite obviously, we have raised sizable theological problems, ones upon which I shall touch only very inadequately. What is the character of God's action? At least three types of interpretation may be observed among the contextualists. One is seen in the Christocentric thinkers who attempt to compress God's work into one major mode of activity. Thus, for Lehmann, it is through Christ a " political " work; God is " making and keeping human life human." [13] Or, for Sittler, God is giving us " the shape of his engendering deed in Jesus Christ." [14] A second type of characterization focuses upon *agapē* as the adequate description of God's action. Thus, for Fletcher, love becomes the key principle. Fletcher writes, " In Christian ethics it is more than a doctrinaire formality to insist that before we ask the ethical question, ' What shall I do? ' comes the *pre*ethical question, ' What has God done? ' " [15] It is significant, however, that

Fletcher puts the question about divine activity in the past tense, and that throughout his book he focuses *not* upon the present activity of God but upon *love* as the absolute ethical principle.

A third and, in my judgment, more adequate characterization is found in Niebuhr's writings, namely, a theocentric and Trinitarian understanding. While it is readily affirmed that the distinctively Christian apprehension of God is through Jesus Christ, nevertheless, God's activity cannot be compressed into Christocentric confines. Better, we should say God is at work creating, judging, and redeeming, or in more traditionally Trinitarian terms, creating, redeeming, and sanctifying. Further, while *agapē* may be the most inclusive value-description of the divine activity, unnecessary problems creep in when we (as Fletcher appears to do) come close to identifying love and God. (Recall Niebuhr's comment in describing the virtues of Jesus: " It was not love but God that filled his soul." [16]) There is a tendency to substitute love as a value or principle for the living divine reality. Further, as the history of Christian ethics should teach us, insofar as this is done the understanding of love's content tends to lose its richness and strength, becoming unduly acculturated. For example, when the principle of love actually functions as the supreme ethical referent, how frequently love as participation in God's ordering-governing-judging work is underestimated while other expressions of love are emphasized.

A further crucial issue is the matter of interpreting the divine activity. Here the question shifts from that of the modes of divine activity to that of the meaning of *God's* action in relation to *man's* action. Again, without the full exploration this deserves, perhaps we can make a beginning by assuming two things. One, God's action toward men is personal action. He has freely chosen to deal with his human creatures as persons. He does not coerce in a mechanistic fashion nor determine finite events in ways which would undercut human freedom. Two, God is not an occasional God, present in some events but absent in others. Assuming these patterns of activity, we can affirm that God's activity is the activity of intention. His will is never forced upon the moral agent; yet, God is present with intention in even the most tragic of moral situations. God's concrete will in a specific situation will be an expression of his loving consistency in creating, governing, redeeming, and sanctifying. Responding to that intent, the deciding man finds guidance toward meeting the true needs of the neighbor.

At once it becomes apparent how relational (can we even say "incarnational"?) such an interpretation of divine activity is. For, God's action is unfulfilled if it remains his intent alone, without the human response. The relation between self and neighbor can become the expression of God's act. But still it is God's act, as in the Pauline paradox, "I worked harder than any of them, though it was not I, but the grace of God which is with me" (I Cor. 15:10b). James Sellers recognizes the difficulty many of us have thinking in these terms when he says, "For the constructive purposes of Christian ethics (as opposed to, say, liturgics or cosmology), no act of God comes to bear in human life except in and through human acts. That, for some reason, is harder for us to accept than the co-equal truth, cheerfully sworn by, that 'the Word of God' in Scripture is expressed in human words." [17] Thus, in the emancipation of the slaves, the Christian interpreter sees Lincoln's response to the divine intent. Historians will agree, of course, that there was ambiguity in this human action (as is characteristic of all human action). Nevertheless, God's activity in judgment, promise, and fulfillment can be affirmed here.

If my moral decision depends upon the interpretation of and response to God's action, it also depends upon my interpretation of and response to my neighbor's needs.

This second element of the ethical triad must be interpreted broadly. My neighbor is my friend; he is also my adversary. He is a single person; he is also the corporate group. He is human; but the neighbor in the ethical sense may also be animal or inorganic being. The concept "neighbor" potentially includes all of created being apart from the self.

I must know my neighbor's needs. The moral decision depends in no small measure upon a concrete knowing of the neighbor. Here the conjunction of ethical and technical knowledge again becomes apparent, as does the debt of the decision maker to all those (including the behavioral and natural scientists) who further his understanding of the neighbor. But what is the neighbor's need? Regarding the human neighbor, it may or may not be, in any given situation, identical with his subjective feeling of desire. To some extent, my knowledge of his needs depends upon his ability to communicate those needs to me. But are we not notoriously subject to misunderstanding our own real needs? The unmarried couple may be persuaded that they would be meeting each other's true needs in sexual intercourse, when in fact their real needs as persons may go far beyond and even counter to the desires of the moment. We seem to be aware that to meet the other's needs means somehow to contribute toward the fulfillment of his potentialities. But his potentialities are not completely self-evident. Thus, the neighbor point of the triangle is driven back to the God point, for it is not only through scientific investigation but also through God's revelation as Creator that we know the potentialities of created being; it is not only through interpersonal human communication but also through God's revelation in Jesus Christ that we know what constitutes true man and authentic human need.

The third element of the ethical triad is the self. The self, as we have seen, is thoroughly social and (contrary to many of the individualistic assumptions made in the debate over contextualism) does not enter the decisional situation unequipped. Each of the self's communities of loyalty, each of his reference groups, each social role, will contribute to the structure of his selfhood. To be sure, the Christian may be shaped more decisively by groups other than the church, though we must also assume it possible that some definitive moral shaping may take place within the Christian community.

The contextualist, therefore, is driven to give considerable attention to that elusive reality, the conscience. Lehmann writes, " It is the *conscience* — theonomously understood — which forges the link between what God is doing in the world and man's free obedience to that activity." [18] In the *koinōnia* the conscience is shaped to receive an imaginative sensitivity to what God is doing. But, I would suggest, such sensitivity is not only knowledge of God's past and present revelation. It further depends upon that personal security which allows one to be open to the claims of another, whether God or neighbor or God through neighbor. The ultimate source of such security is in God's grace, but it is also a grace that is mediated, however imperfectly, through the interpersonal relationships within the *koinōnia*.

Again, we must recognize that the ethos of the Christian community (just as that of any human community) has a certain content. Gustafson has described the way in which meanings and understandings are internalized by the self through the church's symbolic formulations in Bible, history, liturgy, polity, and so forth.[19] Miller likens the church to the family, and each family has its traditions, heirlooms, and family lore — all of which carry and give structure to its ethos.[20]

In addition, each human community develops certain patterns of response toward broad types of situations, and such response-patterns may be appropriated and internalized by the member. The church is no exception, and it is here that the question of moral law and principle needs consideration. I think it is more than mere intellectual juggling to propose that we associate moral law primarily with the self-dimension rather than with the God-dimension in the moral triad, though still recognizing their interrelatedness. Insofar as we associate the moral law *in the first instance* with God, we diminish our ability to perceive the fresh activity of the living God, and perhaps subtly and unintentionally, though I think almost inevitably, we begin to respond more to the law than to the Lawgiver, more to the order than to God's ordering activity. By perceiving moral principle and law as in the first instance part of the self and the self's community, less as " God's law " and more as the church's structured response to the actions of the living God, at once we are reminded to maintain a greater humility about our principle-formulations, and also we are reminded that the social effectiveness of moral principles depends upon their internalization within the deciding self. The problem of those ethics which associate moral law with the God element of the triad is not only the tendency to absolutize the relative. It is also the problem of " closing the gap " between the divine claim and the human situation. If my ethical orientation is primarily to principle (whether I formulate this in terms of natural law, Christ-transformed natural law, middle axioms, or whatever), then I also tend to assume that a rational moral nature in the self closes the gap. If, on the other hand, I associate moral law primarily with the responding social self, then *community* becomes the bridge between divine claim and human situation. It would seem to follow that the problem of relating Christian and non-Christian ethics is not solved so much by the assumption of a common rational nature in men as by the recognition that there are elements of common communal experience. There are recognitions that the human community or, more broadly, the community of being, is enriched by one type of action and diminished, thwarted, or unfulfilled by another.

At this point a distinction adapted by Paul Ramsey from the work of John Rawls appears helpful.[21] Ramsey distinguishes three types of ethical orientation: "act-agapism," "summary-rule agapism," and "general-rule agapism." Act-agapism means that the moral decision is made simply by getting clear about the facts of the situation and then asking what is the most loving thing to do. Summary-rule agapism allows for the development and utilization of principles or rules on the basis of past experiences in making direct application of agape to particular situations. Summary rules, then, are summaries of what has *usually* been found to be the loving act in certain types of situations. Ramsey himself rejects both of the above in favor of general-rule agapism, the affirmation that certain acts are inherently wrong because of the lovelessness that is always in them, and other acts, contrariwise, are always right. There are no exceptions to general rules. If an exception seems necessary because the most loving act in a particular situation would break the general rule, then this only demonstrates that this general rule has not been adequately defined.

The position which I am advocating is similar (though not quite identical) to what Ramsey calls summary-rule agapism. Sheer act-agapism, we have seen, fails because of its unwarranted individualism concerning the self and the self's communities; it fails to take seriously enough the continuities of moral experience which *are* there; it is unduly optimistic regarding both the individual's moral wisdom and the breadth of his moral experience.

But general-rule agapism, in my judgment, fails as well. Is it actually possible to formulate a general rule which admits of no exception, *unless* that general rule *were* to become in effect an expression of the central tenet of Christian ethics itself, that is, the claim on the self of faithful response to God's activity in meeting the needs of the neighbor? Is, as Ramsey suggests, cruelty always inherently loveless? Or in some tragic moral situation may an act of lesser cruelty appear, as a result of the most careful moral calculation, necessary to avoid a greater cruelty? I think it conceivable that participation in God's judging and restraining activity may in some cases involve the lesser evil without a man's necessarily losing the sense of moral tragedy. An ethics of general rules, I fear, tries to escape the recognition of moral tragedy; it is more prone to bow to the individual's desire for personal purity above social responsibility; it cannot do justice to the paradox that the moral actor may need to pray for God's forgiveness in the very moment that he is, to the best of his understanding, responding faithfully to God's claim upon him.

The difficulty with general rule ethics is, I believe, always rooted in its wedding to an intrinsicalist, objectivist value theory. The two are partners. Together with the other difficulties, suggested earlier, in nonrelational value theory, there is also the stubborn tendency toward self-justification and defensiveness in the moral life. The assumption that a certain act is (no matter what the situation) intrinsically good (or bad) seems to lead more readily to a concern for correct behavior than to the concern for responsible service, even though it is intended otherwise. If virtue somehow exists objectively, a man is more inclined to be concerned about whether or not he *possesses* such virtues, to the detriment of his concern about the quality of the relationship with his neighbor. If a nation understands justice as a quality which it can possess, the fires of the crusading mentality will more likely be fed than if, on the other hand, its main concern is the creation of the just *relationship* with other nation neighbors in the human community.

In contrast, then, to that of general rules, the notion of summary rules (or, better, summary principles) expresses most adequately one important dimension of the self's " equipment " in decision-making. These summary rules are the patterns of moral wisdom which are part of the Christian's conscience through the mediation of the Christian community. They are experientially based, historically grounded patterns which the Christian takes with great seriousness even while realizing that they are earthen vessels. However, the vessels are not made of summary-rule *agapism*, in the sense that these are patterns of response to the *principle* or *law* of love. Rather, they are summaries of tried and tested communal responses to the loving *God*, in his manifold activity.

III

Much of the popular-press discussion of " the new morality " has, I am afraid, done a grave disservice to serious Christian contextualism. Each element of the ethical triad, in such discussion, becomes truncated. The living God is reduced to the principle of love. Distinction between the neighbor's desires and his needs is overlooked, and the neighbor is frequently abstracted from the wider web of his relationships. The self is understood as an asocial, ahistorical individual who enters the decisional situation unequipped, save for his intuition and pragmatic judgment. Whenever Christian contextualism succumbs to these pitfalls, it deserves the strident criticism which some have given.

But I have tried to argue for the viability of a contextualism based upon a richer understanding of the ethical triad. It is not simply that vast middle ground between the Scylla of legalism and the Charybdis of antinomianism. It is more precisely that which attempts to avoid the lesser Scylla of general-rule thinking and the lesser Charybdis of responsible-love-without-adequate-structure.

Obviously, many challenges can be put to this kind of contextualism. Does it encourage self-deception and sinful rationalization? But no ethical method per se can defend itself successfully against the sin of its user. The objectivist may express his sin more in defensive rigidity (in the face of rapid social change) or in self-justification (in the completion of good acts and the possession of virtues). The subjectivist is particularly prone to the rationalization of desire as need, and the sinful severing of the self from the communal bonds. The contextualist is sinner, too, but he does have the advantage of a method forcing him to take seriously the community of forgiveness and the community where there may be " a testing of the spirits."

Does such ethics of the context tend toward conservatism in its efforts to be relevant to society? Again, no *methodological* defense against this peril is complete. Yet conservatism and cultural religion are not the exclusive perils of a relevance-seeking contextualist. We have only to recall how relative and historically conditioned the various systems of natural law appear in a time of rapid social change. Is not the only defense against cultural conservatism the continuing openness of the Christian and the church to the radical intentions of the living God, whose actions are self-consistent and who conserves the best he has brought into being, yet who is always doing the new thing?

Does contextualism assume too great a maturity on the part of the individual? Does it make unwarranted assumptions about the degree to which he is willing and able to think ethically and use freedom responsibly? To be sure, maturity and the ability to use freedom reflectively and responsibly are never automatic possessions of persons. Yet, persons can grow into responsible relationships if they are surrounded by a community which mediates the guidance necessary at various stages, the gracious security necessary for moral creativity, and the forgiveness for his failures in the risks of freedom. We need to encourage, I believe, that style of ethics which encourages rather than inhibits maturation, and which also reflects most adequately the actual dynamics of human decision-making.

Does this approach take seriously enough the problem of interpreting the activity of God in our time? Though we do not agree with the " God is dead " theologians, is there not a sense in which God's hiddenness in our secularized age makes any ethics of response to divine activity unworkable, simply because people are too confused about what God is doing, or whether he is doing anything at all? Perhaps there is a twofold danger with which any age of Christians must come to grips: either saying too much or saying too little, either presumptuous certainty about the divine activity or paralyzing humility about the impossibility of knowledge. But we who do confess faith in the living God cannot reduce him to a principle, law, or goal, or to a past revelation alone.

Finally, is contextualism a method at all? It is not, if by "method" we are asking for solutions to difficult moral problems. But a method cannot decide; a person can. It is a method, however, if by this we mean a manner of disciplined reflection upon the meaning of relationships among God, the self, and the neighbor. It is a way of clarifying the loyalties and faiths with which we decide and by which we live.

In an age of particularly rapid social change we are abundantly aware of the risks of moral failure. We are also aware of the perils of moral irrelevance. The creative, reconciling, and sustaining act of the Christian responding to the divine intent in meeting his neighbor's need is always risk taken in freedom. In our freedom we remain both finite and sinful, hence in need of God's forgiveness. But that forgiveness is intended for those willing to take the creative moral risk, and not only for those who, eschewing risk, would strive for moral security in an existence which can never be made secure by human systems or achievements.

7.
CHARLES E. CURRAN
— "Dialogue with Joseph Fletcher"

WHAT IS THE PRECISE AREA of practical disagreement between the proponents of situation ethics and traditional Catholic moral theology? Disagreement centers on the existence of negative, universal prohibitions concerning ethical conduct. Catholic theology has traditionally upheld such norms whereas situation ethicians claim that love is the only absolute. . . .

However, there are vast areas of practical agreement. Catholic theology realizes that the majority of man's moral decisions are not based on the application of determined, universal norms to particular cases. Catholic theologians teach that the negative, universal norms merely serve as the boundary lines within which the ethical life of the Christian must be lived. Certain actions are not in keeping with the new life received in Christ Jesus. Just as there are certain actions that a mother would never perform, so too there are certain actions which a Christian should never do. Within these extreme limits all ethical decisions are arrived at in a situationalist manner.

In the past, Catholic life has often suffered from legalism. The Catholic was the one who obeyed the laws of God and the church. However, today all realize the horrible caricature in reducing the Christian life to the observance of a few negative commandments. Catholic theology, however, has always taught that a human law, by its very nature, admits of exceptions. Since human laws are based on what generally happens for most people, they must admit of exceptions. Even concerning the natural law, most moral decisions are not based on uni-

From the article "Dialogue with Joseph Fletcher," by Charles E. Curran, in *The Homiletic and Pastoral Review*, Vol. LXVII, No. 10 (July, 1967), pp. 821–829. Used by permission.

versal norms, for the norms are generally negative and merely tell us some few things that we must always avoid. The universal laws cannot positively tell us the exact and fitting decision to make in the particular situation. The number of such negative, universal norms is quite few. Even the prohibitions against killing and abortion have been limited to direct abortion and direct killing.

The dialogue over situationalism must avoid caricatures and false arguments. For example, some situationists show the absurdity of an absolute norm against lying.[1] In certain situations it seems that man must tell a lie; for example, the captured soldier who is asked about vital information. However, the defenders of an absolute prohibition against lying can come to the same conclusions as situationists. It all depends how one defines a lie! If the malice of lying consists in the violation of my neighbor's right to truth and not in the conformity of the spoken word with my thought, then principlists and situationalists can agree on the question of truthtelling in particular situations.[2]

Frequently, the opponents of the new morality will accuse the situationists of anarchy and antinomianism. Such charges are false. The situationist is a very responsible person who is honestly striving to respond in a Christian manner. Situationists do not believe that man can do whatever his whim and fancy might wish. Christians are always obliged to do the most loving thing in the particular situation.

Occasionally, situationists propose the problem in terms of love versus law. Joseph Fletcher inaccurately states the problem in terms of the opposing methodologies of legalism and situationalism.[3] Such a formulation of the problem is totally unfair. The principlist would never admit that the law or principle should always be followed even when love would demand something else. The question is not one of law versus love. Rather, the proper question is: Does love demand constant, uniform ways of acting? Are there certain actions which are always incompatible with love? Most situationists would admit some general ways of acting that are always incompatible with love; e.g., real disrespect for neighbor. The problem centers on the very few, specific, universal prohibitions. Likewise, the two positions cannot be characterized as code morality versus wisdom morality. To admit that certain actions are incompatible with Christian existence does not mean that one subscribes to code morality. Charges and countercharges of antinomianism and legalism do not help to clarify the rather limited but none the less real differences between situation ethics and traditional Catholic moral theology.

. . . I will consider three difficulties I find in the ethical presuppositions enunciated by Fletcher; the notion of love or *agapē*, extrinsicism or nominalism, and pragmatism.

According to Fletcher *agapē* or loving concern is the only norm for the Christian. *Agapē* describes the complete willingness to give oneself to others the same way that Christ has given himself for us. *Agapē* is distinguished from romantic love (*erōs*) and friendship love (*philia*) precisely because *agapē* is incompatible with any aspiring or self-seeking love. Reciprocity, mutuality, and friendship do not enter into the notion of *agapē*. Fletcher seems to draw too exalted a picture of *agapē*.[4] He definitely does not solve the age-old problem of the relationship between *agapē* and proper love of self. His description of *agapē* appears to be even ahuman and would always demand the heroic on the part of man.

Paradoxically, the exalted notion of *agapē* does not seem to enter into the final decisions made by the Christian situationist. Is *agapē* really as important as Fletcher says? One could start with a very human idea of wisdom or justice and come to the same practical conclusions as Fletcher. . . .

Secondly, an extrinsic or nominalistic approach to

ethics. Fletcher denies that there are any values at all. There are only things which happen to be valued by persons.[5] Extrinsicism maintains that all meaning and value come from outside the thing itself. I maintain that earthly realities do have a value and meaning in themselves apart from the meaning given them by the intention of a particular person. The whole theory of incarnational spirituality reminds us of the importance of the things of this world. . . .

. . . Perhaps here again Catholic theology has overexaggerated the meaning of intrinsic morality. Intrinsic morality does not mean the object in the abstract is always right or wrong. Rather, the whole moral complex, the situation, if you will, is right or wrong apart from the intention of the person. Perhaps there is not as much disagreement with Fletcher on this point as there might seem to be at first sight.

Thirdly, pragmatism. . . . Fletcher tries to wed pragmatism and *agapē,* but I do not think they are totally compatible. Pragmatism is success oriented in the sense of producing successful results as quickly as possible. Pragmatism will do anything to achieve its purpose. . . .

To be pragmatically Christian means to bring about the success of true *agapē,* but the Christian notion of success lies in the shadow of the cross of Christ. The Paschal mystery is the success story for the Christian, but such a life requires a dying to self. Is there enough room for the cross and suffering in the system proposed by Fletcher? Even the theological advocates of the secular city realize the need for the transcendent judgment of Christianity. The secular city with all its pragmatism can set up its own false idols which have to be criticized in the light of the Christian message.[6] I do not think that Christianity and a totally pragmatic outlook are entirely compatible. If by pragmatic, one means only that the Christian must find the most creative ways of showing *agapē* in the modern world, I agree. But too often the very connotations of pragmatism seem opposed to Christian ethics.

What can moral theology learn from a dialogue with Joseph Fletcher? At the very least situation ethics has been a good corrective for traditional moral theology. The average Christian makes almost all his ethical decisions within the boundary lines of the Christian life marked off by the few negative, universal prohibitions. Creativity and not conformity must be more present in the lives of most of us Christians. Situation ethics is a constant reminder to avoid the pitfalls of a shallow legalism.

Joseph Fletcher's methodology does reflect a way of looking at reality which is more suitable to modern man than the approach frequently employed in moral theology. The classical philosophy underlying much of moral theology tends to emphasize the permanent, the essential, the unchanging, and the substantial. Modern man places more emphasis on the historical, the particular, the individual, the changing, and the relational. The classical approach is primarily deductive; whereas modern man tends to be inductive. The inductive approach is more probing and less dogmatic than the deductive. I do not conclude that there are no absolute, negative norms of ethical conduct; but the modern way of looking at reality is less favorable to such norms than the older, classical world view. . . .

. . . In general, I think that within the continuity of traditional moral theology I can substantially agree with many, although not all, of the practical solutions mentioned by Professor Fletcher in his writings. However, I have definite reservations about some aspects of his methodology as mentioned above; and I feel uneasy at the general tone created in his attitude of exceptions to general rules. Fletcher makes the exception the rule! Perhaps such an attitude comes from the obviously polemical nature of his controversy with his opponents. In reacting to them, he seems to overreact.

How is it possible to find substantial agreement from within the Catholic tradition with many of the conclusions reached by Professor Fletcher? Catholic theology has admitted a distinction between formal sin and material sin. Material sins are actions which are wrong, but because of mitigating circumstances are not imputable to the person. Such actions are objectively wrong, but not subjectively sinful. On a popular level the existence of that distinction is shown in the remark that there is all the difference in the world between what the priest says in the pulpit and what he says in the confessional. Certainly no confessor would act harshly toward the woman who bore an adulterous child to free herself from the concentration camp and the danger of death.

Catholic moral theology also acknowledges the possibility of choosing the lesser of two evils where there are no other viable alternatives in a conflict situation. Therefore, the actions which Fletcher would call good, Catholic theology would say are objectively wrong, but not subjectively sinful or they are the lesser of two evils. But I think that Catholic theology might even go farther. How?

. . . How can moral theology come to grips with ethical decisions in sin-filled situations? I believe that a theory of compromise is in continuity with the tradition of Catholic theology. In the face of the sinful situation, man must do the best he can. The destructive and disruptive influence of sin frequently prevents man from doing what he would want to do in the given situation. The businessman might be forced to make kickbacks in order to stay in business. The laborer might have to kick in so much a day to be hired. The word compromise seems to fit such situations quite well. From one viewpoint the act is good because it is the best that one can do. However, from the other aspect the act is wrong and shows the presence of sin in the given situation which the

Christian is continually called upon to overcome.

Fletcher will object that a compromise theory is typical of an intrinsic approach to morality. I agree. However, his own approach seems to dismiss too easily the sinfulness and the wrong present in the situation. When a woman is forced to have an abortion to save her life there is something wrong in that situation. When one must kill to protect innocent victims of mass hatred, there is something sinful and wrong about the situation. When a woman in Harlem is deprived of every source of human happiness except having a child out of wedlock, there is something wrong with the situation. Those sinful situations must be overcome. Fletcher dismisses the whole problem too easily by saying that the particular action is not wrong. Under one aspect, the action is not wrong; but under another aspect, the action is wrong and manifests the sinfulness of the situation. The notion of compromise tries to do justice to the total situation. Compromise also indicates that the person cannot be entirely at ease in making such a decision. In a sense the Christian must always have an uneasy conscience. Every such decision indicates that sin is forcing a person to do what he would not do under other conditions.

Catholic theology with such a theory of compromise could better speak to the reality of the world as we know it. Such a theory recognizes the truth in many of the dilemmas brought forth by the situationists, but at the same time the theory of compromise looks beyond the predicament of the individual conscience to the social reality of the total situation.

8.
WALTER G. MUELDER
— " Moral Law and Christian Social Ethics "

. . . In contrast and opposition to ethicists who try to fit
cases into previous or prescriptive moral laws. Lehmann stresses the transforming power of a concrete exception and cites from the New Testament the man
healed on the Sabbath Day, the woman taken in adultery, the "good Samaritan," and the "prodigal son"
as vivid instances of the way Christianity specializes in
the exception. He is not referring to exceptions which
prove the rule, but to ones that suspend the rule and
break new ethical ground. "Transvaluation means that
the ethical inadequacy of accepted norms and values has
been exposed by ethical insights and directives integrally
related to the concrete ground of decision." To do this we
may respond, Very good! Yet a question must be pressed.
Does not the new insight claim to have general significance? Does it not belong to subsequent knowledge
about what God is doing in the world? in *all* the world,
not just in the *koinōnia* of the Christian church? Does not
the way the concrete situations were handled by Jesus
give attitudinal guidance by redefining a norm which is
relevant to a whole range of other situations? A new
ethical generalization, attitude, motive, or insightful
norm has become part of subsequent ethical judgment:
" Go do thou likewise."

On these issues Barth seems to have grasped the universal implications of humanity in Jesus Christ more
radically than Lehmann has expounded them, for Barth
is not confined by the *koinōnia* of the church. " On the
basis of the eternal will of God we have to think of
every human being, even the oddest, most villainous, or

From the chapter " Moral Law and Christian Social Ethics," pp. 17–
22, in *Moral Law in Christian Social Ethics,* by Walter G. Muelder.
Used by permission of John Knox Press.

miserable, as one to whom Jesus Christ is Brother and God is Father; and we have to deal with him on this assumption. . . . On the basis of the knowledge of the humanity of God no other attitude to any kind of fellowman is possible. It is identical with the practical acknowledgment of his human rights and his human dignity." By arguing in this way Barth lays the foundation for a common ground morality that cuts across faith lines and all cultural lines. This emphasis radically corrects the exaggerations of his earlier theological position which stressed the eternal qualitative difference between time and eternity.

From the standpoint of the present writer one of the most successful efforts at presenting the Christian category of love coherently with an understanding of the elements making up discriminating judgments is that by Joseph Fletcher. A presentation and brief evaluation of six propositions which he regards as the fundamentals of Christian conscience will serve to clarify a number of issues relating moral laws to Christian ethics. For Fletcher the category of love, *agapē,* is the primordial or axiomatic value. This *summum bonum* cannot be reached except by an act of faith. Christian moral judgments are *decisions,* not conclusions; science and logic are only auxiliary to evaluation and choice.

The six propositions are as follows: (1) " Only one thing is intrinsically good, namely, love; nothing else." (2) " The ultimate norm of Christian decisions is love; nothing else." (3) " Love and justice are the same, for justice is love distributed." (4) " Love wills the neighbor's good whether we like him or not." (5) " Only the end justifies the means; nothing else." (6) " Decisions ought to be made situationally, not prescriptively."

In commenting on these propositions, we must note how the meaning of each one and all of them together embody laws which will be systematically detailed in later chapters. First of all, Fletcher argues that values

exist only in response to persons. Value is not an absolute, independent existence but is always "value for a
person." He approvingly quotes Brightman that "in
personality is the only true intrinsic value we know or
could conceive; all values are but forms of personal experience." Love is "goodwill at work in partnership
with reason, seeking the neighbor's good radically, nonpreferentially." Augustine was right in reducing the
whole Christian ethic to the single maxim: "Love and
then what you will do," not, however, "Love and do
what you please!" This principle is too radical to be a
prescriptive legalism; it shares its power with no other
kinds of laws, natural or supernatural. It is, thus, the ultimate ideal which controls all other values and choices.

The category of love so interpreted contains an axiological law which commands a critical use of reason in
relation to ideals like justice and the "more or less"
which is relevant to concrete situations. Since justice is
love distributed, it requires a consideration of the claims
of self and those of the plurality of "neighbors." So
conceived, justice and love are not (as in Brunner and
Niebuhr, says Fletcher) independent categories. In seeking social policy love acknowledges both person and
community and the reshaping of subordinate principles.
"Justice," Fletcher argues, "is Christian love using its
head — calculating its duties." It is attitudinal, not emotional. It is volitional, conative. It considers consequences and makes preferential judgments. When
Fletcher says that "love's method is particularity," he is
affirming in effect a "law of specification." Love includes
the laws of concrete moral responsibility.

The situationism of Fletcher is marked off from that
of Lehmann in the following strategic formula: "*The
indicative plus the imperative equals the normative.
What is, in the light of love's demands, shows what ought
to be.*"

Though oriented by faith in theological decision,

Barth, Lehmann, and Fletcher proceed differently in handling concrete decisions. Of the three contextualists or situationists Fletcher shows the greatest understanding of the place of the empirical in moral judgments. The relation of theological to philosophical and scientific disciplines involved in the above theories and their implications for moral law requires further analysis than the exposition has thus far provided. . . .

It is often acknowledged that law cannot evoke a non-existent ethic or one that has become uncouth, obsolete, or irrelevant. Scientific validity and moral propriety must be sought together and reconciled through the worth of persons. It is persons who must make the transition from one cultural stage to the next. " In all technical change," writes Margaret Mead, "even when it seems to be concerned with tools, machines, and other impersonal objects, the individual person is both the recipient of change and the mediator or agent of change. His integrity as a person, his stability as a personality, must be kept ever in focus as the living concern of all purposive change."

What sort of creature, then, is man? How is person related to community? What bearing do philosophical and scientific thinking have on moral law which does justice to persons in community? It is one of the theses of this book that if the contextual ethic of a Barth, a Lehmann, or a Fletcher is to be concretely relevant to decisions, it must be aware of all the empirical aspects of these situations and must be corrected and disciplined by moral laws which command the person to choose coherently at the logical, the axiological, the personalistic, and the communitarian levels.

9.
JAMES A. PIKE — *Agapē* Is Not Enough

FACTS in the real world around us, not authoritative laws imposed from the outside, are these: persons count more than things; the well-being of persons requires certain conditions. Some of these conditions can be brought about by self-help, some by mutual arrangement, some by the gift of others. The fullest gifts and most wholesome way of giving — for donor and receiver — is *love*.

But love is a fuzzy word. What kind of love? More and more familiar is the distinction between *erōs, philia,* and *agapē*. Hence the following definitions are not meant as an analysis of the three kinds of love, but as a reminder before we confront the crucial question, " What kind of love? "

Erōs is the love of the lovable; the object of the loving is the source of it.

Philia is the affection which arises between people because of mutual interest or focus; an outside factor is its source.

Agapē is the love of the apparently unlovable. (Professor Joseph Fletcher says: " We can say quite plainly and colloquially that Christian love is the business of loving the unlovable, i.e., the *unlikable* " in the *Situation Ethics*, p. 105.) Its source is in the one loving — from duty, or in response to being so loved by God or man.

Christian moral theologians, basing their view on New Testament texts, give *agapē* the highest marks. (*Ibid.,* p. 49.) Code ethicists include the requirement of it among the rules, some proponents of the new morality

From the chapter " What Preserves Persons? " pp. 70–73, in *You and the New Morality,* by James A. Pike. Copyright © 1967 James A. Pike. Used by permission of Harper & Row, Publishers, Inc., New York.

set it forth as the sole ethic. *But it is not the best brand of love, either for the lover or loved.* It is not enough. . . .

. . . But it has been said that *erōs* can't be commanded; *agapē* can. We are to love (agapeistically) people we don't like. What can be achieved by command and what is the good, however, are not the same thing. *Agapē* is not only not the full good; it partakes of evil. In its " pure " form, without admixture of *erōs* or *philia,* it is a " putting down " of the person thus " loved." (Dr. Fletcher says, "Pinned down to its precise meaning, Christian love is benevolence, literally.") It supplies a sense of goodness and well-doing to one person while *belittling* the other. For it to be recognizably operative it is intrinsically requisite that the other be assessed as unlovable, unworthy, undeserving, *no good.*

Whatever specific immediate needs of the agapeized one are being met and however well they are being met, the deepest need — to be respected as a person — is not only *not* being met, it is being intensified.

But the supporters of *agapē* as the highest love — and they are legion, including both the conventional and the situation ethicist — would answer that part of the *agapē* package by recommending the concealment of this write-off, this disrespect, out of concern for the other person. There are two difficulties with this:

1. This would mean that hypocrisy is built in — is part of the very nature of *agapē*. To tell the truth presents a different problem from making an existential decision, where all the factors are weighed in a given context. . . . Dishonesty is inherent in full *agapē*. Thus there are harmful effects on the actor: habituation to deceit, increase of resentment — hidden or open, and diminution of a posture of candor in life.

2. The feigned liking of another is not uniformly successful, especially in relationships which are ongoing if for even a short time. Respectful words and even responsive action, however carefully designed, do not al-

ways successfully hide the basic disrespect, the inner estimate that there is nothing in the other worth responding to. Even when there is the best possible "cover," the one on the receiving end of *agapē*, whether by intuition or extrasensory perception, or because of perceiving occasional cracks in the cover, can *know*. And when he does know, there is resultant humiliation, sense of inferiority, and resentment — all of which can combine to increase his apparent unlovability.

In being realistic about these factors, we do not mean to overstate the case. The plain fact is that there are many, many encounters in which a person with particular needs does not in any way attract the person or persons equipped to meet those needs. And the needs ought to be met. Meeting needs is the exercise of positive ethics and to that extent *agapē* is a good thing. But obviously it is not good enough.

10.
PAUL RAMSEY — A Riposte and Excursus

. . . OUR AUTHOR calls his own pragmatism "neopragmatism" (*SE*, p. 41) [*SE stands for Situation Ethics*] largely because he has come again to hold this view, which is evidently progress. To be plainspoken, pragmatism is " a *practical* or *success* posture " (*SE*, p. 42), and that seems enough to warrant the posture. " Our attempt to be situational " is described in apposition to our attempt " to be contemporary " (*SE*, p. 43). " Our milieu and era " are unfriendly to law (*SE*, p. 46). Four theories of conscience lie side by side in all thought upon this subject, but "situationalism takes none of them seriously " (*SE*, p. 53) — not even seriously enough to refute

From the chapter " The Case of Joseph Fletcher and Joseph Fletcher's Cases," pp. 156–159, in *Deeds and Rules in Christian Ethics*, by Paul Ramsey. Copyright © 1967 by Paul Ramsey. Reprinted with the permission of Charles Scribner's Sons.

them before adopting a purely prospective view of the function of conscience, which I suppose is equivalent to saying that this is correct because prospective. " The whole mind-set of the modern man, *our* mind-set, is on the nominalists' side " (*SE,* p. 58) , which is enough said in behalf of mind-set even if it could be demonstrated to be a species of thoughtlessness. The words " benevolence-malevolence " have sometimes heretofore been used with " a more direct and deliberate meaning than Christian situation ethics *cares to adopt*" (*SE,* p. 63, italics added). Our "normative relativism . . . waves good-by to legalism and dogmatism " (*SE,* p. 67) . " No twentieth-century man of even average training will turn his back on the anthropological and psychological evidence for relativity in morals." (*SE,* p. 76.) None should, of course, turn his back upon or wave good-by to such evidence; but a number of twentieth-century men of more than average training have not thought the evidence conclusive, and certainly not conclusive to the ethics Fletcher wishes to declare to be the policy of every true inmate of the twentieth century. Where Cicero affirmed that "only a madman could maintain the distinction between the honorable and the dishonorable . . . is a matter of opinion, not of nature," * Fletcher counterdeclares: " This is nevertheless precisely and exactly what situation ethics maintains " (*SE,* p. 77) . The new morality is " the emerging contemporary Christian conscience " (*SE,* p. 77) ; " people are, in any case, going to have to grow up into situation ethics, no doubt about it " (*SE,* p. 82) , since, I suppose, this is the wave of the future. The " generalization argument " is a " fundamentally antisituational gambit, . . . a form of obstructionism, a delaying action of static morality " (*SE,* p. 131) , even though Fletcher should know that a number of reputable philosophers believe this to be a fundamental principle of ethics.[1] " Modern Christians ought not to be naïve enough to accept any other view

of Jesus' ethic than the situational one " (SE, p. 139),
even though W. D. Davies' monumental study of the
Sermon on the Mount contains, with no *systematic* ax
to grind, a great deal of historical evidence to the contrary.[2] Still, " *Situationsethik* more and more openly wins
a place " (SE, p. 146) not only among nonfundamen-
talist Protestants, but, when you think about it, "in
effect most men are situationists and always have been! "
(SE, p. 147). After that sweeping, comforting statement,
a better truth is told, advertently or inadvertently: " Situationism . . . is the crystal precipitated in Christian
ethics by our era's pragmatism and relativism," to which
acculturation of Christian ethics Fletcher pays his highest tribute: " It is an age of honesty, this age of anxiety
is " (SE, p. 147).

We can, then, riposte upon Fletcher his own account
of classical Christian ethics' resistance to the situational
love ethic: " by any and every tactic " (SE, p. 36). This
volume's exhibition of the situation in theological ethics
could best be described as a standoff, an opposition of
declaratory policies or of persuasive appeals, and not a
grappling with one another over intellectual issues and
ethical warrants. I myself have a higher opinion of traditional ethics than to suppose that, say, its sexual ethics
can appropriately be dealt with by making any use of
the label " marital monopoly " (SE, p. 80), but evidently Fletcher does not. This would still not be the
way to do Christian ethics even if we had to give ourselves rational arguments where before there were none.

The foregoing excursus upon " the case of Joseph
Fletcher " is by no means an inappropriate introduction
to his ethics or to his cases, since so much depends for
this book's suasion upon appeals to the reader's like-
minded prejudices in favor of individualistic freedom,
normlessness, traditionless contemporaneity, and modern
technical reason.[3] I would be the first to grant, however,
that there is little to incline the mind toward rational

conviction one way or another insofar as I have simply riposted *ad hominem* explanations of Fletcher's ethics to his own *ad hominem* charges against all legalists and intrinsicalists, and insofar as I have suggested various cultural or personal idiosyncratic reasons why his ethics fails to fulfill the promise of his initial definition of situationalism and in fact turns out to be an act-situationalism.

* This is as good a point as any to indicate a glaring dyslogic in Fletcher's book, and one that is a rather characteristic misstep made by theologians who wish to protect some revealed norm of ethics from any admixture or connection with an ethics based on " natural " justice. " The attempt to study nature and discern God's will in it," Fletcher writes, " is only a hoary old sample of the ' naturalistic fallacy ' of deriving *ought* from *is.*" (*SE*, p. 76. The author had himself just derived *the relativity of morals* from anthropological and psychological evidence!) Now, if the naturalistic fallacy *is* a fallacy it counts as well against the foundation of Fletcher's ethics. It counts against his statement that " the key category of love (*agapē*) as the axiomatic value is established by *deciding* to say ' Yea ' to the faith assertion that ' God is love ' and *thence by logic's inference to the value assertion* that love is the highest good " (*SE*, p. 49, italics added). The case is not altered by using more pious expressions such as " we understand love in terms of Jesus Christ "; or by using the jargon of pre- or meta-ethics: " Before we ask the ethical question, ' What shall I do? ' comes the *pre*ethical question, ' What has God done? ' " (*SE*, p. 157). Philosophers from David Hume to G. E. Moore who have been proponents of the naturalistic fallacy have known that it counts against any type of theological ethics as well as against so-called " naturalistic " ethics. One has either (1) to refute or otherwise reject the naturalistic fallacy (and then the way is open for either a Christological or theological ethics *or* for an ethics of " nature ") or (2) to accept the naturalistic fallacy and then develop an ethics wholly upon some normative foundation, because the way is closed to either a supernaturalistic or a naturalistic ethics of any sort. One cannot be a theological moralist and at the

same time invoke the naturalistic fallacy to get rid of hoary old opponents; that weapon would cut the ground from under one's own position. Yet this is a device used by both Joseph Fletcher and N. H. Søe, both Barthians of some sort who, however, refuse to engage seriously in the "prolongation" of *agapē* into special ethics lest "nature" or intrinsicalism be admitted.

If the fact that God is love is one good reason why I should love and if the fact that Jesus Christ first loved us is one good reason why I should be thankful and why Christian ethics is a *eucharistic* ethics (*SE*, p. 156), then the deep propensities of human nature, etc., may be one good reason why I should do X. The naturalistic fallacy admits of none of these statements; it happens also to be by no means unanimously admitted to be a fallacy.

11.
ELTON M. EENIGENBERG
— "How New Is the New Morality?"

WE SHALL pose a simple problem in the area of interpersonal relationships. Three days ago Cynthia had given a rather important letter to her husband, Fred, to drop into the mailbox on his way to work. Fred is reading the evening paper. He hears Cynthia, busy in the kitchen washing dishes, call out: "Fred, you mailed that letter the other day, didn't you?" An hour and a half earlier Fred had been hanging his topcoat in the hallway closet when the back of his hand had brushed against a slight bulge in one of the pockets. "What could that be?" he said to himself. Investigation revealed it was the letter he had forgotten to mail. "No use making a fuss," he confided to himself. "I'll be sure to mail it in the morning. Cyn will never know the difference." And now she was asking. "Was she psychic or something?"

From the article "How New Is the New Morality?" by Elton M. Eenigenberg, in *The Reformed Review*, Vol. XX, No. 3 (March, 1967), pp. 11–23. Used by permission.

An answer had to be given immediately, of course. But before we hear Fred's response, let us expand the slight interval between question and reply into a space big enough to include the whole range of factors which are operative in the production of answers like " Yeah, took care of it! " " Sorry, I forgot. I'll take care of it in the morning." A vague, blurred " Uh-huh, mm. Don't bother me now, I'm in the sports page, dear." " Quite sure, hon." These factors will be of various kinds, including the physiological. Whether Fred had his favorite dessert tonight might well be the deciding factor in his resolution to tell Cynthia the truth or not. The history of their relationship together, especially in the subtle interplay of sensitive psychological factors, will have a good deal to do with the way Fred replies.

But we're going to give Fred credit for being a man of some ethical integrity. We still don't know what he will say. Cynthia had always thought him so reliable. He is ethical enough, however, to want to do the right thing — at least, that is, in the long run. We'll hand Fred over to the theorists for a little while and see what they can do with him.

Professor Joseph Fletcher of the Episcopal Theological School in Cambridge, Massachusetts, and perhaps the most radical exponent of the new morality in this country, declared recently that there are " at bottom just three lines of approach to moral decision-making." [1] At the one extreme is the antinomian or lawless approach. It produces spontaneous decisions. Christians of this stripe will usually claim that they are guided directly by the Holy Spirit and are therefore " above the law." Even general principles of morality are repudiated. Existentialists like Jean-Paul Sartre claim to make moral decisions with " autonomy " and " instantaneity." Each " moment " of existence is completely discontinuous from every other, so there can be no generalizing about our decision-making. Bultmann's " radical obedience," with its discerning of the demand of God in the moment of decision, is of the same kind.

If Fred's ethical stance were that of the antinomian type, we really don't know what he would reply to Cynthia, for to claim to know in advance what God would direct Fred to say (supposing Fred to be a Christian who relied on God for guidance), would be to usurp the divine prerogative. If Fred is an atheistic existentialist, our guesswork would be equally fruitless, for who can tell what kind of response will be served up by instantaneous insight into the moral wisdom that fits the moment?

At the opposite extreme from the antinomian Fletcher finds the legalist. This man works with predetermined general "laws" of morality.[2] He turns many of his legalistic rules into absolutes. This is "law ethics." One is obedient to prefabricated "rules of conduct." Principles are treated as rules rather than as maxims. Classical Christian ethics has been of this kind, says Fletcher. It has been characteristic of "the natural law of Catholic morality," and of "the scriptural law of Protestant morality."[3]

If Fred's morality is of this legalistic kind, the question, "What does the law require?" will be operative in his consciousness at the point of his wife's question. It may not be explicit at all. If Fred's Christianity has been conditioned by years of legalistic accents, in which the "Thou shalt's" and the "Thou shalt not's" have controlled the way life was lived from day to day, the question, What does the law require? may now have only an instinctive functioning, like that of a conditioned reflex. All of this does not mean that Fred is going to blurt out a craven and apologetic, "I'm sorry, dear. I forgot to mail your letter. Please forgive me."

Precisely because Fred's primary frame of reference morally is not a person, but a law; not a *who*, but a *what;* is he able to make immediate adjustments within the legal apparatus as it stands over against his own conscience. In the instance before us, the necessary adjustment may call for a " white lie," for which amendment or atonement will not be too difficult, on the strength of the rationalization that a white lie does less damage than the dark truth. Fred may dimly remember that the Bible said somewhere, " Do not lie to one another " (Col. 3:9a) , or he may recall Paul's instruction, " Putting away falsehood, let every one speak the truth with his neighbor " (Eph. 4:25). He will not remember, however, that Paul added to the latter: " For we are members of one another " (*ibid.*) . He is too imbued with the legal spirit to understand that a lie brings a serious disruption into a person-person relationship, that the real question is not, What law am I breaking, but How does my lie injure this person before me?

Fletcher finds both these styles of morality completely unacceptable. He recommends, instead, the approach of the new morality. His favorite term for this moral stance is " situation ethics." [4] Hear him as he speaks of it:

> In this moral strategy the governing consideration is the situation, with all of its contingencies and exigencies. The situationist enters into every decision-making situation armed with principles, just as the legalist does. But the all-important difference is that his moral principles are *maxims* of general or frequent validity; their validity always depends upon the situation. The situationist is prepared in any concrete case to suspend, ignore or violate any principle if by doing so he can effect more good than by following it. As Dietrich Bonhoeffer said in his prison-written *Ethics,* after conspiring to assassinate Hitler, " Principles are only tools in the hand of God, soon to be thrown away as unserviceable." [5]

It should be noted that Fletcher, in a more recent writing, has softened his accent on " principles," moving them into a more secondary position. " The new mo-

rality," he says, " subordinates principles to circumstances." [6] Perhaps Fletcher has felt the force of criticism
other new moralists have laid against the necessity of
beginning the attack on ethical problems with even so
handy an instrument as principles. Douglas A. Rhymes
insists that we must start with the person rather than
with the principles.[7] Bishop John A. T. Robinson declares, " We are not here as Christians with changeless
principles to *apply* to an alien process." [8] Antagonism
against principles per se has not reached the loathing
point, however, of the Cambridge professor of Christian
ethics, who fairly spat: " Principles! I wouldn't have the
filthy things around the place." [9]

The new moralists are united in opposing any ethics
which puts a code of laws, rules, principles, or explicit
regulations *prior* to, and *external* to, individuals in situations requiring ethical decision. To do so is to derive
" right " and " wrong " at second hand, as Bishop Robinson has said.[10] God gave the commandments or laws to
Moses on the mountaintop, in this view. Coming directly from heaven, they are eternally valid for human
conduct.[11] " Certain things are always 'wrong' and
'nothing can make them right', and certain things are
always 'sins', whether or not they are judged by differ-
ing human societies to be 'crimes'." [12]

In the persistent emphasis of the new moralists upon
the rejection of prior and external legal elements in the
resolution of ethical problems, and in their demand that
all ethical situations be viewed as being between, or
among, persons, one can detect the powerful influence of
the existential movement upon their thought. Prof.
James M. Gustafson of Yale University has remarked
that he cannot detect a difference between the situational
ethics of the new morality and existentialist ethics.[13] Not
the existentialism of a Sartre or Bultmann, but one
which wants to do some justice, at least, to the complex

of factors which make any human experience the integral thing it is.

On the positive side the new morality insists that the only absolute is that of love. Love alone is able to discover the deepest need of the other person. " Love's casuistry," says Robinson, " must cut deeper and must be more searching, more demanding, than anything required by the law, precisely because it goes to the heart of the individual personal situation." [14] Love respects the unique, individual person unconditionally. It penetrates to the center of the concrete situation and asks what the predicament at that point demands. In this kind of involvement, Robinson avers, there can be no " packaged moral judgments," for " persons are more important even than ' standards '." [15]

We have neither the time nor space to record samples of the paeans of praise raised by the new moralists to the Great Absolute, Love. Paul's " Love bears all things, believes all things, hopes all things, endures all things " (I Cor. 13:7) finds frequent iteration in one form or another in the writings of the new morality. It is more important at the moment to seek to be fair to the new moralists by attempting to discover what *content* love has in their estimation. Critics seem to find the new morality to be at its most vulnerable precisely here, and not without reason. The new moralists have been least scientific when they have allowed themselves to be carried away with ecstatic avowals of the high virtue of love. Further, their frequent condemnation of laws and rules, because these have a built-in content, ready to be applied, has seemed to say that any and all content is to be scorned. Professor Tom Driver, in an essay entitled " Love Needs Law," puts the new moralists' accent on love in the category of " free-floating ideals." [16]

The *content* the new morality is opposed to is that which is in existence prior to the particular ethical problem. The love which is called into play arises *after* the ethical predicament has become apparent. The content of the first is legalistic, abstract, applicable to many cases of the same general kind. The content of the second is particular, concrete, and uniquely fitted to the special instance to which it is applied as a healing medicine. The first is deductive in its approach, starting with general principles, ready to be applied. The second is inductive, starting with persons. The first regards some things as being always inherently evil; other things as always inherently good. The second sees nothing as being inherently good or evil, except love (translated as " personal concern "), and indifference or actual malice.[17] The content of the new morality approach is nothing less than a kind of sheer goodness, but as Fletcher has said, " Goodness is what *happens* to a human act, it is not *in* the act itself." [18] To put it in another of Fletcher's statements: " *Goodness or rightness is a predicate of actions, not a property of them!* " [19]

Now back to Fred and Cynthia. Let us assume that this couple had been attending a class in their church engaged in studying the ethical approach of the new morality. Douglas Rhymes has indicated that such instruction might well be necessary, to train people in the making of "mature decisions." [20] Let us also assume that of late the emotional relationship between Fred and Cynthia had been growing somewhat cold. The old " electricity " just wasn't there anymore.

But Fred understands that he ought not try to solve the problems of the moment with the energy a once-vibrant love might be able to furnish. Right now he must look upon Cynthia as a unique person needing his deep concern for her well-being, and he must see himself in very much the same light. The spiritual and moral health of their relationship may be significantly affected by his decison to tell the truth or to tell the lie. Let us assume that Fred concludes that their relationship cannot now stand the test of truth-telling. The fabric of their mutuality has worn too thin for that. Six months ago it might have been different. " Yes, dear," Fred calls. " I took care of it."

We shall now pose a more complicated problem in the sphere of interpersonal relationship. Bob and Betty have been dating one another for about a year. For some time their relationship had been warmly cordial, with only an occasional kiss to remind one another that they were, as some folk quaintly put it, of " opposite sexes." However, more recently Bob and Betty had been pressing cordiality to somewhat perilous limits. Tonight they had attended a church dance and were now ostensibly on the way home.

But the night was yet young, and Bob's heart being full of love for Betty, he decided to park at the lake shore. Betty found herself in immediate agreement with the idea, and as this ageless story goes, one thing led to another until Bob found himself demanding from Betty, in the name of an eternal love that knows no dying, and with the incoherence such situations invariably call forth, the ultimate gift she was able to give him.

The new morality has been charged by its critics with being obsessed with such situations — and more than that, with encouraging a bland permissiveness in the area of sexual relationships. The new moralists have been forced to become highly defensive at this point. Their moral scheme, they have said, has to do with moral problems of every kind, from the simplest difficulties in personal relationships to the question of American involvement in South Vietnam. Bishop Robinson has protested that the new morality has become identified in the popular mind with an " invitation to sexual licence," with himself as the author of it.[21] Douglas Rhymes remarks on the same theme, but adds that the new moralists have had to say much in the area of sex because it is in this field of personal morality that most needs to be done to " Clean up " the church's attitude and restore it to the sense of the wholeness of man in which the use of his sexuality is part of his wholeness. We would wish to see a view of sexuality which is *not* perpetually asking the question, " Is premarital intercourse wrong? " but rather seeing all sexual as other moral problems in the context of daily living, of the persons involved, and as a responsibility for maturity of decision and action. All such problems will be seen as to be solved in such a way that God may bring the maximum of maturity into the individual life. Such a method would mean that the church might look more realistically at the problem of the homosexual and ask the question, " How is he to express his sexuality to the greatest degree of wholeness for himself and others? " rather than just go on with the dreary and often totally unrealistic counsel of enforced celibacy. It might also mean that we would have a more helpful answer to the people whose marriage has gone dead than again a demand for a future total celibacy which is likely to be as impossible as undesirable.[22]

Some of the new moralists have been insistent that their approach, if followed through faithfully, will actually reduce sexual license. The logic of that claim is clear. If love's careful estimate of the need and welfare of the other person is always made, if, as Fletcher says, we are " who-askers " (that is, who will be helped or hurt) rather than " what-askers " (that is, what does the law prescribe) ,[23] the vast amount of sexual practice in and out of marriage which simply " uses " the other person will be eliminated.

Robinson declares that love's gate is strict and narrow, its requirements infinitely deep and penetrating.[24] It would be triflingly easy for Bob to ask, in his relation to Betty, " Why shouldn't I? ", and then answer, " Because it's wrong," or " Because it's a sin." It is far more demanding of one to ask, " Do you love her? " or " How *much* do you love her? " and then accept " *for himself* the decision that, if he doesn't, or doesn't very deeply, then his action is immoral, or, if he does, then he will respect her far too much to use her or take liberties with her. Chastity is the expression of charity — of caring, enough." [25]

What follows on the lake shore between Bob and Betty is closed to our sight. As far as general outcomes are concerned, they either did or they didn't. But as far as preliminary factors are concerned, the possibilities are many. If both had studied their textbooks in the new morality well, and had accepted the conclusions both rationally and emotionally, the conclusion of the matter is uncertain. They might have, or they might not have — depending upon love's directive, one in which the comprehensive need and welfare of Bob and Betty are properly calculated (this is " love's casuistry "). And calculations must take into account the far reaches of time, not just the span of an evening at the lake shore, with, perhaps, tomorrow's regrets.

That's the one extreme. The other is a rigid legal apparatus in which Bob and Betty, admonished a thousand times by parents, Bible, church, and the personal tragedies of others, that certain things, like the thing proposed now by Bob, were *dead wrong,* and that acquiescence to them could bring only terrors in this life and in the world to come, heroically flee the lake shore before it is too late. Between the extremes lie the sad mixtures and confusions thrust upon young people by the sophisticated relativisms of the times. These are the broken norms of the present. Besides these there are a multitude of imponderables at work in both persons, like emotional strength and tone, the firmness of the rational threshold, biological structure and condition, the subtle power of perfumes and ointments, factors of empathy, today's success or failure, relative distance to the married state, and who knows what else. Only an all-knowing God, fully cognizant of the delicate balance among all the factors, or their lack of it, might predict with accuracy the evening's outcome.

How New Is It?

We have given only two examples to illustrate the special strategy of the new morality. The same basic procedure might be followed through with problems from any ethical area whatsoever. While sexual practice in all of its ramifications provides the most dramatic focus for illustration, the implications of the new morality in every sphere of moral activity must be acknowledged and studied. There has been a method in our madness in providing this extensive discussion of new morality methodology before raising our principal question, How new is it? That question cannot be dealt with properly until one has seen something of the stark contrast between traditional approaches to moral problems, Catholic and Protestant, and what is now being proffered as " new," and yet as very old.

The insistence of the new moralists that their ethical scheme is not "modern" at all, but is the true ethics of the New Testament, needs our careful examination. If the claim is a true one, we ought in all honesty and integrity give up our present ethical stance if it is not in substantial agreement with that of the new morality. We are concerned, after all, with being as Biblical as possible. Bishop Robinson remarks about the new morality, " Of course, it is nothing new at all. . . ." [26] Fletcher observes that the new morality is not a new entity in itself, nor is it new in its method or approach.[27] That the new moralists are convinced that their ethics is not really new is evidenced best by the fact that frequent reference is made to the New Testament, especially to

Jesus, in support of their views. Naturally this always involves interpretation, but no special difficulty is experienced by the new moralists in finding the New Testament people to be in essential agreement with themselves.

If the claim that the new morality is quite old is true, it will have to be understood as " new " only in the sense of being a recovery of the original — of a very old original — and hence practically " brand new " for our time. If the claim is not true, the new morality will have to be accorded a new phenomenon, one which belongs to that large number of " new things " which the world of our times has delighted to bring forth.

It will be well to exonerate the new moralists at the outset of any possible charge of having unworthy motives in claiming an ancient origin for their views. They appear to make the claim in sincere conviction that they are recovering for our times the true New Testament point of view. They argue their case with the zeal and dogmatism of convinced partisans. Naturally, everyone likes to find some corroboration in ancient wisdom for his present scheme of ideas. This may well be both because there isn't supposed to be anything new under the sun, and because it seems awfully presumptuous to offer a cynical world anything at all that doesn't have a handsome pedigree attached.

The new moralists are not to be held responsible for the invention of the title of their ethical method. It came in the first instance from one of the method's chief enemies, Pope Pius XII, who, in an allocution on April 18, 1952, denounced what he called " existential " or " situational " ethics.[28] The pope protested that such a method might be used to justify a Catholic leaving the Roman Catholic Church if he felt it might bring him closer to God. Birth control might be defended on the claim that thereby personality was enhanced. On February 2, 1956, the Supreme Sacred Congregation of the

Holy Office gave the title, "the New Morality," to it, and banned it from all Catholic academies and seminaries. Professor Fletcher and others would like very much to drop the ambiguous title and call the method "situation ethics."

A qualifying word must be interjected here about the criteria which may be used in determining whether the new morality can be identified with the original ethic of the New Testament. Plainly, a point-by-point identification cannot be required. At the most we can insist upon agreement in the more central features. Even then, it is not at all easy to make comparisons between moral situations which are centuries apart. The complexities of modern moral situations frequently tend to obscure the ethical factors at work. In many a contemporary instance, for example, one must first attempt to decide whether he is being confronted primarily with a moral problem or with a medical one. On the other hand, the Biblical moral situation is completely free of theorizing, while contemporary moral situations are usually thoroughly attended by rival theories of explanation.

We shall ask at the very beginning of our comparison of the New Testament with the new morality whether the "situational" idea of the first is the same as that of the latter. According to the new morality the situational is not that merely which provides a situation of one kind or another. It would be hard indeed to conceive of an ethical problem which was not bound up in what we commonly understand as a situation. By situational the new morality means a structure of event in which moral solutions are produced out of empirically known situational elements, all of this under the control of the norm of love.

As an instance of this kind of thing Fletcher cites Matt. 12:3-4, where it is recorded, with Jesus' approval, that David and his companions entered the house of God and ate the bread of the Presence.[29] This was an unlawful act. Only the priests might eat that holy bread. Thus Jesus left no doubt whatsoever that " *the ultimate norm of Christian decisions is love: nothing else.*" [30] Love transcended the demands of the law. The act was right and good because the genuine needs of persons were served. The " need situation," guided by the considerations of love, furnished its own right course of conduct.

What Fletcher fails to observe, however, is that David's act with respect to the bread of the Presence did not abrogate the law with respect to it. The ceremonial law would continue to be observed as a divine requirement upon the people. The people would observe the rule with faith and love in their hearts toward God, or they might look upon it as an unnecessary tyranny. Most probably simply accepted it as a logical feature of the apparatus of religion. In any case it was right conduct before God to observe the rule. David's act illustrated that the ceremonial law was not absolute. In exceptional circumstances real human need might set the law aside temporarily — especially if one were a highly regarded person being chased about by a neurotic king. General ethical principles cannot be based upon such exceptions. They have their foundation, rather, in the approved forms of behavior. Except, of course, the general principle that exceptions can, in many instances, be allowed.

Robinson takes up the matter of Jesus' attitude toward the Fourth Commandment, that relating to the use of the Sabbath.[31] It was this same problem which was at issue in the case of David and the bread of the Presence. Robinson argues that against the counterclaim of " doing good," " the Sabbath regulation, as regulation, was null: law and love were simply incommensurable." [32] The incident in Luke, ch. 13, in which Jesus healed an infirm woman on the Sabbath, is selected as an illustration. In this situation Jesus berated his pharisaical opponents for their hard legalism, asking whether " this woman, a daughter of Abraham whom Satan bound for eighteen years," should not be loosed from the bond on the Sabbath Day (v. 16).

Does Jesus' heated response to the legalists of his time really prove that the Sabbath regulation, as regulation, was null, and that law and love were " simply incommensurable "? It must not be forgotten that Jesus' attack in these matters was mainly against the Pharisees' terrible corruption of the law, in which they had made it, not as Psalm 19 declares, something that revived the soul and rejoiced the heart, but an intolerable burden which no man could bear. God had intended the Sabbath to serve man at the point of his deepest needs. His law in these matters was a sign of his wonderful convenant love for his people. If the people kept God's law with a like love in their hearts, they would use the Sabbath for the blessing of man's life. Love does not abrogate the law, but lifts it to the plain of the service of God and man.

In another place Robinson points up the situational character of the Sermon on the Mount.[33] Jesus' moral precepts in that Sermon are not to be understood legalistically, prescribing what all Christians must do under any and all circumstances. He does not pronounce some course of action to be universally right and others universally wrong. Rather, " they are illustrations of what love may at any moment require of anyone." [34] This need not be disputed. But what Jesus says in the Sermon has to be related meaningfully to what he remarks near its beginning, that he had not come to abolish the Law and the Prophets but to fulfill them. Not an iota or dot would pass from the law until all was accomplished (Matt. 5:17-18). His own precept and example indicated that this fulfillment came, not when God's law was converted into a generalized love, but when love became the methodology in which the law's demands spelled " obedience in freedom " for Christ's people.

Robinson remarks that the parabolic character of much of Jesus' ethical teachings should save us from regarding them as literal injunctions for any situation, or as universal principles applicable to every situation.[35] Ethical decisions do not precede the problems; the context of the problems provides decisions — when love controls. So also in Jesus' teaching on marriage. His words do not mean that divorce is always the greater of two evils.[36] They do say that love, " utterly unconditional love, admits of no accommodation; you cannot define in advance situations in which it can be satisfied with less than complete and unreserved self-giving." [37] The implication is that in some instances the greater love will require the dissolution of a marriage. A lesser love, or the lack of it altogether, may insist upon its continuance, even if this requires the perpetuation of an intolerable relationship. The plea is that in such manner God's law is served.

Our only concern at this point is to ask whether Robinson has come by his conclusion about the permissibility of divorce by sound interpretation. If divorce is permissible in some instances, is it because the rule concerning the ideal permanence of marriage (Jesus: " The two shall become one. . . . What therefore God has joined together, let no man put asunder," Matt. 19:5-6) has been annihilated by the claim of love? Is not the allowance of divorce rather a sign of the deep tragedy of much of human existence, that sinful man cannot always live by the law of God, and that therefore love must woefully sue the law to allow another sorry exception to its demand? Is not the law of God heightened in its beauty and power when in pity the exception can be allowed — but the ideal remains? The sorry situation does not produce its own ethical decision. It is given from the outside, as it were.

Robinson is more concerned than the other new moralists to insist that the law has not been abrogated, not really. It is merely destroyed *as law*.[38] Law, he says, belongs at the boundaries of situations, not at their center.[39] But if it has been destroyed as law, what is it that stands at the boundaries? The Bishop has been very ambiguous in all of this. He seems reluctant to let law go altogether, yet whenever he sets it by the side of love, it pales into insignificance. Perhaps the reason for this is that he has never really distinguished carefully between law per se and the legalistic use of the law. He is very much opposed to the second, and regularly he seems to be destroying the first in the name of the second.

Inherent in the new morality's accent on situationalism is the insistence that laws, rules, and regulations do not properly exist *prior to* ethical situations as norms to which deeds must then conform. Can this be proved from the New Testament? We have seen how the new moralists have attempted to do so, far more by simply asserting it than by straightforward exegesis. Robinson alone gives much effort to the work of interpretation — and he is regularly controlled by his powerful " love premise." It becomes necessary at this point to raise the critical question whether the new moralists have not made the fundamental error of making a part to be the whole.

There can be no doubt that the methodology of New Testament ethics is that of love. God's own primary mode of securing his ends was by love! He requires the same of his people. But love is not *everything!* It is the divinely appointed way of serving God in trustful obedience; it is at the same time a dynamic force of great power. It is, however, the will of God that must be done; or better, God must be served in faithful obedience. His revealed will concerning that which delights him is his law. And so the law must be obeyed. That law is fulfilled when it is obeyed through love's instrumentality. Jesus himself said that he did not come to destroy the law, but to fulfill it. He did so with a love unsurpassable in its depth and embrace. Love as instrument is secondary, and functional to that primary thing, God's revealed will. In a great many instances it stands prior to man's obedience — or his disobedience.

It is perfectly true that the church has too often served the purposes of the law, including revealed law (or, the will of God), with a loveless heart. The law has too often been separated out as a thing in itself. It has been constructed into ponderous codes and frightening legal systems. It has stood over against hapless Christians like an awesome giant, demanding an obedience no one could proffer. So impossible were its demands the Roman Catholic Church determined that only a small minority of her people, the clerics and the religious, were able in some measure to live by the utmost requirement. All the rest were committed to the small attainment of mere conformance to explicit commands of the Scriptures. There is much in Protestant history that is as equally unwholesome. The church always stands in need of correctives over against this gigantic mistake. But the answer is not found in taking legalism's opposite, Love, and making it everything, creative even of its own contents.

The content for a Christian situationalism is the will of God that must be done in love. Paul does not let his fellow Christians think that love can be understood without the specific detail which the life of Christian love demands. His letters have many references to the kind of morality required of God's people in this world, and much of this is in the form of specific commands, exhortations, ethical directives. Of course he did not spell out Christian ethics in the form of codes or tables of rules. But ordinary Christians, which most of us appear to be, want the details. We want to know how love works itself out in specific ways in Christ's church and in the community of the world. The Bible does not fail us here.

From many possibilities in the epistles of Paul we may select Eph. 4:25-32 to serve as an example of Paul's manner of speaking about the requirements of the Christian life. In the first twenty-four verses of the chapter he has set forth the *context* and *situation* of the Christian life in a beautiful and powerful way. It is life in the love of Christ. But it is also life in the loving obedience of Christ. So he tells the Christians to put away falsehood and to speak the truth, " for we are members of one another " (v. 25). They are not to sin in the expression of their legitimate anger, for this gives the devil his opportunity (vs. 26-27). Those who had been given to stealing are to stop it and get down to honest work with their hands, " so that [they] may be able to give to those in need " (v. 28). Christians are not to engage in " evil talk," so that their speech " may impart grace to those who hear " (v. 29). They are not to grieve the Holy Spirit by bad conduct, and so it will be well if they put away from them bitterness, wrath, clamor, slander, and malice, and to be, instead, kind, tenderhearted, and forgiving, " as God in Christ forgave you " (vs. 30-32).

An illustration of Paul's exhortations and demands in the area of the sex life can be found in I Cor. 6:9 to 7:40. Certainly there is not found here a code of rules standing by itself, or " over against " the Christian community with the police power of civil law behind it. Nevertheless, obedience to Christ in this area demands loving adherence to certain rules and principles which promote the spiritual and moral health of both the Christian person and the Christian community. The Bishop and his friends have declared that it is love *or* rules. The apostle seems to be saying that Christ is best served when love for him and other persons follows ways which God in his Word has approved for the good of all. Some of these ways say quite definitely what is permitted in sexual behavior, and what is not. This is how Christ and love are served.

Our conclusion is that the new morality is, after all, quite new. There are significant enough differences between it and the New Testament to make us refuse to accept its deliverances as a faithful rendering of the same. A factor we have not had space to discuss, but a very important one, is the very great difference between the communicative power of New Testament ethics and that of the new morality. The latter can speak meaningfully only to a very few — those who are able to master its dialectic. It is a specialists' ethic, a precious thing for an intellectual elite. One must go to a class to learn its technique. The common people heard Jesus gladly, and while they frequently gave little attention to his moral directives for life in the Kingdom, they were able, at least, to understand what they were. So with the writers of the New Testament. They have been understood by millions down through the centuries. Too often their ethical directives have been converted into hard legalisms. That was mostly a corruption of the method, not of the content.

Jesus and the apostles spoke to men where they were, on the level of their appreciations. God's demands were made as his will was revealed. The grace of God was promised and given — so that those who wished to obey might have at their disposal the means by which to obey. Forever there was a falling short of the goal — and always the exhortation to keep trying. The new morality is incredibly naïve. It takes a fellow and a girl at the lake shore — and demands of them a miracle of objective evaluation of a deeply passional situation, and with that, decision-making at a rational level the UN would be proud of. People aren't made like that, and so God had to make a lot of things pretty clear beforehand.

12.
HARVEY SEIFERT — " The Promise and *Peril* of Contextualism "

CONTEXTUALISM or " situation ethics " is stirring up quite a storm on the ecclesiastical landscape. We should be grateful for any fresh breezes that blow away accumulated fog so long as they do not also scatter their own particular types of smog. Modern contextualism used responsibly as a corrective may contribute important insights. In its more radical and distinctive forms, however, this may turn out to be one of the most dangerous ethical emphases of modern times.

A great deal depends upon what we mean by contextualism. If one means that for moral choice it is necessary to take into account the realities of the existing situation, there can be no quarrel with the position. It is indeed necessary to gather data, recognize facts, and do empirical research. Before one makes a political decision he had better study the political situation. Before adopting an economic policy he had better become familiar with economic theory. In this sense any responsible person is a contextualist.

Or, if contextualists insist that it is important to be aware of differences between situations and to act differently under varying circumstances, again most persons would surely agree. Any parent who has ever brought up two children recognizes that accomplishing the same goal requires some modification in approach because of differences in personality. Circumstances do alter cases. Even " Thou shalt not kill " cannot be regarded as an infallible rule in defense against a marauding madman. Suicide may be heroism if it saves others on a lost Arctic

From the article, " The Promise and *Peril* of Contextualism," by Harvey Seifert, in *The Christian Advocate*, Vol. 10, No. 24–25 (December 29, 1966), pp. 11–12. Copyright © 1966 by The Methodist Publishing House. Used by permission.

expedition with supplies running low. We need to be extricated from too rigid or archaic rules and we need to learn a proper humility about our conclusions. A certain flexibility is necessary if we are to be completely true to all complexities.

Insofar as contextualism dramatically protests against utopianism or legalism we had better listen carefully. One cannot immediately read off from a rule book a prepackaged prescription for the perfect action in every concrete situation. Life is too complex, ambiguous, and changing for that. Furthermore, it is only realistic to recognize that love requires us to seek a variety of goals, such as freedom and order, or justice and peace. In pursuing one, it may be necessary to compromise another. The most moral act is always the one which is the best possible under the circumstances.

In all these respects contextualists make important contributions, but in none of these respects are they unique. Other important ethical schools of thought also recognize all these factors. The so-called principlist, for example, can also include the characteristics of the context as an important part of his analysis. He retains all the values noted above for contextualism by insisting that principles be applied not singly but as a *system* to indicate the course of action which maximizes the expression of love in the concrete situation.

The uniqueness of contextualism as an ethical position is to be found in its tendency drastically to minimize the place of principles. Modern situation ethics is allergic to generalized guiding rules — and this is where its sickness lies. An epidemic of this disease could have mortal consequences for both church and culture.

This distinctive emphasis of contextualism can be seen in terms of the three sets of factors usually considered to enter into ethical decision. The first of these are theological realities, including, for example, the character of God, the potentiality of man, or the overarching norm of love. The second is a system of ethical prin. ciples, goals, guidelines, middle axioms, or whatever similar terms might be preferred. The third set of factors is the sociological data describing the specific concrete situation within which choice is made.

The contextualist tends to move directly from theological realities to concrete situations, stressing the dangers and minimizing the use of principles. His theory tends to eliminate the disciplined relating to any concrete choice of principles like order, freedom, or equal opportunity, or of general statements about the profit motive, national sovereignty, or premarital sex relations. He is so impressed by the decisive differences between circumstances that he stresses the freedom of the Christian man imbued with the disposition of love and acting pragmatically in each unique situation.

A first major criticism of the distinctive emphasis of contextualism is that it leaves the norm of love too nebulous to be meaningful. Outgoing concern for others gives little guidance until we ask *what* in general is to be sought for others. Principles or middle axioms are necessary to spell out such meanings. Unless they are given an important place in ethical analysis, the concept of love can easily be given all kinds of curious meanings. " Love " can then be used as Stalin used the concept of peace, or as Eichmann used the concept of duty — to rationalize private interests and desires. Either we give meaningful content to love by a system of principles or we leave conduct essentially unguided by love, except possibly in some erratic or intuitional sense.

Especially is this true in a culture which presents unprecedented problems and complex situations. To think that a good man will directly know what to do under modern circumstances is naïve. One might require less elaboration of the goals sought by love in the simple situations of a comparatively static society as, for example, in the case of the good Samaritan. But how is one to recommend a solution to the Vietnam problem without some very careful work on the social goals which lie between the overarching norm of love and the realities of the concrete situation? Without such summarizing generalizations we remain basically ineffectual in the crucial processes of modern decision-making.

A second major defect of the contextualist position is that it tends to overlook likenesses among circumstances. Situations are not filled to the brim with uniqueness. They are also shot through with common characteristics, especially as they appear in the same common environment of modern times or of the Western industrial world or of finite men with similar needs. It is possible to group acts into classes of situations. One can define types of murder, for example, and say something which is generally applicable about each of them. Contextualists often seem to see this in some fields. They may be willing to make ringing general declarations about the meaning of " freedom now " in race relations or poverty. Yet they are unwilling to do the same thing about matters like smoking and sex, even though frequently the ambiguities and complexities of race and economics may be even greater than those of cigarettes and sex.

When there are unusual cases they should not be treated as if they were typical. That would be to make rules out of exceptions. For example, Joseph Fletcher cites the case of a German mother in a Russian prisoner-of-war camp who could gain release and rejoin her family by becoming impregnated by one of the prison guards. Should she choose this way out? One might agree with Fletcher's affirmative conclusion. Yet it does *not* follow from this that each sex experience is decisively unique or that generalizations about extramarital sex give little help. The problem for American young adults is not posed by an extremely rare foreign captor. It is instead a problem which in its significantly important aspects is common to thousands of persons.

One can speak to this common problem in some quite specific terms.

The similarities between situations become especially apparent if society as a whole is taken into account rather than restricting observations simply to the individual actor or to the few persons directly involved. If one goes beyond extreme individualism to a cultural viewpoint, he will recognize that the undesirable consequences of some acts for society as a whole outweigh any advantages they might have for the individual participants. One can make statements about extramarital sex relations on this ground which he might not make so long as he was considering only the two partners to the act. The same thing is true if one takes long-run consequences into account, rather than simply concentrating on immediate effects. Another way of putting this is to say that a responsible use of the context requires that we take all of the context into account. When we do that, in several respects it becomes more easily possible to generalize.

In some cases similarities outweigh differences among situations to such an extent that it is possible even to speak of absolute evils. Under all foreseeable circumstances it would seem to be wrong to use the " doomsday machine," a weapon so destructive that a single use would wipe all human life off the planet. No other human values could be protected by such an intensity of destruction. Or investing resources in diamond-studded dog collars is wrong no matter what the different characteristics of dogs or their owners may be, so long as there are so many persons suffering from malnutrition in the world.

Similarities among situations make it possible to legislate. If we considered every situation completely unique, laws against murder or race discrimination would become impossible. We could not even make a decision in advance to hire a cleaning woman to come in once a week or to route invoices across the same desk as they arrive in the office. Policy decisions as well as statutory law are continuously based on the observation of likenesses which are more significant than differences.

It is sometimes argued that we cannot determine prior to the moment anything about the demand of the moment. To attempt to do so, it has been claimed, is to make man lord and judge where only God should be. God's command is held to be a particular command to a specific man in a unique situation. But this protects the spontaneity of God at the cost of his character. It reads continuity and consistency out of the nature of God. If we believe that God exhibits integrity and dependability and that he does not will contradictions, then we can count on similar guidance from him with respect to acts that are significantly alike. Since the spontaneity of God is always an expression of his character, it is possible to speak of principles or guidelines for conduct.

The moment does not contain everything necessary for decision. In fact, the meaning of the moment cannot even be seen unless it is placed in historical context. The Bible interprets concrete decisions in relationship to the insights of tradition. Man does not need to start over from the beginning each time a similar issue comes up. To suggest that he should is to dehistoricize man. Principles or summarizing rules gather up ethical resources from man's past. Prior reflection is necessary to responsible action. We do not need to make up our minds afresh whether or not we are going to steal each time that we see a car we admire. There may be infrequent occasions on which stealing can be defended, but the burden of proof is always placed on such "exceptions." Strictly speaking, such acts are not exceptions since they are required by other principles which loom as more relevant to the situation when an entire system of principles is coherently applied.

Radical contextualism eliminates the values of a systematic approach to the moral life. When man tries to move directly from love to the situation, he lays himself open to the charges historically leveled against anti-nomianism. His judgments are in danger of becoming capricious and erratic. Personal and social life under such circumstances becomes ethically chaotic.

The claim of Christian ethics is systematic and comprehensive. A total commitment of life to the will of God requires rigorous dedication and continuous discipline. Contextualism can easily lapse into a less demanding and thoroughgoing ethic. There is enough of evil in man that he is tempted to exaggerate the uniqueness of his own circumstances in order that he may yield to impulse. Instead of the more radical demands imposed by consistency with principles, we prefer uncritical conformity to custom. Contextualism can become a cover for conservatism. It easily leads to a relaxed relativism or a too easy acceptance of compromise. Reluctance to accept a responsible code of behavior even down to the fine points like drinking or smoking is refusal to take the ethical task seriously.

When contextualists confront moral choices, they often avoid these traps because they do as a matter of fact use principles in their process of decision. They bootleg in generalized goals like order, or the primacy of personality over property, or efficiency in the management of resources — even though doing so contradicts their distinctive theory. Or they may admit in fine print that they are doing this, yet the rest of their theory goes on as though the footnote had not been inserted. If they did put this admission into big print and make it a significant part of their theory, they would no longer have a distinctive ethical stance. They would find themselves saying much the same thing as the Roman Catholic natural law theologian, or as many principlists among Protestants. They face the horns of a dilemma. Either they maintain a distinctive system which is dangerously inadequate, or they make a more responsible contribution which is less distinctive.

Christian ethics would be better off if contextualists adjusted their theory to fit their frequent practice. Then laymen could more easily recognize that the apparent confusion and controversy in ethics is to a great extent artificial. Instead there is a considerable consensus about the actual practice of decision-making which employs all three of the factors listed above: theological realities, principles, and sociological data. The contextualist's attempt to correct an oversimplified legalism by going to the opposite extreme is no improvement. Extremism is as dangerous in ethics as in politics. Publicizing the more adequately balanced consensus position may be less sensational but it is more sound.

13.
THOMAS A. WASSMER, S.J.
— " Is Intrinsic Evil a Viable Term? "

LET ME EXPLAIN why it appears to me that the term "intrinsic evil" is not a viable term in moral philosophy and why it causes more problems than it attempts to solve or even to explain adequately. I shall try to defend this position by considering the meaning of intrinsically evil and then by examining the representative acts which are usually designated as intrinsically evil. To translate these ideas of mine from one rhetoric to another is to find the principal thrust in Joseph Fletcher's *Situation Ethics*. In his own language this insight is that there are no universal negative prohibitions.

An act is considered to be intrinsically evil if, viewed

From the article " Is Intrinsic Evil a Viable Term? " by Thomas A. Wassmer, S.J., in *Chicago Studies*, Vol. 5, No. 3 (Fall, 1966), pp. 307–314. Used by permission.

just from its moral object, prescinding from circumstances and motive, it is always in difformity with the
proximate norm which is rational human nature. The
moral object of an act is that relationship which it bears
to the norm of morality. The object of an act is the
whatness of the act. For example, homicide has a different moral object than murder; fornication has a different moral object than adultery. If the act is regarded
solely from its object and found to be repugnant to rational human nature (adequately considered), then such
an act is characterized as intrinsically evil. The object
of most acts or, to phrase it more precisely, most acts
viewed just from their objects, prescinding from circumstances and motive, are morally indifferent. Walking,
smoking, even killing are morally indifferent acts considered just from their objects. It is only when walking
is done under certain circumstances and with this or
that motive that walking acquires the moral dimension
of being either morally good or morally bad. Likewise
it is only when smoking is done in excess by someone
whose health may become endangered that the act assumes a moral dimension of good or bad. Incidentally,
this latter example provides a rash of problems because,
while smoking in excess may involve consequences upon
physical health, there is no doubt that it provides psychological good consequences which may well be intended to counterbalance the possible harmful consequences to physical health.

The last example cited above of homicide is a more
interesting one to consider. Homicide, the killing of a
man — just this act viewed from its object — is morally
indifferent. It requires the addition of several factors to
become an act morally evil. Not every variety of homicide is the same. Which circumstances have to be added
to homicide to constitute an act of murder? These are
circumstances that are required even to constitute the
physical integrity of the act of murder. What is inter-

esting is that these very circumstances that change a mere act of homicide into an act of murder also are the circumstances that change the moral object of indifference in the case of homicide to a moral object of evil in the case of murder. What is added to homicide to make homicide a case of murder? Here is where the moral philosopher becomes even more technical and begins to add elements that almost inflate the original moral object of mere homicide. What is murder for the moralist?

Murder for many moralists is unjust killing of another man. What really does this mean? When spelled out it becomes this expanded definition and, as John Hospers says, makes the original moral rule " do not kill " almost diluted into a tautology. This is the articulated meaning for unjust killing or murder: it is the *direct killing of another man on one's own authority outside a case of legitimate self-defense. Direct* killing refers to the act of killing intended as an end or as a means to an end, and *on one's own authority* means that one is exercising right over another person's life which he does not have. By the inclusion of self-defense within the definition, the definer surely wants to exclude this as an act of murder when the assailant is killed. But what happens if someone considers it just punishment for a society to exercise capital punishment? In order to exclude capital punishment as an act of murder when the criminal is killed, does this not compel the advocate of the above definition to include this exception? Murder then assumes this definition: Direct killing of another man on one's own authority outside a case of legitimate self-defense and *capital punishment*. If anyone wants to designate this moral act with its expanded, articulated object, an act morally wrong, he will receive wide acceptance in Western society. However, suppose this definition is offered to the extreme pacifist who takes the moral rule not to kill literally; suppose it is submitted to the Hindu who extends the prohibition against taking life to all forms of life; suppose it were submitted to Dr. Schweitzer?

Now I do not quarrel with the fact that there is general acceptance in many quarters of the definition of murder. What I do suggest is that murder has been so defined that it excludes everything that we do not regard as murder, and it is here where some moralists with one constellation of values will add or subtract cases and other moralists with a different constellation of values will add or subtract other cases. If, then, for us murder is defined as it was above — *direct killing of another man on one's own authority outside a case of legitimate self-defense and capital punishment* — and if this act of murder is then considered to be merely evil from its object, intrinsically evil from its object, just how viable has this notion of intrinsically evil become? Viable for all who accept, but not viable for those who dissent from our own constellation of values, our own value system.

This speculation on the problems that arise from any designation of an act to be intrinsically evil can be extended to include a consideration of similar problems in the cases of suicide, lying, and sterilization. It seems to lead to this conclusion: that the moral philosopher must struggle to develop the most authentic meaning for murder, suicide, lying, sterilization, but after he has constructed such a moral act, he should be very hesitant to designate it as intrinsically evil. Why is this so? Because by characterizing this act with all of its qualifications as intrinsically evil, he has little ground on which to move unless he is willing to reexamine each of the qualifications and admit that the definition is malleable. The problem with the person who readily designates an act to be intrinsically evil is that he will tolerate very little modification within the definition of the moral act as he proposes it. In fact, does not the very term " intrinsic evil " seem to imply that modifications are not in order? However, any student of the history of ethics knows well that modifications are very much in order arising from a more penetrating knowledge of human nature and the complexities of the human act.

An examination of most texts in ethics will reveal a general reluctance to refer to any act as intrinsically evil. Most books mention blasphemy and stop there; others add dishonesty, infidelity, dishonor, but these latter are really dodging the issue because they do not specify the very moral act which *is* an act of dishonesty, infidelity, or dishonor. Any moral act can be built up into something approaching the notion of intrinsic evil if we construct upon the simple moral object of the act a variety of circumstances and motives which will alter its moral species from moral indifference to moral evil. But how far does this construction have to go before we are sure that the moral act is intrinsically evil?

To take sterilization as a further example. *Sterilization in itself* is morally indifferent; *indirect therapeutic sterilization* in the presence of a pathological disorder is morally good; *direct punitive sterilization* would be acceptable to anyone who accepts the De Lugo position on the lawfulness of direct killing of an aggressor in the case of legitimate self-defense. If the De Lugo position warrants direct killing of a criminal in these circumstances, then a fortiori direct sterilization of a criminal can be allowed because to intend directly the death of the man himself is something more serious than to intend directly the mutilation of his generative system. The further problem with the moral dimension of sterilization is the question which is the thorny question in the controversy over the anovulants, i.e., if the anovulant results in a sterilization (temporary) , may such a sterilization be *directly* intended in the absence of a pathological condition such as menorrhagia, dysmenorrhea, or an irregular menstrual cycle? In other words, may this kind of sterilization be directly intended, intended as a means for the further good of marital intimacy and in the presence of serious psychological reasons? To say that a direct sterilization is always wrong, to say that only indirect sterilization is licit in the presence of a *physical* pathological condition, is to narrow the area of moral dialogue.

More can be said and should be said about the non-viability of the concept of intrinsic evil. It is hoped that these reflections will stimulate some further discussion on the problem of moral evil in general and on the prudent unwillingness to characterize any moral act as intrinsically evil. Intrinsically evil, applied too freely, can place an albatross around the neck of the user.

From this analysis of mine, carried out in a somewhat different rhetoric, I am inclined to the conclusion that Fletcher is correct and that any attempt to construct such universal negative prohibitions terminates in meaningless tautologies.

Universal negative prohibitions are found principally in the areas of sexuality and human life. It seems to me that even here a case can be made against their status as *universal* negative prohibitions.

14.
JOHN LACHS — "Dogmatist in Disguise"

IT IS by an understandable egotism that we speak of our own age as the one in which codes can "no longer" meet the demands of morality. The facts are, however, that codes have never sufficed to solve a single moral dilemma, and that unthinking adherence to them has never guaranteed the worth of any agent. Decisions

From the article "Dogmatist in Disguise," by John Lachs, in *The Christian Century*, Vol. 83 (November 16, 1966), pp. 1402–1405. Copyright 1966 Christian Century Foundation. Reprinted by permission.

have always been essential to the moral life. But all along most people, indeed most Christians, have refrained from decision-making largely because this necessitates thought. Thus a telling objection to Fletcher's view is that it is altogether impractical. The majority of people are neither willing nor able to deliberate and decide with the care and rational foresight demanded by genuine morality.

The ideal of the unthinking advocate of law-morality is that of a computer divinely programmed with the list — no doubt infinite — of all the individual right actions which may be performed. If we had such a list, our moral problems would certainly be solved. In any problematic situation we should simply check the alternative courses of action which appeared on the list, and hope that in each case the machine would approve at least and at most one such alternative. Fundamentalists have on occasion attempted to use the Bible as such a computer, but the list of right actions derivable from the Bible by even the most careful study is too incomplete and too schematic to give more than general guidance.

What renders laws useful and even indispensable for the person who finds thinking difficult is the unavailability of specific commandments to cover every conceivable situation. Following a code — the Ten Commandments, for instance — does not guarantee that the right thing will be done in every case. But it does ensure that the person who unflinchingly acts by the code will do the right thing much more often than if he acted out of instinct or private " inspiration." If Aristotle was correct in declaring that in any situation there are many ways of doing what is wrong but only one way of doing what is right, the chances of a person's hitting on the right action by following his hunches are not very good. Choice has many advantages over simple adherence to law. It is by no means clear, however, that choice yields actions which have a higher probability of being right than does code-governed behavior. In his legitimate attempt to expose the inadequacies of codes, Fletcher seems to forget their genuine and useful function in guiding the conduct of the many. Decision-ethics cannot become universal so long as human nature remains what it now is.

In ethics as in everyday life we speak sometimes of moral actions and sometimes of moral persons. The word "moral" has different senses in these different contexts. To say that a man is moral might mean that he is likely to do or intend doing the right thing. To say that an action is moral, on the other hand, might mean that it is likely to produce good consequences. Further, if a person is thought moral, he is considered worthy of being rewarded; and if an action is thought moral, it is considered worthy of being performed. Now there is general agreement that a person's moral worth should be determined on the basis of his intentions, his disposition, and his character traits. But there is great disagreement as to what it is that makes an action right. Some hold that certain actions or certain types of action are right in and of themselves, and that any adult with a developed moral sensibility can tell whether an action is intrinsically right or not; and that is the end of the matter. Others maintain that the rightness of an action is conferred on it by the intention of the person performing it. Others — perhaps the majority of moralists — declare that an action must be judged right on the basis of the good consequences it produces.

These are simple but central distinctions in ethics. Yet Fletcher seems to lump them all together. On the issue of what makes actions right, he appears to hold every possible position. He gets off to a good start by denying that an action can ever be right in and of itself (pp. 59–60). But soon we find him retracting this view, in favor of one which maintains that actions are "right *when* or while or as long as they are loving," simply because they are loving (p. 141). Since "loving" is something we do (p. 61), we could simply say, then, that actions are right in and of themselves if they are "loving."

This last might be a defensible position. Fletcher, however, apparently is not satisfied with it. He goes on to explain that the morality of an act is really a function of the purpose we have in performing it. If our purpose is loving, the action is right; if the good intention is missing, even conformity to the moral law will not make the action right (p. 65). This too might be a defensible position if it were held consistently and alone. But it flatly contradicts Fletcher's previous view (that loving actions are intrinsically right) as well as the next view he adopts.

This third and final theory maintains that an action is right if it creates a greater amount of value than any alternative action could create. Actions, we are told, are justified by their "agapeic expedience" (p. 125). This means that they are right when their consequences are good or when they help create the greatest possible amount of love in the world (p. 156). Fletcher is quick to discern the close similarity of this view to utilitarianism, and with the qualification that the ultimate value is love not pleasure, he hastens to ally himself with Bentham (p. 95). Thus, by a few bold contradictions, he succeeds in combining in the same book Bishop Joseph Butler's view of intrinsically right actions, Immanuel Kant's insistence on the central importance of intentions, and John Stuart Mill's plea for the primacy of consequences.

If I had no theory about the cause and cure of such miscellaneous contradictions, it would be pointless or unkind of me to dwell on them. Let me say then that the reason Fletcher is unclear about the morality of actions is that he is confused in his concept of love. Love is central in his "new morality." The presence of love, he says, is pivotal in the moral life, and in ethical theory everything hinges on it. Yet nowhere are we told in detail what love *is*. Instead, we are given an astounding series of half-developed and contradictory indications. Love is first said to be something we do: it is thus (1) an action or a way of behaving (p. 61). This definition is quickly revised: love becomes (2) a characteristic of certain human actions and relationships (p. 63). Again it is (3) the purpose behind the action (p. 61). Toward the end of the book it becomes (4) the motive behind the decision to act (p. 155). Elsewhere, love is (5) an attitude of persons, (6) a disposition to act in certain ways, (7) a preference for certain values, and (8) goodwill or a conative predisposition to take certain attitudes (pp. 61, 79, 104, 105). And it is also said to be (9) a relation, (10) a formal principle, and (11) a regulative principle (pp. 60, 61, 105).

Surely love cannot be all these things. If love is (1), it cannot also be (2), since actions cannot be the characteristics of actions. If love is (9), it cannot also be (4), (5), and (6), since relations are not motives, attitudes, or dispositions. If love is (3), it cannot also be (10) and (11), since no conceptual dexterity can identify purposes with principles. This central confusion about love explains why Fletcher is confused about the morality of actions. For if he holds that love, which he considers the only ultimate value, is (1) a kind of action, he is naturally led to the position that right actions are right intrinsically; that is, simply by virtue of their being loving regardless of their antecedents and consequences. If he maintains that love is (3) a motive, (4) a purpose, or (5) and (8) a conative attitude, he must obviously embrace the view that the value of an action derives from the intentions or personal traits of the agent who performs it. And if he avers that love is (9) a relation between persons, he will inevitably adopt the opinion that the morality of an action must be judged by its tendency to bring about such ultimately valuable relations.

Although he presents no clear ideal of its nature, Fletcher is admirably single-minded in maintaining that love alone is unconditionally good. In consequence, it is difficult to take seriously his assertion (p. 34) that situation ethics is a method only. In fact, situation ethics is both more and less than a method. On the one hand, to designate something as the *summum bonum* is to do far more than merely providing a method of making moral decisions. If love is the only thing good as an end, we know not only *how* to make choices; we also know *what* to choose. On the other hand, to bid us make decisions is to fall vastly short of providing a method for decision-making. The injunction "Take the circumstances into full account" does not amount to a description of a procedure which would reduce decision-making to an ordered sequence of steps. Nor is it helpful to introduce the hedonistic calculus. That approach never brought much order or mechanical regularity to moral deliberations. Rechristening it "agapeic calculus" merely compounds its own problems with the difficulties of specifying the nature of love and measuring its extent and intensity.

By an exercise of Christian benevolence one might attribute all these weaknesses to the difficulties inherent in working out a revolutionary new Christian ethics. The reason Fletcher's view appears revolutionary is obvious: Fletcher claims to be a relativist. Now no one loses sleep over relativity in physics; yet the bare mention of relativity in the realm of values evokes an outcry which brands the moralist as a radical. However, most of the great systems of Christian ethics have been relativistic. In theological ethics, the good has traditionally been conceived as relative to God's will or God's intellect, or to the total configuration of God's nature. In natural-law ethics, excellence is conceived as relative to and determined by the essence of existing types of being. Such traditional relativisms upset no one. After all, it would be an exaggeration to call Augustine and Aquinas radicals today. Relativisms which establish fixed and universal values appear to be generally welcome. What motivates the rejection of other sorts is the fear that they might make values varied, changeable, and individual. Most Christians are instinctive dogmatists firmly convinced that unanimity in belief and uniformity in behavior are indispensable conditions of the moral life.

Fletcher announces his bold break with the dogmatists, and promptly rushes headlong into the most unstable and absurd relativism. He quotes Cicero's remark that only a madman would hold the difference between virtue and vice to be a matter of opinion (p. 77), and then cheerfully introduces himself as such a man. In short, his position seems to be the Protagorean one: that anything is good and any action is right for the individual, so long as he honestly thinks so. A view magnificent in its simplicity. Fletcher gives a fair sample of its wisdom when he says that " if people do not believe it is wrong to have sex relations outside marriage, it isn't " (p. 140).

But surely this is not Fletcher's basic view. He is quite explicit in maintaining that love is good intrinsically, that it is supremely valuable whether anyone thinks so or not. A person who says that love is not good or that it is good only because he thinks so, is simply wrong. And here for a moment Fletcher displays his colors. Love, it turns out, is good not only independently of opinion; it is " always good and right . . . regardless of the context " (p. 60). As the end of all ends, love is an absolute and unchanging value; its goodness is neither relative nor contingent (p. 129).

Here Fletcher's vaunted relativism and contextualism vanish. The nature of the agent and the context in which he operates, says Fletcher, have no influence on *what* is valuable; they only govern *how* something of value may be best achieved. Thus their relevance is restricted to moral means. In other words, the good is fixed and unalterable, and in any moral situation firm, discoverable causal laws make possible the production of a definite amount of good; the moral agent's obligation is simply to discern the good and to discover the means by which it may be realized. The nature of the good, the quantity of good realizable in a given situation, and the means to such maximal achievement all being fixed and determinate, virtually no room is left for choice, decision, and the varieties of individual conscience. Thus it becomes easy to separate the sheep from the goats. Those who are intelligent enough to recognize the good and industrious enough in their pursuit of it are morally justified; the others must be condemned for a failure of intellect or will. Residual credit may be given those who earnestly try, without success, to make the right decisions; but the fact remains that their decisions are wrong, their choices mistaken, and their values confused.

It should be clear by now that what lurks behind the new morality is the old dogmatism. To render the old moral dogmas acceptable, they are dressed in today's garb. There is much talk of relativism, and on some individual moral issues concessions are made. Free love, abortion, euthanasia appear to be condoned. At first the reader thinks that a genuinely Protestant view of morals, insisting on the primacy of individual conscience, is about to emerge. But in the end Fletcher seems to believe that the values *he* favors are objective and universal, and that no one else's values have any legitimacy. This urge to disclose the universal good and this ambition to prescribe values for everything that lives and moves are prime characteristics of the dogmatist, who in his vast immodesty presumes that he may speak for others in the matter of moral commitment and values. It is no surprise, then, to find Fletcher delivering imperial judgments on sundry moral situations. He seems to take it for granted that every reflective person will agree with him, or at least tacitly to demand agreement. From his point of view, every moral problem has its solution; and when the solution is not provided — as in the case of the four problems he leaves us with at the end of his book — we shall find it ourselves if we have been attentive students of the new morality. Thus the making of moral decisions is like elementary mathematics: a search for right answers. The skilled moralist always gets the right answer. But woe befalls the man who, in this game for the highest stakes, has not learned the rules and so makes a mistake.

Nowhere is Fletcher's promise of a genuinely Protestant, individualistic ethics fulfilled. A fruitful Christian relativism is indeed not impossible. Not, of course, the Protagorean relativism that Fletcher flirts with; for if values were relative to opinion, our lives would fall into a disconnected series of momentary commitments. No value could be consistently judged lesser or greater, and belief would float erratically about, unattached to any firm basis in compelling fact. Still, opinions about the good must touch the world of facts somewhere, and the contact can occur only in living, judging persons. If we were omniscient, we would share God's knowledge of whatever universal norms the unchangeable divine nature might dictate. As it is, we must be content with the modest conviction that values vary with the nature of finite individuals.

Such might be the complexion of a warm, generous, Christian relativism. The theory that values are relative to a universal human nature does violence to the facts of man's plasticity and straitjackets the rich variety of his perfectibilities. The theory that the good is individual, however, sounds alien harmonies. Christian humility debars us from judging the lives or ways of others; Christian love demands that we accept their different goods as of equal legitimacy with our own, and that we permit, even help, them to seek each his own perfection. The theoretical basis of such loving toleration is that natures differ, that one's values are a function of one's nature, and that a unanimity greater than constitutional likeness allows is useless in morals and unnecessary for harmonious social existence.

For a human being caught in this valley of doubt, there can be no higher morality than to live by the most inclusive values his nature dictates. The test of his achievement — and its reward — is the satisfaction without which life has no meaning, and in whose presence one can feel no lack. Fletcher hints at this view when he says that all ethics are happiness ethics and that everything turns on what it is that makes the individual person happy (p. 96). If we add to this the criterion (also briefly hinted at by Fletcher, on p. 140) that self-realization should not be allowed to proceed at the expense of hurting others, we have the rudiments of a sane value-relativism that may revolutionize Christian ethics. Minor concessions on issues of sex or business practice cannot save the old dogmatism, nor can they do justice to the radical love message of Christianity. The " new morality " will have to be a relativistic ethics of total toleration. And there will be little that is new even in that, for it is simply the all-forgiving love-ethics of Christ.

15.
VERNON L. WEISS — Read Fletcher Aright!

SIR: It isn't often that I feel like taking on one of the writers for my favorite periodical, but John Lachs's critique of Joseph Fletcher (Nov. 16, 1966) was just too much. I too found some things with which to disagree

From a Letter to Editor, by Vernon L. Weiss, in *The Christian Century*, Vol. 83 (December 14, 1966), p. 1542. Copyright 1966 Christian Century Foundation. Reprinted by permission.

in Fletcher's *Situation Ethics;* I could even agree with some of Lachs's criticisms. But the Fletcher [whom] Lachs spends most of his space bludgeoning bears only the remotest relationship to the Fletcher that I read! . . . As a pastor who is currently using *Situation Ethics* as the basis for a course with members of my parish, I first hit the roof while reading the paragraph which ends " Fletcher seems to forget their [the codes'] genuine and useful function in guiding the conduct of the many." Lachs's implication seems to be that Fletcher would have us ignore all codes completely as inadequate and untrustworthy. This position smacks of the antinomianism that Fletcher puts down almost as positively as he does legalism; his position is made clear when he writes, " The situationist enters into every decision-making situation fully armed with the ethical maxims of his community and its heritage, and he treats them with respect as illuminators of his problems " (p. 26). In his hurry to accuse Fletcher of forgetfulness, it seems that Lachs forgot something himself — to read the first chapter of the book he was criticizing.

I punished my already sore head against the ceiling once more when I read that " the reason Fletcher is unclear about the morality of action is that he is confused in his concept of love." Maybe so. Fletcher does not define it with the hair-splitting accuracy available to the user of a powerful philosophical vocabulary. But my class of noncollege adults and I certainly learned a whale of a lot more about the New Testament concept of love from Fletcher than we'll ever learn from the kind of philosophical gobbledygook with which Lachs clobbers us in the section of his article which follows. It is clear to me, at least, that if Fletcher seems to cover a good bit of ground with his concept of love, that is precisely because agape *does* cover a lot of ground. It would also appear that if Lachs's objections to Fletcher's " loose " use of the term " love " are valid, then the New Testa-

ment is also in line for criticism on the same grounds.
" Surely," says Lachs, " love cannot be all these things."
I'm not so sure, and neither, I think, were the New
Testament writers.

Fletcher's view is, says Lachs, " the Protagorean one:
that anything is good and any action is right for the
individual, so long as he honestly thinks so." To sub-
stantiate this point, he quotes Fletcher: " ' If people do
not believe it is wrong to have sex relations outside
marriage, it isn't ' (p. 140) ." But what Lachs doesn't
tell us is that the rest of Fletcher's sentence runs as follows, " unless they hurt themselves, their partners, or
others "! And then Fletcher goes on to say, " This is, of
course, a very big ' unless ' and gives reason to many to
abstain altogether except within the full mutual commitment of marriage." Just as Fletcher says, that is a
very big " unless." But Lachs ignores this, and would
not have us even know that Fletcher considers it.

Lachs's petulant and sometimes petty reaction to
Fletcher reminds me of the reactions several years ago
by four theologians to J. A. T. Robinson's *Honest to
God*. In the course of their several lectures on the topic,
they all made it clear that Robinson really didn't have
anything to offer because (1) he didn't say anything
new and (2) he didn't say it as accurately as the various
specialists would have liked. This was, of course, during
the time when Robinson was selling like the proverbial
hotcakes. In summing up the four lectures, the master
of ceremonies (a former editor of *The Christian Century*) said to the lecturers, " Well, now, if what Robinson said has been old hat to you theologians for a generation, why hasn't the church heard it before? " The
same could be said of Lachs's criticisms of Fletcher:
maybe he didn't say it perfectly, but he said it in a way
that the church is finally able to listen!

Fletcher has taken a subject that has left many a good
scholar hanging on the ropes, gasping for understanding,

and made it clear enough that ordinary pastors and their parishioners can catch some glimmer of understanding. Why pillory him for a few inaccuracies, if indeed he is guilty of them? Far better for him to have oversimplified on the far side of complexity than to have stopped short of it in the childish simplicity of traditional legalism. The church has had all too much of that. Better, too, a few inaccuracies than to have bogged down in the midst of theological and philosophical complexity. Few would wish to follow him there. Thank you, Joseph Fletcher, for your help. And thank you, too, John Lachs, for one clear line at least — your last: " For it [a relativistic ethics of total toleration] is simply the all-forgiving love-ethics of Christ." And that's funny, because that's what I thought Fletcher was writing about all along!

V

REFLECTION AND REPLY

by

Joseph Fletcher

THE OLD MORALITY with its classical absolutes and universals is a form of Pharisaism. Its purpose is to follow the law (moral norms), even though staying as close to love as possible. The new morality, for which situation ethics is the appropriate method, follows love (freedom to put human need before anything else), staying as close to law as possible yet departing as far from it as need be. Jesus taught this situationist kind of freedom from moral law. He held that morals were made for man, not man for morals.

In *The Shaking of the Foundations*, Tillich said of Jesus: " The burden he wants to take from us is the burden of religion. It is the yoke of law, imposed on the people of his time by the religious leaders, the wise and the understanding, as he calls them in their own words — the Scribes and Pharisees, as they are usually called. Those who labor and are heavy laden are those who are sighing under the yoke of the religious law. And he will give them the power to overcome religion and law; the yoke he gives them is a ' new being ' above religion." [1] Tillich should have completed his last sentence, " and moral laws."

The conflict between Jesus and the orthodox Jews was not " theological " in the sense of differences about doctrine. It was ethical. He spearheaded a *moral* revolt. He was a Jew, not a Christian — but a Jew whose morality was centered on love instead of law. Then Paul took up his cause and theologized it by adding to Jesus' new moral teaching a new teaching about who this Jesus was. He preached a faith about Jesus, not the faith of Jesus. Later, among the Greeks converted by Paul, there were some who wanted to follow a third ethical line, i.e., ignore law altogether. These were the " God-directed " who denied that they needed moral guidelines of any kind. Most of the Christians, however, soon forgot Jesus' bid for freedom and slid back into the legalism he threw out. One recalls the young Nazi's devout cry before World War II: " We Germans are so happy. We are free from freedom."

Here we have the three primary models for ethical strategy: legalism, situationism, and extemporism. Our language may change but the shape of the problem stays much the same. We may be more sophisticated conceptually, but the argument is still the old one, in modern dress. One critic has asked whether a codeless love is the only alternative to a loveless code. The reply must be a clear Yes.

I confess that the main thrust of *Situation Ethics* was against legalism. This was because almost all people in our Western culture, especially Christians, are and have been legalistic. They hang on to certain eternally invariable rules of conduct as absolutely valid and universally obliging regardless of the situation. They think there are some things (allegedly learned directly from God) that are always right or always wrong. Yet the recent hippies' ethics, a hang-loose-baby ethics in wild reaction, and its sophisticated support by existentialist writers and philosophers may soon become influential enough to call for a second corrective treatise, aimed in *their* direction.[2]

The thing to note is that situation ethics is in the middle, between moral law and ethical extemporism. One is bound by its principles, the other has none. (Professionals speak of "rules ethics" and "act ethics.") Situation ethics is a victim of polarization — the easiest and silliest of tools used by those who oversimplify life's relativity and fluidity.

If you refuse to give intrinsic validity to moral principles, you are assumed to have none. Even my German publisher, before I knew what he was up to, retitled *Situation Ethics* as *Moral ohne Normen?* [3] The old morality's advocates (Catholic and Protestant) see the new morality camp as cryptoantinomian, while the non-principled and "way out" spontaneists see them as soft legalists. The *via media* is a dangerous path, and I suppose we really are, in some degree, fifth columnists in both of the polar camps. We cannot absolutize both love and law, and the New Testament makes it perfectly clear which one to choose.

We are all in debt not only to Edward LeRoy Long for tracing the modern debate, in his account included in this volume, but also to John Giles Milhaven, S.J., and David J. Casey, S.J., for their "Introduction to the Theological Background of the New Morality." [4] Noting Father Milhaven's remark, quoted earlier in Part III, that *Situation Ethics* was "too popular" for some and "too pedantic" for others, the debate is, I think, steadily finding its own level.

So — as Harvey Cox says, situation ethics is not new. Let's say it is a *re*newed cause. Look again at Vernon Weiss's tale about what happened to John Robinson, and the chairman's question, "Well, now, if what Robinson said has been old hat to you theologians for a generation, why hasn't the church heard about it before?" If the new way of looking at belief (e.g., Robinson's) and the new way of looking at mission (e.g., Cox's) and the new situationist way of looking at ethics are all old stuff, why all the fuss? Does old hat mean long accepted, long rejected, or what?

Ouwerkerk in Holland puts it this way: " The fact alone that situation ethics is still a recurrent and almost obtrusive problem and is once again attracting attention in the context of secular ethics . . . is, to say the least, significant. If, leaving all incidental matters aside, we state the essential problem of situation ethics as: ' How can I know God's will in the world? ', then we are immediately faced with certain categories which Catholic moral theologians have also debated *without as yet arriving at any solution*." [5] (I added the italics; let's add Protestant ethicists to Catholic moral theologians.)

Let me repeat again and again that *Situation Ethics* advanced a methodological thesis — about how to do ethics. It did not enter into the " content " problem. I personally would adopt nearly all the norms or action-principles ordinarily held in Christian ethics. I refuse, on the other hand, to treat their norms as idols — as divinely finalized. I can " take 'em or leave 'em," depending on the situation. Norms are advisers without veto power. Situationism is a form of relativism as to both norms themselves and as to their use; for Christians it is a Christianly motivated form of ethical relativism. It decides what's good by the facts, not by ideal abstractions. The insistent demand to spell out the " content of love " masks an insistence on norms as prefabricated decisions. To " fill up " love with rules or laws is to slip back into a new form of legalism.

An atheist could be a situationist, or an egoist, or a vitalist — anybody who, no matter what his formal imperative may be (love, self-interest, life, or whatever), cuts his coat to fit each situation. Lots of atheists, for example, make love their imperative, and often they outdo Christians in their faithful service to it — even if their reason (motive) is neither Christological nor theological.

In Cox's happy phrase, *Situation Ethics* like *The Secular City* (and *Honest to God*) has helped in the "democratization of theological conversation." We have seen that ethics, even theological ethics, is still of interest and concern to people on the pavement and in the pews, as well as to the professionals. These things are not so esoteric in our culture as they were thought to be.

Nor are the professionals themselves unable to break loose from traditional rhetoric and ideas. On the contrary, behold the situational or contextual positions taken by Protestant contemporaries Lehmann, Sittler, Cox, Kaufman, Rasmussen in America; Robinson, Rhymes, Montefiore, and Williams in England; Bultmann and Thielicke in Germany. Among American Catholics, an outstretched hand comes from Johann, Milhaven, Wassmer, Curran, and such Catholics abroad as Bishop Simon in India, Louis Monden in Belgium, and Archbishop Hurley of South Africa. Incidentally, it is a mistake to include Rahner, Gilleman, and Häring, since they are all still too tied up in the old natural law metaphysics, even though they try to follow Teilhard de Chardin in treating natural law as evolving in a dynamic way rather than in the old static "given" ontology. Still and all, it makes a pretty grand roster.

If I had to pick the one difference among situationists or contextualists that is most important, I'd say it is the epistemological issue. How do we know what the good is in any situation — the most loving or concerned or human-helping thing to do? Ouwerkerk puts it theologically: How can I know *God's* will? Or, in Paul Lehmann's language, How am I to identify the "activity" or "politics" of God in the world at a given time and place?

Take James Nelson's "summary-rule agapism." It is,

of course, mine too. But I want to explain why, in Nelson's words, I focus "not on the present activity of God but upon love as the absolute ethical principle." *It is because I simply do not know and cannot know what God is doing.* People never have agreed about it — not even, maybe especially, in the church. This is the Achilles' heel of Paul Lehmann's *koinōnia* ethics. It was for a while pretty fashionable in neoprophetic circles to talk smoothly about "looking around" and seeing "what God is up to" and acting according to his will (his "political activity"). This starting point is losing lip service, inevitably. After all, the Christian has no inside track cognitively. What is special about him is his faith, not his knowledge.

It is tricky enough to decide what course is the most loving one, but I can do it with more or less assurance. However, to assert in a civil war, for example, or a strike, or in any complex "gray area," that God is on this or that side is plainly demonic, idolatrous, or psychotic. My faith in God is not some kind of tracer ink with which I can splatter God, so that I may find him when I look for him in spite of my humanly limited perception or God's own *absconsum*. Love I can do, but God's will I can do only through love. As Eric Berne, author of *Games People Play,* has said, what we "have to do about problems is make decisions. But people want certainty. You cannot make decisions with certainty. All you can do is compute likelihoods. People don't like that." [6]

What is God doing? There is only one way for a Christian to answer. Look at Christ and ask, "Does this or that action fit his perfect love?" This then forces upon us the question, "What is love?" or "What is it to love or to be loving?" And for this there is no law — only a rule-of-thumb: "Seek the best welfare and deepest happiness of the most people in the situation."

I know "love" (*agapē*) first as an empirical and experiential thing. Then I recognize it in Jesus and by faith I (not all who know love) find Jesus " the most " and go on to believe in a God exemplified by Jesus. Then I come, thereafter, to reunderstand love in terms of Jesus and the kind of love he made manifest.

I say with Nicolas Berdyaev: " The gospel morality of grace and redemption is the direct opposite of Kant's formula; . . . you must *not* act so that the principle of your action could become a universal law; you must always act individually, and everyone must act differently. The universal law is that every moral action should be unique and individual, i.e., that it should have in view a concrete living person and not the abstract good. Such is the ethics of love. Love can only be directed upon a person, a living being, and not upon the abstract good. To be guided in one's moral action by love for the good and not for men means to be a Scribe and a Pharisee and to practice the reverse of the Christian moral teaching." [7]

Insisting on man's fallibility, which is not denied or disputed, as if it makes agapeic concern impossible or unworkable, pulls the rug from under all ethics, except sheer egoism. It also undermines the Christian view of man and redemption.

Still, given all the loving disposition in the world, we need common sense and knowledge and logic to put it to work successfully. This is why I, for one, cannot go along with any inspiration or intuition theories about conscience. Conscience is a function of personality, it is not a faculty or " gift "; it is not a moral radar or guide, like a remora on the nose of a big fish. It is something we do, not something we have; we have to speak of it in verb terms, not in noun terms.

Harvey Cox's reference to our " rediscovery of experience " has some basis in fact and as such is welcome, but I cannot let it pass without a warning to those (not Cox) who may take it to be an imprimatur on subjectivism. I would like to add to what he says about it that "experience" must be understood empirically, not religiously or mystically or sentimentally. Let's rule out the transrational dreams of both intuition and inspiration. Father Milhaven puts it well: "It is empirical evidence, not direct insight into what something is, but the observation, correlation, and weighing out of numerous facts, which reveal the value of most human acts." [8] I would only want, as a situationist, to change Milhaven's "most" to *all*.

This new-old morality is part of a larger movement, of course. It is a breakthrough which has to be seen in a broader context along with the new theology and the new evangelism; a three-pronged drive reflecting the pluralism and empiricism and relativism of "mature" men in the modern age. All three have sloughed off the classical metaphysical apparatus of a priori assumptions and ontologically "grounded" axioms and norms. We just do not reason deductively or syllogistically anymore.

Some critics have been shrewd enough to recognize that situationism is, by traditional standards, a little "weak" on the side of guilt, "sin," repentance, and forgiveness. Its sharp distinction between remorse or contrition, and regret, is bound to narrow the range of the forgiveness business. It holds that sins are offenses against love (i.e., against God), but if love in any situation calls for violation of a moral law, no sin is committed that needs excuse or remission. If an act is loving, it is good and therefore right. If it is loving, it is right and therefore good. In each case it depends upon *the situation,* and upon *how we understand it.*

If we misunderstand it and act accordingly, that is cause for regret but not for remorse. If we act unlovingly, that is cause for remorse as well as regret. Only in the latter case is there any cause for penitence, *mea culpa, peccavi.* For a legalist some actions, such as stealing or ending a pregnancy — no matter how lovingly done — would be cause for remorse as well as regret, thus calling for penitent confession and forgiveness. But the only guilt and sin in situation ethics is in being unfaithful to love. (False guilt leads to cheap grace.) Like Abelard in the twelfth century, the situationist says sturdily that those who crucified Christ according to their own consciences were guilty of no sin. If this intentional idea of sin had been held by the old-morality churchmen, their anti-Semitism would have been harder to perpetrate.

This admittedly reformist theory comes down to this: a loving but mistaken action is cause for regret; a loving but correct action is cause for joy; an unloving action, whether a correct or a mistaken reading of the situation, is cause for remorse. Thus remorse follows a betrayal or cheating of loving concern, while regret follows a cognitive but not moral failure. This is a shift away from the penitential systems of both Catholicism and Protestantism. Other things, like this one, will come clearer as the dialogue proceeds.

One gratifying feature of the debate is the Roman Catholic contribution. On the whole, Catholics have been warmer, if anything, than Protestants. I tie this to their superior training in moral theology and casuistry. The order of sympathy runs, on the thermometer, downward from " secular " opinion through Catholics to Protestants. One roadblock has been the matter of labels, due to Karl Rahner's earlier misunderstanding of situation ethics. He polarized, supposing that since we depart from the traditional intrinsic-legalist morality we therefore are existentialist and nonprincipled.[9] In more recent years he has corrected himself somewhat. " This age," he wrote in 1967, " will not be content solely with a Catholic universal ethics of essence which in itself does not touch the moral difficulties of the present time, nor with a purely Protestant situation ethics which is always in danger of degenerating into an empty formal ethics of mere subjectivity of an existentialist kind." [10]

Thus Rahner acknowledges that situation ethics is not existentialist, even though it *might* degenerate into it. He speaks as if only Catholic ethics is universal and "essential" (intrinsic, given), but so is Protestant Scriptural legalism. And his early description of situationism in his *Theological Dictionary* as "an exaggerated existentialism" was obviously hasty and unconsidered. But there are bridges, things like Aquinas' statement in *De malo:* "The just and good . . . are formally and everywhere the same, because the principles of right in natural reason do not change. . . . Taken in the material sense, they are *not* the same everywhere and for all men, and this is so by reason of the mutability of man's nature and the diverse conditions in which man and things find themselves in different environments and times." [11] Our task is somehow to rescue Rahner from his "formal sense" and moral "essence."

Dialogue of this order is more promising than is shown in some conservative Protestant denominations. One group circulated a statement on *Moral Responsibility: Situation Ethics at Work* indicating that this was a well-written book of serious consequence in the field of Christian ethics, that it would sell well, but probably would be quite controversial. The suggestion was made that every pastor should read the book but that the church's bookstores would be bound to be criticized for selling it. The stores were advised therefore to stock the book but not to promote or catalog it.

An inventory of the pro and con material to date suggests two sets of questions. Situationists need to wrestle with them as much as their opponents do. The first one lists seven questions raised directly by situation ethics. (See Father Milhaven's original statement of them, in Part III.) In my own language, they are:

1. Are there no absolutes besides love?
2. What do maxims (not laws) tell people?

3. How do they help decision makers?
4. How are they " summaried " or generalized?
5. What determines a loving action?
6. What is love's purpose and demand?
7. Is there a hierarchy of " good's " in *agapē?*

To these we might add another list of seven, more indirectly raised but quite relevant:

1. Whether freedom and responsibility go together necessarily;
2. Whether human actions are inherently or only accidentally good or evil;
3. Whether human actions should be duty bound or goal oriented;
4. Whether an ethics of " response to need " is an alternative to duty and goal ethics;
5. Whether the spirit of ethical norms comes first, or their letter;
6. Whether the control and authority of moral actions is internal or external to the agent;
7. Whether men have moral capability and potential (and whether a negative answer does not rule out all morality).

Meanwhile let's remember Richard Reinhold Niebuhr's remark somewhere that it is not the business of theologians to form a Society for the Protection of God. Neither is a Society for the Protection of Good needed. Situation ethics is not (repeat: *not*) a " Death of Good " movement.

One of our quagmires in this debate is the failure, on all hands, to see the distinctions between kinds of principles. " Pure agapism " by making love the only rule is said by several critics to be inconsistent with its rejection of all principles. However, the love commandment is a " formal " principle, whereas such principles as " Do not fornicate " or " Keep your promises " are normatives. " Always act with love " is indeed an absolute and universal, but it is a formal ethical principle — imperative, hence ethical. But it is not substantive, i.e., it does not say what love is. It is not normative, i.e., it does not tell us how we are to do it. In lawyers' language, the love rule does not stipulate. It is not prescriptive. It points in a certain direction, toward human need and personal welfare, but it does not supply its own nuts and bolts. It is a strategy amenable to changing tactics. It leaves its footwork to the situation — and to the decision maker.

Our problem is to bring people to *really* accept and proceed on William James's statement of it: " There is but one unconditional commandment, which is that we should seek incessantly, with fear and trembling, so to vote and to act as to bring about the very largest total universe of good we can see." [12]

In the lexicon of old-fashioned ethics, *agapē* is a " virtue " — it is virtual, not actual. " It does not specify." It does not supply ready-made decisions; it only motivates them — as other formal imperatives such as egoism or class interest or nirvana do. But what is good, i.e., loving, in any situation must be decided by rationality and knowledge. Love says why we act, what for; then calculation combines the facts and their logic to tell us what to do or how to act. It does not, to use John Bennett's terms, " as such provide any illumination concerning what is good," except in concrete situations. *In concreto*, not *in abstracto*. I repeat my formula: The imperative (love) combined with the indicative (empirical data) determines the normative (the good thing to do). " The indicative plus the imperative equals the normative." In this process (" conscience ") , maxims of conduct or normative generalizations help, illuminate, suggest. But love is not, as Ramsey thinks, inprincipled. Neither is it unprincipled. It is supraprincipled. Love produces moral principles, but moral principles cannot produce love in *any* form — agapeic concern, philic affection, or erotic passion.

It is a very simple kind of reasoning that charges contradictions on the basis of semantic differences. Another
"contradiction" charged against us is that we claim to
be relativistic about morals (and indeed we do), yet we
make love absolute. But consider. We cannot relativize
things unless there is something against which everything
else is relative. All values or behavioral norms in "pure
agapism" are such in relation to loving concern. It is
the *summum* and *primum bonum.* As Gordon Kaufman
points out, "Does not every relativistic theory presuppose a standpoint from which it itself is formulated and
which is assumed to transcend every standpoint which it
claims to be relative?"[13]

To Norman Langford's complaint about "ethics in
cold blood" it would seem that the situationist's reply
is: "All right, we accept that. Cold calculation for love's
sake is indeed the ideal model. But careful calculation
does not eliminate caring or concern. It presupposes it."
And psychologically it is impossible to completely de-
emote or dehydrate intellect, anyway. If the computer is
really an analogue for the mind, then let's remember
that emotion is its electricity. Just enough makes the
computer work, too much burns out the circuits and
connections (the synapses) — whether wired or printed.

The "warmer" love's calculations are, the more apt
they are to be only interpersonal or even individualistic.
Situation ethics calls for careful calculation on a wide
range — social concern or "general utility." It has the
scope of political sensitivity and imagination. It looks
with suspicion on Mario Savio's "gut" ethics because it
can so easily slide into sentimentality and group egoism.
So-called "love-ins" may too often be spontaneous drop-
outs, no less asocial because they are group-warm and
authentic in their "feelingness." (I hope this kind of
viewpoint does not make me a stodgy and merely decorous Anglican.)

Agapeic situationism is a social ethic. It aims at the

most good for the most people possible. So many critics and discussants, however, have voiced doubt on this score that they ought to have some reassurance. Professor George Abernethy at Davidson College in North Carolina once told me that I should be more careful to guard against a merely local or in-group or just " *meum-tuum* " conception of " the situation " — and that since remote as well as immediate interests and consequences are always at stake, I might better speak of " the *network* of situations." Let it be so. As Cox says, I must next prepare an analysis of situation theory as a method for social ethics, showing some of its practical uses and results. What the social scientists call " defining the situation " is hazardous, not only as to data and logic, but as to the pervasive factor of perception — which is so personal. It is this problematic side of free ethical decision which tempts people into arguments for transcendent or intrinsic morality.

Social situationism has already been foreshadowed in the proposition that love and justice are the same thing. My, my, how that has stirred up the dovecote! But I mean it literally. If an action or policy is loving, it will be just. The more just, the more loving; and vice versa. They do not complement each other. They are each other. Loving concern, using its head, seeks the widest distribution of benefits, and that's what justice is. When Fanon contemptuously rejects all hogwash about " love," *I do too,* because it is the kind of love that is something other than justice. It is sentimental love — interpersonal but not political. All revolutionaries have had to say to a paternalistic *status quo,* " We don't want your love, we want justice." I do too. As Fanon says, " no professor of ethics, no priest," has taken the " native's " place on the bottom.[14]

But there is another side of situation-focused love, and we should be straightforward about it. Only in this way will its merits or weaknesses be fully explored. This other side is what troubles John Swomley as a pacifist. Situation ethics as it copes with social justice (what other kind is there?) is *not doctrinaire or ideological*. That is, it hangs loose about all normative moral principles whether they deal with interpersonal or social affairs, in the secular city, nation, or world. On the question of the ethics of warfare, for example, situationists cannot be pacifists or militarists. They are situationists. They stand for *selective* conscience. All depends on the concrete and particular war. John Bennett, who has *pro forma* expressed greater sympathy for "principled ethics" than for situation or contextual ethics, has acted according to the latter in opposing the U.S. war in Vietnam while supporting Israel's war in the Middle East. He calls, rightly, for "contextual" judgments (he used the term).[15] Be not a dove, nor a hawk, but an owl.

The situationist does not go in for isms — pacifism, militarism, capitalism, socialism, and so on. He is not doctrinaire about conflict (Marx) or cooperation (Weber) theories of social process. All isms are out. The situationist agrees with Daniel Bell — "In the end there is nothing but process." We cannot fix values in *given* principles — social or personal. As Bell, spokesman for the secular version of "the end of ideology," says, an ideologue is a man running down the street crying that he has an answer, who has a question? This is exactly what the warning in Eric Hoffer's *The True Believer* is all about.[16] The fanatic absolutizes his beliefs and his "principles." This is why, using a phrase of Martin Luther King's, the church is more often a taillight than a headlight.

Freud saw it all in his own way. "In the development of mankind as a whole, just as of individuals, love alone acts as the civilizing factor in the sense that it brings a change from egoism to altruism."[17] In terms of his three-story model of the human psyche we may say that "id" is extemporist, the force of impulse and spontaneity, "superego" is domination by and even crippling slavery to external rules and laws of feeling and conduct, while the wholesome and creative personality is the one in whom there is sufficient "ego" strength to mediate successfully in the tension between unprincipled behavior on the one hand and overprincipled "conscience" on the other. Freud designed psychoanalysis as a therapeutic tool to make the unconscious id conscious and the superego realistic. He proposed, in effect, that where id was should be ego, where superego was should be ego. In this language, ego is responsibility, free response to situations. Legalistic ethics and spontaneist ethics, both, reverse this lifeline.

Somewhere in the White House, supposedly in the cellar, is a Situation Room. It holds the "hot line" to Moscow. Its staff are in touch by all communications equipment with all branches of the government, military systems, intelligence operations, news services. In constant touch. They pool their knowledge, daily re-relating the data, being able to say at any time what the situation is on any score when asked, especially by the President. That is the kind of "room" every moral decision maker needs. That is a pretty good model of conscience.

CONTRIBUTORS
AND
REFERENCES

CONTRIBUTORS

BARNETTE, Henlee H., Professor of Christian Ethics, Southern Baptist Theological Seminary, Louisville, Kentucky. Has been a pastor in North Carolina and Kentucky, and once taught at Samford and John B. Stetson Universities. B.A., Wake Forest College; Th.D., Southern Baptist Theological Seminary. Author: *The New Theology and Morality*, 1967. Baptist.

BENNETT, John Coleman, President, Union Theological Seminary, New York, formerly dean and professor of Christian ethics. Coeditor of *Christianity and Crisis*. B.A., Williams College; M.A., Oxford University; S.T.M., Union Theological Seminary, New York. Author: *Social Salvation*, 1938; *Christian Ethics and Social Policy*, 1946; *Christianity and Communism Today*, 1961; *The Christian and the State*, 1958; *Foreign Policy in Christian Perspective*, 1966; *et al*. United Church of Christ.

Cox, Harvey Gallagher, Associate Professor of Church and Society, Harvard Divinity School. Once taught in Andover Newton Theological School. Fraternal worker, Gossner Mission, East Berlin (1962–1963). Codirector of the Center for the Study of Religion and Society, Woods Hole, Massachusetts. B.A., University of Pennsylvania; Ph.D., Harvard University. Author: *God's Revolution and Man's Responsibility*, 1965; *The Secular City*, 1965; *On Not Leaving It to the Snake*, 1967.

CROSS, Wilford Oakland, Professor of Christian Ethics and Moral Theology, Nashotah House, Wisconsin. Once taught philosophy in Washington and Jefferson College and University of Pittsburgh, Daniel Baker College, and University of the South. Has been a parish priest. Frequent contributor to magazines and journals. B.A., University of Illinois; Ph.D., Columbia University. Episcopalian.

CURRAN, Charles E., Associate Professor of Moral Theology, Catholic University of America, Washington, D.C. Once taught in St. Bernard's Seminary, Rochester, New York. B.A., St. Bernard's; S.T.L. and S.T.D., Gregorian Institute, Rome; second S.T.D., Academia Alfonsiana, Rome. Author: *Christian Morality Today: The Renewal of Moral Theology*, 1966. Two works, one a symposium, now in preparation.

EENIGENBERG, Elton Marshall, Dean, Western Theological Seminary, Holland, Michigan, and since 1963 Professor of Christian Ethics and Philosophy of Religion. He has been a pastor in churches in the East and Midwest. B.A., Rutgers University; Ph.D., Columbia University. In 1968 he will publish a book on Christian ethics. Reformed Church.

FITCH, Robert Elliott, recently retired as Dean, Pacific School of Religion, Berkeley, California. Had taught in City College, New York, Pacific University, and Occidental College. B.A., Yale University; B.D., Union Theological Seminary, New York; Ph.D., Columbia University. Author: *Preface to Ethical Living*, 1947; *The Limits of Liberty*, 1932; *The Decline and Fall of Sex*, 1957; *Odyssey of the Self-centered Self*, 1961. United Church of Christ.

FLETCHER, Joseph, Robert Treat Paine Professor of Social Ethics, Episcopal Theological School, Cambridge, Massachusetts. Once taught in St. Mary's College, Raleigh, University of Cincinnati, Graduate School of Applied Religion, and was Dean, St. Paul's Cathedral, Cincinnati. B.A., University of West Virginia; B.D., Berkeley Divinity School; S.T.D., London University-Kenyon College. Author: *The Church and Society*, 1930; *Christianity and Property*, (ed.), 1948; *Morals and Medicine*, 1954; *William Temple*, 1963; *Situation Ethics*, 1966; *Moral Responsibility*, 1967; *et al*. Episcopalian.

GREEN, Joseph F., Editor, specialized books, Broadman Press, Nashville, Tennessee. B.S., Texas Wesleyan College; M.A., Baylor University, Th.D., Southwestern Baptist Seminary. Contributing editor, *The Church Musician*. Author: *Faith to Grow On*, 1960; *Biblical Foundation for Church Music*, 1967. Baptist.

GUSTAFSON, James Moody, Professor of Christian Ethics and Chairman, Department of Religious Studies, Yale University. B.S., Northwestern University; B.D., University of Chicago; Ph.D., Yale University. Author: *Treasure in Earthen Vessels,* 1961; Coauthor with H. R. Niebuhr and D. D. Williams, *The Advancement of Theological Education,* 1957; wrote " Christian Ethics," in *Religion* (ed. by Paul Ramsey), 1964. United Church of Christ.

HILTNER, Seward, Professor of Theology and Personality, Princeton Theological Seminary, and consultant, Menninger Foundation, Topeka, Kansas. Once taught at the University of Chicago, was executive secretary of pastoral services, Federal Council of Churches. B.A., Lafayette College; Ph.D., University of Chicago. Author: *Religion and Health,* 1943; *Pastoral Counseling,* 1949; *Sex Ethics and the Kinsey Reports,* 1953; *Preface to Pastoral Theology,* 1958; *et al.* Presbyterian.

LACHS, John, Professor of Philosophy, Vanderbilt University, Nashville, Tennessee. Once taught at College of William and Mary, has held the Danforth-Harbison Award for Distinguished Teaching (1967–1968). B.A. and M.A., McGill University; Ph.D., Yale University. Author: *Animal Faith and the Spiritual Life,* 1967; *Marxist Philosophy: A Bibliographical Guide,* 1967. Episcopalian.

LANGFORD, Norman F., Editor in Chief, Board of Christian Education, The United Presbyterian Church U.S.A., Philadelphia, Pennsylvania. Once a tutor in the University of Toronto, and then a pastor in Canadian churches. B.A. and M.A., University of Toronto. Author: *The Two-edged Sword,* 1945; *The King Nobody Wanted,* 1948; *Fire Upon the Earth,* 1950; *Barriers to Belief,* 1958. Presbyterian.

LEHMANN, Paul Lewis, Auburn Professor of Systematic Theology, Union Theological Seminary, New York. Has taught in Elmhurst College, Eden Theological Seminary, Wellesley College, Princeton Theological Seminary, Harvard Divinity School. B.A. and B.Sc., Ohio State University; B.D. and Th.D., Union Theological Seminary, New York. Author: *Ethics in a Christian Context,* 1963; contributor to various journals. Presbyterian.

LONG, Edward LeRoy, Jr., Professor of Religion, Oberlin College, Ohio. Has taught in Virginia Polytechnic Institute, and summer sessions at Union. B.C.E., Rensselaer Polytechnical Institute, B.D., Union Theological Seminary, New York; Ph.D., Columbia University. Author: *Christian Response to the Atomic Crisis*, 1950; *Science and the Christian Faith*, 1954; *Conscience and Compromise*, 1954; *The Christian as a Doctor*, 1960; *The Role of the Self in Conflicts and Struggle*, 1962; *A Survey of Christian Ethics*, 1967. United Church of Christ.

McCORMICK, Richard Arthur, S.J., Professor of Moral Theology, Bellarmine School (Loyola University), Chicago, Illinois, and an associate editor of *America*. Serves on the National Catholic Commission on Catholic-Methodist Dialogue. Has taught in Ignatius High and John Carroll University, Cleveland, Ohio, and West Baden College in Indiana. B.A. and M.A., Loyola University; S.T.M., Gregorian University, Rome. Contributes extensively to magazines, journals, and symposia.

MILHAVEN, John Giles, S.J., Professor of Pastoral Theology, Woodstock College, Maryland, and lecturer in medical ethics, Georgetown University. Taught in Canisius College, Buffalo, before studying in Enghien, Belgium, and then in Germany. B.A. and M.A., Woodstock College; Ph.D., University of Munich. Author: several papers in journals; now working on a book with " a positive approach to situation ethics."

MILLER, William Robert, Book Publishing Consultant, Lecturer at the New School for Social Research, New York. Once editor of *Fellowship*, active in the Fellowship of Reconciliation, efforts to stop capital punishment, etc. Ph.D., New School for Social Research. Author: *Non-Violence, A Christian Interpretation*, 1964; (editor) *The New Christianity*, 1967; *Ethics in Action*, 1968; *Goodbye, Jehovah*, 1968. United Church of Christ.

MUELDER, Walter George, Dean, School of Theology, and Professor of Social Ethics, Boston University. Has taught philosophy and ethics in Berea, Kentucky, University of Southern California, and was a Lowell Lecturer. Leader in social and ecumenical affairs. B.S., Knox College; S.T.B. and Ph.D., Boston University. Author: *Development of American Philosophy* (coauthor L. Sears), 1940; *Religion and Economic Responsibility*, 1953; *Foundations of the Responsible Society*, 1959; *Methodism and Society in the Twentieth Cen-*

tury, 1961; *Moral Law in Christian Social Ethics,* 1967; *et al.* Methodist.

NELSON, James Bruce, Associate Professor of Church and Society, Theological Seminary of the Twin Cities, Minnesota. Served congregations in the East and West before teaching. B.A., Macalester College; B.D., M.A., and Ph.D., Yale University. Contributor to various magazines and journals. United Church of Christ.

PIKE, James Albert, Associate, Center for the Study of Democratic Institutions, Santa Barbara. Retired Bishop of California. Has taught in University of California and Catholic University of America; was Dean of St. John's Cathedral, New York, and chairman of the Department of Religion, Columbia. B.A. and LL.B., University of Southern California; J.S.D., Yale University; B.D., Union Theological Seminary, New York. Author: *Doing the Truth,* 1955; *Beyond the Law,* 1963; *A Time for Christian Candor,* 1964; *You and the New Morality,* 1967; *et al.* Episcopalian.

RAMSEY, Paul, Harrington Spear Paine Professor of Religion, Princeton University. B.A., Millsaps College; B.D. and Ph.D., Yale University. Author: *Basic Christian Ethics,* 1950; *War and the Christian Conscience,* 1961; *Nine Modern Moralists,* 1962; *Deeds and Rules in Christian Ethics,* 1967; *et al.* Edited *Religion,* 1965, in Princeton Studies in Humanistic Scholarship. Methodist.

ROLEDER, George, Professor of Social Science, Mt. San Antonio College, California, and a licensed marriage and child counselor. Active in clinical pastoral work. Has served various West Coast churches. B.A. and B.D., Wartburg College; M.A., Claremont Graduate School. Lutheran.

SEIFERT, Harvey Joseph Daniel, Professor of Christian Social Ethics, Claremont School of Theology, California. Formerly taught in University of Southern California; served on national church boards. B.A., Evansville College; M.A., S.T.B., and Ph.D., Boston University. Author: *Fellowship of Concern,* 1949; *The Church in Community Action,* 1952; *Ethical Resources for International Relations,* 1964. Methodist.

SMITH, Harmon L., Assistant Professor of Christian Ethics, Divinity School, Duke University. Has been active in the civil rights movement as well as scholarship. B.A., Millsaps

College; B.D. and Ph.D., Duke University. Doctoral dissertation on William Temple. Methodist.

SWOMLEY, John M., Jr., Professor of Christian Ethics, St. Paul School of Theology, Kansas, and editor, *Current Issues*. Formerly Executive Secretary, Fellowship of Reconciliation, worked for the American Friends' Service Committee, National Council Against Conscription. B.A., Dickinson College; M.A. and S.T.B., Boston University; Ph.D., University of Colorado. Author: *The Military Establishment*, 1964, and various monographs and articles. Methodist.

WAGNER, C. Peter, Professor of Ethics, Emmanuel Bible Institute, Cochambamba, Bolivia.

WASSMER, Thomas A., S.J., Professor of Moral Philosophy, St. Peter's College, Jersey City, New Jersey. Has held various study and research grants, was Scholar in Residence, Episcopal Theological School, 1966–1967. B.A., Fordham University; Ph.D. and S.T.L., Weston College; M.A. and Ph.D., Fordham University. Author of more than 35 articles and papers in magazines, journals, and encyclopedias in the U.S. and abroad.

WEISS, Vernon L., Pastor, John Day Valley Parish, Mt. Vernon, Oregon. Has studied in Germany. B.S., Oregon State University; B.D., San Francisco Theological Seminary. Presbyterian.

YOUNG, John P., Counselor-at-law in Bronxville, New York. Episcopalian.

REFERENCES

IV. ASSAYS AND ESTIMATES

EDWARD LeROY LONG, JR.

1. Durant Drake, *The New Morality* (The Macmillan Company, 1928).

2. G. E. Newsome, *The New Morality* (Charles Scribner's Sons, 1933).

3. John A. T. Robinson, *Christian Morals Today* (The Westminster Press, 1964), p. 8.

4. Ignace Lepp, *La Morale nouvelle* (Paris: Éditions Bernard Crasset, 1963). This work has been translated into English by Fr. Bernard Murchland, C.S.C., and published in 1965 by The Macmillan Company under the title *The Authentic Morality*. Within the text, however, the phrase "the new morality" is used.

5. Cf. Karl Rahner, "On the Question of a Formal Existential Ethics," *Theological Investigations:* Vol. II, *Man in the Church,* tr. by Karl H. Kruger (Helicon Press, Inc., 1963), pp. 217–234.

6. Cf. John C. Ford, S.J., and Gerald Kelly, S.J., *Contemporary Moral Theology:* Vol. I, *Questions in Fundamental Moral Theology* (The Newman Press, 1962), especially Chs. 4 to 8.

7. Emil Brunner, *The Divine Imperative* (The Westminster Press, 1947).

8. Karl Barth, *Church Dogmatics* (Edinburgh: T. & T. Clark, 1957 and 1961).

9. Dietrich Bonhoeffer, *Ethics* (The Macmillan Company, 1955).

10. In recent years the thought of Rudolf Bultmann has become better recognized in America as part of the European contribution. It seems difficult to explain why some Continental theologians become known on this side of the Atlantic while others remain relatively unnoticed. Why, for example, have the works of N. H. Søe (*Christliche Ethik* [Munich: Chr. Kaiser Verlag, 1942]) and Hendrick van Oyen (*Evangelische Ethik* [Basel: Friedrich Reinhardt] 1943) attracted such little interest?

11. In John A. Hutchison (ed.), *Christian Faith and Social Action* (Charles Scribner's Sons, 1953), pp. 93–116.

12. Nels Ferré, "Theology and Ethics," in *Minutes of the Presbyterian Educational Association of the South,* 1951, pp. 47–77.

13. George Forell, *The Ethics of Decision* (Augsburg Publishing House, ca. 1954).

14. Joseph Sittler, *The Structure of Christian Ethics* (Louisiana State University Press), p. 50.

15. H. Richard Niebuhr, *The Responsible Self* (Harper & Row, Publishers, Inc., 1963).

16. Paul Lehmann, *Ethics in Christian Context* (Harper & Row, Publishers, Inc., 1963).

17. Joseph Fletcher, "The New Look in Christian Ethics," *Harvard Divinity Bulletin,* Vol. 24, No. 1, pp. 7–18.

18. John A. T. Robinson, *Honest to God* (London: SCM Press, Ltd., 1963).

19. Joseph Fletcher, "Contemporary Conscience: A Christian Method," *Kenyon Alumni Bulletin,* Vol. XXI, No. 3 (July–Sept., 1963), pp. 4–10.

20. Joseph Fletcher, "Love Is the Only Measure," *Commonweal,* Vol. LXXXIII, No. 14 (January 14, 1966), pp. 427–432. This issue also carries a commentary by Father Herbert McCabe (pp. 432–437) and a second exchange between the two men (pp. 437–440).

21. Joseph Fletcher, *Situation Ethics: The New Morality* (The Westminster Press, 1966).

22. Harvey Cox, *The Secular City* (The Macmillan Company, 1965).

23. Ronald Gregor Smith, *The New Man: Christianity and Man's Coming of Age* (London: SCM Press, Ltd., 1965).

24. Gayraud S. Wilmore, *The Secular Relevance of the*

Church (The Westminster Press, 1962).

25. Paul Lehmann "Chalcedon in Technopolis," *Christianity and Crisis,* Vol. XXV, No. 12 (July 12, 1965), pp. 149–151.

26. Robinson, *Christian Morals Today,* p. 10.

27. Douglas A. Rhymes, *No New Morality* (London: Constable & Co., Ltd., 1964, and the Bobbs-Merrill Company, Inc., 1965).

28. Harvey Cox, "Maturity and Secularity," *Religion in Life,* Vol. XXXV, No. 2 (Spring, 1966), p. 216.

29. Douglas A. Rhymes, "The New Morality: What, Why — and Why Not," *Religion in Life,* Vol. XXXV, No. 2 (Spring, 1966), p. 173.

30. Robinson, *Honest to God,* p. 112.

31. Fletcher, *Situation Ethics,* p. 50.

32. Robinson, *Honest to God,* p. 105.

33. Lepp, *The Authentic Morality,* p. 54.

34. Fletcher, "Love Is the Only Measure," *Commonweal,* Vol. LXXXIII, No. 14 (January 14, 1966), p. 431.

35. Lehmann, *Ethics in a Christian Context,* p. 347.

36. Robinson, *Honest to God,* p. 116.

37. Fletcher, *Situation Ethics,* Ch. 4.

38. Robinson, *Honest to God,* p. 115.

39. Fletcher, "Contemporary Conscience: A Christian Method," *Kenyon Alumni Bulletin,* Vol. XXI, No. 3 (July–Sept., 1963), p. 4.

40. Robinson, *Christian Morals Today,* p. 10.

41. James Gustafson, "Context Versus Principle: A Misplaced Debate in Christian Ethics," *Harvard Theological Review,* Vol. 58, No. 2 (April, 1965), pp. 171–202.

42. Max Stackhouse, "Toward a Theology for the New Social Gospel," *The Andover Newton Quarterly,* New Series, Vol. 6, No. 4 (March, 1966), p. 16.

43. Consider, e.g., Häring's treatment of these matters in *The Law of Christ: Moral Theology for Priests and Laity:* Vol. I, *General Moral Theology* (The Newman Press, 1961), pp. 294–300.

44. Paul Ramsey, "Deeds and Rules in Christian Ethics," *Scottish Journal of Theology Occasional Papers,* No. 11 (Edinburgh: Oliver & Boyd, Ltd., 1965), p. 4.

45. Robert E. Fitch, "A View from Another Bridge," *Re-*

ligion in Life, Vol. XXXV, No. 2 (Spring, 1966), pp. 182–186. See especially the concluding section of this article.

46. Herbert Waddams, *A New Introduction to Moral Theology* (London: SCM Press, Ltd., 1964).

47. Bernard Meland, "A New Morality — But to What End?" *Religion in Life,* Vol. XXXV, No. 2 (Spring, 1966), p. 195.

48. John R. Fry, *The Immobilized Christian: A Study of His Pre-Ethical Situation* (The Westminster Press, 1963); see p. 10.

HENLEE H. BARNETTE

1. Robert Moskin, "Morality U.S.A.," *Look,* Sept. 24, 1963, p. 74.

2. Harlow Shapley, "Stars, Ethics, and Survival," *Religion in Life,* Vol. XXX (Summer, 1961), p. 341.

3. Thomas C. Oden, *Radical Obedience: The Ethics of Rudolf Bultmann* (The Westminster Press, 1964), p. 25; Rudolf Bultmann, *Jesus and the Word* (Charles Scribner's Sons, 1958), pp. 75 ff.; and Rudolf Bultmann, *Jesus Christ and Mythology* (Charles Scribner's Sons, 1958), pp. 11–21.

4. Rudolf Bultmann, *Theology of the New Testament,* tr. by Kendrick Grobel (Charles Scribner's Sons, 1951), Vol. I, pp. 19–21.

5. Bultmann, *Jesus and the Word,* pp. 71–72.

6. Bultmann, *Theology of the New Testament,* Vol. I, pp. 18–19.

7. Bultmann, *Jesus and the Word,* p. 115.

8. Oden, *op. cit.,* pp. 48–56

9. Rudolf Bultmann, *Essays: Philosophical and Theological* (London: SCM Press, Ltd., 1955), pp. 95 ff.

10. Robinson, *Honest to God.*

11. David L. Edwards (ed.), *The Honest to God Debate* (London: SCM Press, Ltd., and The Westminster Press, 1963).

12. Robinson, *Honest to God,* p. 76.

13. *Ibid.,* p. 82.

14. Fletcher, *Situation Ethics,* p. 34.

15. Robinson, *Christian Morals Today,* pp. 12–13.

16. *Ibid.,* p. 46.

17. *Ibid.,* p. 16.

18. *Ibid.,* pp. 36–37.

19. *Ibid.,* pp. 25–26.

20. *Ibid.,* p. 40.

21. Robinson, *Honest to God,* p. 115.

22. *Ibid.*

23. *Ibid.,* p. 117.

24. Fletcher, *Situation Ethics,* pp. 17–39.

25. *Ibid.,* p. 31.

26. *Ibid.,* p. 33.

27. *Ibid.,* p. 52.

28. *Ibid.,* p. 54.

29. *Ibid.,* pp. 69–144; also in brief form in his article " Six Propositions: The New Look in Christian Ethics," *Harvard Divinity Bulletin,* October, 1959, pp. 7–18.

30. Fletcher, " Six Propositions: The New Look in Christian Ethics," *Harvard Divinity Bulletin,* October, 1959, p. 10.

31. *Ibid.*

32. *Ibid.,* pp. 11–12; also Fletcher, *Situation Ethics,* pp. 91, 95.

33. Fletcher, " Six Propositions: The New Look in Christian Ethics," *Harvard Divinity Bulletin,* October, 1959, p. 14.

34. *Ibid.*

35. *Ibid.*

36. *Ibid.,* p. 15; see Brunner, *The Divine Imperative,* p. 132.

37. Fletcher, " Six Propositions: The New Look in Christian Ethics," *Harvard Divinity Bulletin,* October, 1959, p. 16.

38. *Ibid.,* p. 17.

39. Fletcher, *Situation Ethics,* p. 148.

40. *Ibid.,* p. 158.

41. Fletcher, " Six Propositions: The New Look in Christian Ethics," *Harvard Divinity Bulletin,* October, 1959, p. 18.

42. Fletcher, *Situation Ethics,* p. 158.

43. Seward Hiltner's review of Fletcher's *Situation Ethics* in *Pastoral Psychology,* May, 1966, p. 55.

44. James Gustafson, " How Does Love Reign? " *The Christian Century,* May 18, 1966, p. 654.

45. Rule-agapism seeks to determine which rules of action are most love-embodying, and act-agapism, which acts are most loving — terms in the ethical typology of William Frankena, *Ethics* (Prentice-Hall, Inc., 1963), pp. 42–44. For examples of Robinson's vacillations between these two positions, see Paul Ramsey, *Deeds and Rules in Christian Ethics* (London and

Edinburgh: Oliver & Boyd, Ltd., 1965), pp. 15–27.

46. Robinson, *Honest to God,* pp. 116–117; Fletcher, *Situation Ethics,* pp. 85–86.

47. James Gustafson, in Martin E. Marty and Dean G. Peerman (eds.), *New Theology, No. 3* (The Macmillan Company, 1966), "Context Versus Principles: A Misplaced Debate in Christian Ethics," p. 70.

48. *Ibid.,* pp. 69–99.

49. J. H. Spencer, *History of Kentucky Baptists from 1789–1885* (J. R. Baumes, 1885), Vol. I, pp. 355–356.

50. Fletcher, *Situation Ethics,* pp. 95–96.

51. Robinson, *Christian Morals Today,* p. 16.

52. Ramsey, *op. cit.,* pp. 94–99.

53. *Ibid.,* pp. 100–110.

54. Bultmann, *Jesus and the Word,* p. 88.

55. Robinson, *Christian Morals Today,* p. 32.

56. See John C. Bennett, "Ethical Principles and the Context," *Year Book 1960–1961,* The American Society of Christian Ethics, Report of the Second Annual Meeting, Evanston, Illinois, ed. by Das Kelley Barnett, 1961, pp. 9–19.

57. See Henlee H. Barnette, *Introducing Christian Ethics* (Broadman Press, 1961), Ch. 10, "Ethics of the Holy Spirit."

RICHARD A. McCORMICK, S.J.

1. Douglas A. Rhymes, "The New Morality: What, Why — and Why Not," *Religion in Life,* Vol. XXXV, No. 2 (Spring, 1966), pp. 170–181. This article is a brief statement of the views expressed in Rhymes's book *No New Morality.* Nearly this entire issue of *Religion in Life* is devoted to the new morality and makes extremely interesting reading.

2. Fletcher, *Situation Ethics* as well as his article "Love Is the Only Measure," *Commonweal,* Vol. LXXXIII (1966), pp. 427–432.

3. Robinson, *Christian Morals Today* as well as *Honest to God,* pp. 103–121.

4. James M. Gustafson, "How Does Love Reign?" *The Christian Century,* Vol. 83 (1966), p. 654.

5. Robert E. Fitch, "A View from Another Bridge," *Religion in Life,* Vol. XXXV, No. 2 (Spring, 1966), p. 186.

6. Tom F. Driver, "Love Needs Law," *Religion in Life,* Vol. XXXV, No. 2 (Spring, 1966), p. 200.

7. Bernard E. Meland, "A New Morality — But to What End?" *Religion in Life,* Vol. XXXV, No. 2 (Spring, 1966), pp. 19 f.

8. Rhymes, *loc. cit.,* p. 178.

9. Paul Ramsey, "Two Concepts of General Rules in Christian Ethics," *Ethics,* Vol. LXXVI (1966), pp. 192–207, at pp. 196–197.

10. *Ibid.,* p. 195.

11. I put it this way because, except for a few absolute negative prohibitions, I believe that Catholic moral theology is quite as situationist as Fletcher at his best.

12. Herbert McCabe, "The Validity of Absolutes," *Commonweal,* Vol. LXXXIII (1966), pp. 432–437 and pp. 439–440, at p. 439.

13. If it can be shown that in one instance the situational suppositions involve an attack on the significance of human behavior, the method has been shown to fail. As Ramsey says: "A single exception to act-agapism and to summary-rule agapism would be sufficient to destroy these positions utterly and to establish general-rule agapism in at least some types of action" ("Two Concepts of General Rules in Christian Ethics," *Ethics,* Vol. 76 [1966] p. 196).

14. Fletcher, "Love Is the Only Measure," *Commonweal,* Vol. LXXXIII (1966), p. 429.

WILFORD O. CROSS

1. H. A. Williams, "Theology and Self-awareness," in *Soundings,* ed. by A. R. Vidler (Cambridge: Cambridge University Press, 1962), pp. 67–101.

2. Robinson, *Honest to God.*

3. Rhymes, *No New Morality.*

4. Lindsay Dewar, *Moral Theology in the Modern World* (London: A. R. Mowbray, 1964).

5. V. A. Demant, *Christian Sex Ethics* (Harper & Row Publishers, Inc., 1964).

6. Arnold Lunn and Garth Lean, *The New Morality* (London: Blandford Press, 1964).

7. Fletcher, *Situation Ethics.*

8. Wilford O. Cross, a review of *Situation Ethics* in *The Living Church,* May 22, 1966, pp. 18, 24.

9. Robinson, *Christian Morals Today.*

10. V. A. Demant, *op. cit.*, Chs. 1 to 4, *passim*.

11. Fletcher, *Situation Ethics*, pp. 164–165. This woman was imprisoned in the Ukraine.

12. Williams, "Theology and Self-awareness," in *Soundings*, pp. 81–82.

13. *Ibid.*, p. 82.

14. *Ibid.*

15. *Ibid.*, p. 81.

16. Alex Comfort, *Sex in Society* (London: Gerald Duckworth, 1963), p. 97.

17. Rhymes, *No New Morality*, p. 25.

18. *Ibid.*, p. 47.

19. *Ibid.*, p. 17.

20. Robinson, *Honest to God*, p. 118.

21. Dewar, *op. cit.*, p. 36.

22. Fletcher, *Situation Ethics*, pp. 89, 91.

23. Robinson, *Honest to God*, p. 115.

24. Fletcher, "Sex and Situation Ethics," *The Living Church*, Nov. 21, 1965, p. 10.

25. Cf. "Therefore love's outreach is many-sided and wide-aimed" and "Love is compelled to be calculating," Fletcher, *Situation Ethics*, p. 89.

26. Robinson, *Christian Morals Today*, p. 18.

27. *Ibid.*, p. 16.

28. Fletcher, *Situation Ethics*, pp. 26, 31.

29. *Ibid.*, pp. 64–68.

30. Hooker's adroit and penetrating language in describing law has not always been appreciated. Taking over the substance of Aquinas' ethic of natural law, Hooker altered the term "natural law" to "the law of reason," at once making this concept rational, historic, subjective, and relative to man's epistemic knowledge; and ruling out, as Aquinas' synthesis had not felt compelled to do, the medieval inheritance of natural law from its Stoic promulgator, Ulpian. This made of natural law a precept, not "according to nature" but according to reason, a flexible, historic guidance, the "measure of behavioural operations" rather than the Stoic maxim "Follow nature" as a deterministic, cosmic, naturalistic system.

31. Fletcher, *Situation Ethics*, pp. 87 ff., e.g., "Prudence and love are not just partners, they are one and the same" (p. 88),

and "Prudence, careful calculation, gives love the carefulness it needs" (p. 89).

32. *Ibid.*, p. 89.

33. *Ibid.*, pp. 29–30.

JAMES B. NELSON

1. See the article by James M. Gustafson in which he makes helpful distinctions among the major contextualists: "Context Versus Principles: A Misplaced Debate in Christian Ethics," *The Harvard Theological Review*, Vol. 58, No. 2 (April, 1965).

2. Niebuhr, *The Responsible Self.*

3. Paul L. Lehmann, "The Foundation and Pattern of Christian Behavior," in *Christian Faith and Social Action*, ed. by John Hutchison (Charles Scribner's Sons, 1953), p. 107.

4. See Gustafson's chapter, "Christian Ethics and Social Policy," in *Faith and Ethics: The Theology of H. Richard Niebuhr*, ed. by Paul Ramsey (Harper & Brothers, 1958), p. 125.

5. *Ibid.*, pp. 126 ff.

6. Lehmann, "The Foundation and Pattern of Christian Behavior," *Christian Faith and Social Action*, ed. by Hutchison. See also his *Ethics in a Christian Context*. Alexander Miller, *The Renewal of Man* (London: Victor Gollancz, Ltd., 1956), p. 48; *The Man in the Mirror* (Doubleday & Company, Inc., 1958), p. 80.

7. H. Richard Niebuhr, "The Ego-Alter Dialectic and the Conscience," *Journal of Philosophy*, Vol. 42 (1945).

8. H. Richard Niebuhr, "The Center of Value," in *Moral Principles of Action*, ed. by Ruth Nanda Anshen (Harper & Brothers, 1952), p. 162.

9. Fletcher, *Situation Ethics*, pp. 59 f.

10. Gustafson, "Context Versus Principles," *The Harvard Theological Review*, Vol. 58, No. 2 (April, 1965), pp. 175 ff.

11. H. Richard Niebuhr et al., *The Purpose of the Church and Its Ministry* (Harper & Brothers, 1956), p. 34.

12. Niebuhr, *The Responsible Self*, p. 126.

13. Lehmann, *Ethics in a Christian Context*, p. 14.

14. Joseph Sittler, *The Structure of Christian Ethics* (Louisiana State University Press, 1958), p. 36.

15. Fletcher, *Situation Ethics*, p. 157.

16. H. Richard Niebuhr, *Christ and Culture* (Harper & Brothers, 1951), p. 19.

17. James Sellers, *Theological Ethics* (The Macmillan Company, 1966), p. 128.

18. Lehmann, *Ethics in a Christian Context,* p. 350.

19. James Gustafson, *Treasure in Earthen Vessels* (Harper & Row, Publishers, Inc., 1961).

20. Miller, *The Renewal of Man,* pp. 89 ff.

21. Paul Ramsey, "Two Concepts of General Rules in Christian Ethics," *Ethics,* Vol. LXXVI, No. 3 (April, 1966), pp. 192 ff. See also his *Deeds and Rules in Christian Ethics* (Edinburgh: Oliver & Boyd Ltd., 1965).

CHARLES E. CURRAN

1. Fletcher, *Situation Ethics,* pp. 64–66; Lehmann, *Ethics in a Christian Context,* pp. 124–132.

2. Father Francis J. Connell could accept the conclusions of Fletcher and Lehmann on truth-telling because Father Connell defines a lie in relation to the other's right to the truth. See Francis J. Connell, C.Ss.R., *More Answers to Today's Moral Problems,* ed. by Eugene V. Witzel, C.S.V. (The Catholic University of America Press, 1965), p. 124.

3. Fletcher, *Situation Ethics,* pp. 17–39. Situationalism or contextualism is a broad term that describes in general those ethicians who deny the existence of absolute, universal norms of conduct. However, there are many different types of situationists. The present paper deals almost exclusively with the situation ethics proposed by Joseph Fletcher.

4. Fletcher, *Situation Ethics,* pp. 79, 80, and most of Ch. 6, pp. 103–119.

5. *Ibid.,* p. 58.

6. Harvey Cox, *The Secular City,* pp. 192–204.

PAUL RAMSEY

1. See, for example, Marcus George Singer, *Generalization in Ethics* (Alfred A. Knopf, Inc., 1961).

2. W. D. Davies, *The Setting of the Sermon on the Mount* (Cambridge: Cambridge University Press, 1964).

3. "The temper of situation ethics is in keeping with the attempt to quantify qualities" (Fletcher, *Situation Ethics,* p. 118).

ELTON M. EENIGENBERG

1. Joseph Fletcher, "Love Is the Only Measure," *Commonweal,* Vol. LXXXIII, No. 14 (January 14, 1966), p. 427.

2. *Ibid.,* pp. 427–428.

3. *Ibid.,* p. 428.

4. *Ibid.*

5. *Ibid.*

6. Joseph Fletcher, "Why 'New'?" *Religion in Life,* Vol. XXXV, No. 2 (Spring, 1966), p. 189.

7. Douglas A. Rhymes, "The New Morality: What, Why — and Why Not," *Religion in Life,* Vol. XXXV, No. 2 (Spring, 1966), p. 173.

8. Robinson, *Christian Morals Today,* p. 18.

9. Alexander Miller, "Unprincipled Living: The Ethics of Obligation," *Christianity and Crisis,* March 21, 1960, p. 29.

10. Robinson, *Honest to God,* p. 106.

11. *Ibid.*

12. *Ibid.,* p. 107.

13. James Gustafson, in "The New Morality," *Commonweal,* Vol. LXXXIII, No. 19 (Feb. 18, 1966), p. 583.

14. Robinson, *Honest to God,* p. 118.

15. *Ibid.,* p. 120.

16. Tom F. Driver, "Love Needs Law," *Religion in Life,* Vol. XXXV, No. 2 (Spring, 1966), p. 200.

17. Fletcher, "Love Is the Only Measure," *Commonweal,* Vol. LXXXIII, No. 14 (1966), p. 430.

18. *Ibid.*

19. *Ibid.*

20. Rhymes, "The New Morality: What, Why — and Why Not," *Religion in Life,* Vol. XXXV, No. 2 (Spring, 1966), pp. 179–180.

21. Robinson, *Christian Morals Today,* p. 8.

22. Rhymes, "The New Morality: What, Why — and Why Not," *Religion in Life,* Vol. XXXV, No. 2 (Spring, 1966), p. 176.

23. Fletcher, "Why 'New'?" *Religion in Life,* Vol. XXXV, No. 2 (Spring, 1966), p. 189.

24. Robinson, *Honest to God,* p. 119.

25. *Ibid.*

26. Robinson, *Christian Morals Today,* p. 22.

27. Fletcher, " Why ' New '? " *Religion in Life,* Vol. XXXV, No. 2 (Spring, 1966), p. 187.

28. In *Acta Apostolicae Sedis,* Vol. 44 (1952) pp. 413–419. The reference to it here is derived from Joseph Fletcher, " The New Look in Christian Ethics," *Harvard Divinity Bulletin,* October, 1959, p. 16.

29. Fletcher, " The New Look in Christian Ethics," *Harvard Divinity Bulletin,* p. 10.

30. *Ibid.*

31. Robinson, *Christian Morals Today,* p. 24.

32. *Ibid.*

33. Robinson, *Honest to God,* p. 110.

34. *Ibid.,* pp. 110–111.

35. *Ibid.,* p. 111.

36. *Ibid.*

37. *Ibid.,* p. 112.

38. Robinson, *Christian Morals Today,* p. 23.

39. *Ibid.*

V. REFLECTION AND REPLY

JOSEPH FLETCHER

1. Paul Tillich, *The Shaking of the Foundations* (Charles Scribner's Sons, 1948), p. 101.

2. J. L. Simmons and Barry Winograd, *It's Happening: A Portrait of the Youth Scene Today* (Marc-Laird Publications, 1967), pp. 6–30.

3. Joseph Fletcher, *Moral ohne Normen?* (Gütersloh: Verlag Gerd Mohn, 1967), Vorwort von Hans Weissgerber.

4. John Giles Milhaven and David J. Casey, " Introduction to the Theological Background of the New Morality," *Theological Studies,* Vol. 28, No. 2 (June, 1967), pp. 213–244.

5. Coenraad van Ouwerkerk, C.Ss.R., " Secularism and Christian Ethics," *Concilium,* Vol. 25 (Moral Theology), 1967, pp. 100–101.

6. Eric Berne, *Games People Play,* as quoted in *Life,* August 12, 1966.

7. Nicolas Berdyaev, *The Destiny of Man* (Harper & Brothers, 1960), p. 106.

8. Harvey Cox, " Towards an Epistemology of Ethics," *Theological Studies,* Vol. 27, No. 2 (1966), pp. 228–241.

9. See Fletcher, *Situation Ethics,* pp. 34–36.

10. Karl Rahner, *The Christian of the Future* (London: Burns & Oates, Ltd., 1967), p. 48.

11. Thomas Aquinas, *De malo,* 2, 4, *ad* 13.

12. William James, " The Moral Philosopher and the Moral Life," *International Journal of Ethics,* April, 1891.

13. Gordon Kaufman, *Relativism, Knowledge, and Faith* (The University of Chicago Press, 1960), p. 120.

14. Frantz Fanon, *The Wretched of the Earth* (Grove Press, Inc., 1966), p. 36.

15. See *The New York Times,* June 24, 1967.

16. Eric Hoffer, *The True Believer* (Harper & Brothers, 1951).

17. Sigmund Freud, *Group Psychology and the Analysis of the Ego,* tr. by James Strachey, International Psychoanalytic Library, No. 6, p. 57.

242

200 20